Asian Gothic

Asian Gothic

Essays on Literature, Film and Anime

Edited by ANDREW HOCK SOON NG

DISCARD

McFarland & Company, Inc., Publishers

Jefferson, North Carolina, and London

LIBRARY OF CONGRESS CATALOGUING-IN-PUBLICATION DATA

Asian Gothic : essays on literature, film and anime / edited by
Andrew Hock Soon Ng.
    p.   cm.
Includes bibliographical references and index.

ISBN 978-0-7864-3335-3
softcover : 50# alkaline paper

1. Gothic literature — Asian authors.   2. Oriental literature
(English) — 20th century — History and criticism.   3. Oriental
literature — 20th century — History and criticism.   4. American
literature — Asian American authors — History and criticism.
5. Supernatural in motion pictures.   I. Ng, Andrew Hock-soon,
1972– .   II. Title.
PR9410.5.A85   2008
809'.91 — dc22   2007051508

British Library cataloguing data are available

Cover image ©2007 Shutterstock

Manufactured in the United States of America

McFarland & Company, Inc., Publishers
  Box 611, Jefferson, North Carolina 28640
  www.mcfarlandpub.com

For my family

Contents

Introduction: The Gothic Visage of Asian Narratives

Andrew Hock Soon Ng

Introduction

David Punter once claimed that the "Gothic is the paradigm of all fiction, all textuality" (1). Overdetermined as this may sound, it rings with a certain validity if we just look at how the Gothic has, in the last forty years, moved from a type of narrative narrowly identified as "canon" Gothic writings, to an aesthetics of confrontation with a range of literary works that convey the terrible and the horrible in their widest senses. In fact, in this short period of time, the Gothic has spawned many sub-species of itself including the postmodern Gothic, and more recently, postcolonial Gothic. This attests to the malleable nature of the Gothic to transcend its own historical, cultural, and geographical parameters (its "canon"). After all, transgressing taboos, complicity with evil, the dread of life, violence, and the return of the repressed (just to name some familiar Gothic themes) are not specific to any culture or people, but are experienced by all throughout history, although of course, the complexities in which these concerns take may vary from culture to culture. But the Gothic has, in recent years, become more than just a particular mode of writing that captures the dark and the strange. It has become a theory in its own right, requiring particular methods and vocabulary to discuss the way in which texts may be read and appreciated. Undoubtedly, much of the Gothic's critical apparatus is supported by affinitive theories such as feminism and especially psychoanalysis, but in the case of the latter, it is arguable that it is also born of, and is a type of, Gothic discourse itself. Maggie Kilgour has noted

1

that "rather than being a tool for explaining the gothic, then, psychoanalysis is a late gothic story which has emerged to help explain a twentieth century experience of paradoxical detachment from and fear of others and the past" (Kilgour 221). Such a view ambiguates the "fictionality" of the Gothic, and suggests that more than just stories, the Gothic is a way in which we conceptualize and articulate "a specific kind of human experience," which is James Farber's definition of aesthetics (2). In other words, the Gothic functions as a method of inquiry into our socio-cultural conditions. Gothic monsters such as the vampire and the Frankenstein creature, for example, should not be read merely as nightmarish configurations of twisted fantasies, but important metaphors for understanding historically-specific socio-political crises. As Jeffrey Cohen posits, "the monster is born only at this metaphoric crossroads, as an embodiment of a certain cultural moment — of a time, a feeling, and a place. The monster's body quite literally incorporates fear, desire, anxiety, and fantasy (ataractic or incendiary), giving them life and an uncanny independence. The monstrous body is pure culture" (4).

This view is corroborated by Glennis Byron in her essay in this volume when she argues that "monsters ... do cultural work." This may go some way in explaining why Gothic tropes are increasingly appearing in discourses outside literature as well. The vampire and the phantom, for example, have been deployed as vital metaphors to address issues in philosophy (such as Moretti's famous essay on vampirism and capitalism, as well as Derrida's later writings which draw on specters to comment on globalization[1]), in postcolonial studies, cultural studies, history and more recently, in international studies as well.[2] When early Gothicists like Walpole, Radcliffe, Lewis and Poe first penned their macabre stories, little did they realize that they were going to be what Foucault would term "founders of discursivity," whose works "have ... produced ... the possibilities and the rules for the formation of other texts ... establish[ing] an endless possibility of discourse [and] have created a possibility for something other than their discourse, yet something belonging to what they founded" (Foucault 114).

It is with this view of "transdiscursivity" in mind that I see the Gothic as a useful critical instrument to interrogate Asian narratives. I once argued in an essay that "Asian literature is rich with narratives of haunting, the uncanny, and the monstrous, but lacks the trope or a critical heritage to discuss these matters" (2006, 75). The Gothic, a Western literary heritage, can, with careful modification and attention to historical, ideological and cultural specificities, be deployed to address this lacuna in the study of Asian literatures. One of the merits of activating Gothic aesthetics in analyzing Asian writings is that it provides new and interesting perspectives that are not limited to a social-realist reading which, to a large extent, has hitherto informed the study of Asian literatures, be they postcolonial texts, Asian-American writings, or national aesthetical expressions such as Chinese literature. This is not to say that such a methodology is outmoded or lacking in effectiveness, but literary studies encourage, even require, a multidisciplinary and multidimensional approach in order to yield multilayered, complex interpretations. By reading such writings through a Gothic lens, often obfuscated and peripheralized concerns (to social-realist analysis) such as the mechanism of the unconscious, the trajectory of trauma, the instrument of violence, and the symbology of monsters, are made prominent, thus layering the narrative with deeper and even alternative significances. The concern that reading an Asian narrative through such a framework would result in a kind of "colonial imposition" should not arise if the framework itself is open to recalibration and resistance by the text under investigation.[3] In other words, as I have argued elsewhere:

> If the Gothic is understood as an aesthetical mode that mutually informs and is informed by cultural, national, racial, sexual, class, historical and ideological differences, its value as a comparative instrument for literary studies becomes undeniable. Instead of being territorialised by a distinct (that is Anglo-American) historical and cultural heritage, this reconstellated approach to the Gothic will significantly open it up to embrace literatures of other lands, as well as sharpen its critical sophistication [2007, 21].

That the discourse of the Gothic is amazingly hybrid and chameleon lends itself (un)familiarly well to such a critical purpose.

Postcolonial and Asian American Gothic

There is already a modest demonstration of scholarship in this regard, most prominently in postcolonial literary studies. While early essays like Gayatri Spivak's "Three Women's Text and the Critique of Imperialism" (1986) and Patrick Brantlinger's *Rule of Darkness* (1988) reveal the insidious prejudices inherent in nineteenth century English narratives which cast the racial others in monstrous terms, thus revealing the ways in which the Gothic can be deployed for colonialist ends, later critics such as Judie Newman argue for the Gothic as a counter-strategy to indict the Western gaze for its fetishistic proclivities. As she notes, postcolonial Gothic should aim at "[rewriting] the fiction of influential predecessors and therefore to deconstruct conventional images of the colonial situation" (Newman 171). Newman's proposal, however, remains largely unexplored.[4] In terms of Asian American literature's relationship with the Gothic, it has hitherto been tacit. This is chiefly to do with the discipline's emphasis on historical and/or sociological (that is, "realist") models to read literature (Ling 19–22), which would regard non-empirical aspects such as the unconscious and psychical wounds as being less worthy of inquiry. It is only recently that psychoanalysis has made its way into Asian American literary studies,[5] indirectly prompting scholars working in the field to question the literature's investment in Gothic tropes such as (especially) ghosts and the fractured family romance.[6] Yet, despite this promising development, the idea of the Gothic as an aesthetical apparatus to read Asian American literature remains an uncomfortable one, perhaps due to stringent demarcations between the Gothic (understood principally as a Western *genre*) and Asian American writings. One obvious example is Cynthia Sau-ling Wong's pioneering work, *Reading Asian American Literature* (1993). Discussing the motif of the double, she acknowledges the motif's prominence in Gothic literature and its usefulness for interrogating Asian American narratives, but stops short of reading these narratives *as* Gothic.[7]

The essays in the first and second parts of this volume seek to redress these shortcomings. In Part I, "Asian Postcolonial Gothic Literature," five essays on postcolonial narratives demonstrate the multiple ways in which the aesthetics of the Gothic and postcolonial writings can converge to mutually illuminate each other. Wendy O'Shea-Meddour demonstrates how, in the hands of a deft writer, the Gothic can be deployed to render a people and their religion into uncanny, unthinking monsters. In her essay "Naipaul, 'Muslims' and the Living Dead," through close reading of Naipaul's travel writings, she argues that a Gothic vocabulary powerfully informs Naipaul's views on Islam and Muslims. Naipaul's equation of Islam with a kind of brainwashing mechanism and its devotees with zombie-like configurations almost reads like a Gothic novel. This may seem sensational and certainly problematic in such a postcolonial and globalized age as this one, but due to Naipaul's influential status as a literary authority, as O'Shea-Meddour intimates, what he has to insinuate can have significant consequences. Glennis Byron's essay "Where Meaning Collapses: Tunku Halim's *Dark Demon Rising* as Global Gothic" takes us to Malaysia and introduces a lesser known cousin of the vampire: the *pontianak*. Like any monster, the *pontianak* (which is always female) highlights certain cultural scissions which, in Tunku Halim's novel — as Byron avers — includes the traditional/modern dichotomy, the East–West clash, and Malay gender politics. Byron also introduces the term "Global Gothic" to indicate the extent in which non–Western writings have appropriated Western symbologies (in this case, the vampire), resulting in interesting interactions between literary configurations that transcend geographical and cultural boundaries to become truly hybridized. In this new textual context, what is local and global can no longer be clearly differentiated, thus rendering any notion of local "reality" diluted of significance. As such, globalization is not just a new site where chimeras are found, but is *the monster* itself.

The cosmopolitan, Westernized space of the city of Singapore is interrogated for its Gothic qualities in chapter 3. In this cosmopolitan state, Tamara S. Wagner argues, the absorptive capacity of the city plots the Gothic in an ambiguous way: sometimes the postmodern city attempts to commodify the exotic and the supernatural, resulting in resistance or appropriation; sometimes the city hides powerful and frightening secrets beneath its dazzling veneer, and of which exposure can prove fatal; and sometimes, the city becomes a dialogical space where ghosts and people can meet halfway and exist together (un)comfortably. Wagner deliberates that such a divergent take on the Gothic in Singaporean literature is partly to do with its colonial legacy (including the English language), partly to do with the nation's imperative to pursue tradition and modernity in equal measures (which inevitably results in schizophrenia), and partly to do with the rapid pace of urban existence which can lead to anomie and angst. Chapter 4, Paula K. Sato's reading of Meiling Jin's poetry collection in *Gifts from my Grandmother*, provides an interesting reappraisal of postcolonial Gothic by reversing the hero/monster binarism. Sato demonstrates that a very different Gothic story unfolds when the "monster" is enabled a subjective position and its "evil eye" activated. The notion that the East is mysterious, other and hence potentially threatening are dissolved and are revealed to be prejudices of whiteness and Western ideology. In this reversed calibrations, what Sato calls "counter-Gothic," whiteness and the West become the monster instead and their will-to-victimize is made manifest. In the last essay in Part I, "Encrypted Ancestry: Kazuo Ishiguro's *The Remains of the Day* and Its Uncanny Inheritances," Hilary Thompson demonstrates Ishiguro's intertextual playfulness which draw on Proust and the Gothic to comment on the narrative's ethical position, its ambiguous, even paradoxical, Orientalist tendencies, and its reflections on time and aging. While it is not exactly a Gothic novel, Ishiguro, who confesses that he is "fascinated with stock figures and cultural storehouses of images" (in Thompson in this volume), certainly borrows many of the characteristic Gothic repertoire, such as the mansion, the evil foreigner (M. Dupont), homosexual panic (as theorized by Sedgwick[8]), and the demise of the patriarchal order. So meticulous is Ishiguro's raiding of the Gothic larder that he even "uncovers" an often missed feature and transcribes it into his novel: the conflation between the Gothic and things Chinese that grew out of boredom of the vogue of chinoiserie during the eighteenth century. Thompson shows how Ishiguro capitalizes on this convergence to great comic effect. And by way of comparative reading that extends the Gothic-chinoiserie affinity, Thompson also briefly analyzes Borges's "The Garden of Forking Paths" to, again, comment on literary representations of time and identities.

What is interesting about these five representative essays on postcolonial Gothic is the way they exemplify the Gothic's flexibility to adopt divergent, even contradictory ideological positions. Whatever these positions are however, the Gothic helps to shed important light to the postcolonial condition and its multifarious complexities. On the one hand, it can be deployed, as O'Shea-Meddour's essay evinces, as a neo–Orientalist bedfellow to incriminate a particular people and religion as monstrous configurations; on the other hand, it can be used to counter such an imposition (Sato's essay, and Thompson's as well, to an extent). Or, in the case of Byron's and Wagner's essays, it can show the extent to which cross-cultural borrowings of certain metaphors and devices can affect concepts of local and global, tradition and modern. These essays, in my view, go some way in realizing Judie Newman's proposal for innovative approaches to postcolonial Gothic studies.

In Part II, "Asian American Gothic Literature," four essays focus on Asian American literature and their Gothic dimensions. These essays directly evoke the Gothic as the theoretical framework from which to interrogate writings by Maxine Hong Kingston, Sky Lee, lě thi diem thúy and David Henry Hwang. One particular motif which, interestingly, seems to feature rather prominently in Asian American writings (and certainly in the texts discussed) is the "ghost," especially ancestral or familial ones. But the way in which ghosts are featured in these texts diverges considerably from the way they are employed in, based on Dani Cavallaro's argument, Western Gothic. According to Cavallaro, "Ghost stories are a vehicle through which writers and readers may confront the destructive undercurrents of the pride, corruption and jealousy that treacherously course beneath the apparently respectable surface of family life" (80), thus suggesting that ghosts metaphorize the rupture of family romances, and transform such romances into tales of unrest. But the way Asian American writers endorse ghosts (or "spirits" to suggest familiarity) often intimates redemptive capacities and demonstrates how friendships and family ties do not cease with death, but continue in different dynamics into the afterlife. Also, ghosts in Asian American writings are invoked to encourage payment of debts. As Bliss Cua Lim notes with regards to the contemporary ghost film, "the haunting recounted by ghost narratives are not merely instances of the past reasserting itself in a stable present, as is usually assumed; on the contrary, the ghostly return of traumatic events precisely troubles the boundaries of past, present, and future, and cannot be written back to the complacency of a homogenous, empty time" (Lim 287). In Asian American literature, ghosts often return not to take revenge, but to seek remembrance and reparation in order to *free those who have forgotten* from their ancestral and historical debts. Trauma and psychic ruptures are often the result of the failure to perform one's obligation to the family, and the ghosts of the dearly departed return to gently cajole the subject into remembering his or her arrears, and to heal.

Nieve Pascual Soler's essay on Sky Lee's novel, *Disappearing Moon Café*, squares precisely with such a view. Contesting the Western notion of mourning, which entails a level of forgetting after a period of bereavement as constitutive of a healthy form of experiencing loss, Soler argues that for Confucian Chinese, mourning is a lifelong performative due to an adherence to the virtue of filial piety. In psychoanalysis, such a prolonged form of mourning is known as melancholia, which to Freud, Nicolas Abraham and Maria Torok, is abnormal and aberrant. Lee's complex novel, in the end, stands as a "testimony of incorporation," at once converging the body of the narrator, Kae, with the body of her text (her written testimony), and dialectically interweaving the "I" with the voices of departed family members (ghosts). As such, the narrator and her writing become haunted sites which sustain the memory of the dead. It is a Gothic novel but one which does not view death and ghosts as threats, but integral to one's personal survival and history.

The next two essays in Part II, Carol Mejia-LaPerle's "The Ghostly Rhetoric of Autobiography" and Belinda Kong's "The Asian-American Hyphen Goes Gothic," discuss what is now considered the Ur-text of Asian American literature, Maxine Hong Kingston's *The Woman Warrior*, and make somewhat related conclusions to that of Soler's essay. In her evocative essay, Meija-LaPerle problematizes the notion of autobiography and argues for the genre's ambiguity especially with regards to Kingston's narrative. After all, if this testament marks the confluence of many voices (and there are many ghosts in Kingston's text), of which the narrator's is just a conduit, could *The Woman Warrior* be rightfully termed an autobiography? More crucially, and to recast the argument slightly differently, if autobiographies are, to an extent, about unearthing dark and painful memories, conjuring possibly dead people, and relieving the self from perhaps unspoken burdens, is not the practice of writing the self already a haunted (or haunting) enterprise? If this is indeed the case, then LaPerle's point that the autobiography is a Gothic text is indeed innovative. Finally, drawing on critical works on the American Gothic, LaPerle's essay also seeks to situate Kingston's work as a unique American Gothic experience. Belinda Kong's essay continues in a Gothic interrogation of Kingston's narrative. Arguing against the dominant view of the novel as a *bildungsroman* progressing from Asian "other" to American "self" *via* the troubled stretch of the hyphen, Kong argues that the contesting ideologies in the narrative is more that of between being Chinese and being Chinese-American. According to Kong, Chineseness is invested with spirits, and as long as they are not surpassed, will trouble the "Chinese-American soul with contempt and pity" (Kong in this volume). As such, it is not a Western gaze that others the Asian, but Chineseness that worries the hyphenated identity. Kong also analyzes Vietnamese writer lě thi diem thúy's debut novel, *The Gangster we are all Looking for,* and argues for an endowment of haunting in the hyphen itself, effectively transforming the ghost into the self's other, or double. lě's narrative refuses to cathect the ghost of the dearly departed but, as in Soler's essay, inscribes it melancholically within the protagonist's psyche as a form of indelible debt of love. As such, the hyphen is the ghost that constantly reinstates the subject in her originary (Vietnamese) history even as she moves on to forge a new identity in America.

Perhaps unsurprisingly, the Asian American writers who invite ghosts into their narratives are all women. Women, according to Diana Wallace, have always been partial to tales of the supernatural, but because her argument centers around Western writers, her view fails to account for the invocation of ghosts outside that paradigm. According to Wallace, ghost stories afford women writers with "special kinds of freedom [such as] to offer critiques of male power and sexuality which are often more radical than those in more realist genres" (Wallace 57). This is only partly true of Kingston's and Lee's stories, and even less so in lě's novel, suggesting that the ghost story, at least for Asian American writers, does more than merely function as critique of patriarchy and exploration of female entrapment within domestic ideologies. For these writers (and certainly many other Asian American writers such as Amy Tan and Nora Okja Keller), ghosts are not just figurative devices, but literalizes as helpmeets and guardians which assist the liminal subject in her transition across the difficult hyphen. Haunting is not something to be dreaded but, placed in an Asian perspective, represents filial piety, familial attachment, continuity and reparation.

Kimberly Jew's essay is an interesting diversion from the other Asian American–centric essays in this collection in that she focuses on plays by an Asian American playwright which do not refer to the Asian American experience. Considering David Henry Hwang's *The Sound of a Voice* and *The House of Sleeping Beauties,* Jew argues in her essay "Gothic Aesthetics of Entanglement and Endangerment" that although there is a very pronounced Orientalizing tendency in Hwang's deployment of the Gothic to represent Japan, there are enough technical elements embedded in the plays that may suggest that Hwang's strategy is much more subtler than meets the audience's eyes. By breaching the "fourth wall" of the theatre with his stage directions, the audience's sense of safeness and exclusion from what is going on "over there" (the stage, Japan) is problematize to indirectly involve it in not only an Orientalist collusion, but an uneasy feeling that what is going on "over there" is possibly happening at our doorsteps as well.

The Gothic Worlds of China, Japan, Korea and Turkey

The final five essays in this collection make up Part III, "The Gothic Tradition in Chinese, Japanese, Korean and Turkish Literature." Before introducing the essays, I briefly outline the affinities these national literatures have with horror that would provide a useful framework from which to discuss the efficacy of approaching them as Gothic.

The macabre has long been staple in Asian art and literature, but due to certain historical developments, ghosts and demons can sometimes find themselves exorcised from the national agenda, forcing them to lie dormant and invisible until a more conducive time permits their return. Such is the case of China. Despite its rich and long history in horror stories, the Cultural Revolution launched in 1960 ensured that literature which did not support the political imperative to glorify party leaders and progressivism were relegated to the margins.[9] After the Cultural Revolution and the fall of the Gang of Four (that is, four of the most notorious party members, including Mao's widow, Jiang Qin, who have launched many wasteful campaigns — both resources and lives — during the Cultural Revolution), an innovative mode of fictive expression known as New Wave Fiction, practitioners of which include writers such as Mo Yan, Su Tong, Can Xue and Jia Pinghwa, came to dominate the literary scene of China. Much of this fiction can be defined as Gothic because of its unabashed representation of excess, horror, terror, and violence. Characters who inhabit the world of New Wave writings are often extravagantly grotesque configurations; generically, many such narratives resemble postmodern *bricolages* that converge realism, the fantastic and the horrific.[10] Whether they be tales of the supernatural, the fantastic or the grotesque, one important feature in New Wave fiction is its utilization of the body as a metaphor of resistance. The body marks the split and wounded nature of the subject, which in turn, announces the "body's revolt against the rigid inscription of social meaning and instrumentalization. It is a scrambling of the dichotomous of self and other, private and social — an undermining of the dominant universe of representation and order" (Ban Wang 246). It is as if such bodies, which have for so long been obfuscated by the *status quo* of the Mao regime, are now returning with a vengeance.

The two essays that begin this section focus on Chinese narratives. While the first essay, "Reading Shi Zhecun's 'Yaksha' against the Shanghai Modern" by Hongbing Zhang, locates the Gothic in a short story written in 1932 by Shi Zhecun, the second one, Amy Lai's "'Disappearing with the Double': Xu Xi's 'The Stone Window,'" reads the Gothic in a very recent tale by Hong Kong based writer Xu Xi. What this evinces is the presence of chilling narratives in China which, despite being temporarily halted during the mid-twentieth century, have always been complexly and deeply woven into the fabric of the Chinese imagination. These two stories, as in many Gothic works, reveal entrenched socio-cultural crises during crucial moments of historical shifts that leave subjects beleaguered by a sense of displacement. According to Hong, the impetus behind Shi Zhecun's horror is the difficult negotiations between East and West, tradition and modernity, and rural and urban that were increasingly impacting Shanghai before the Second World War. Such bifurcations left the modern self bereft of any existential bearings. In the tradition of the Chinese "strange tales,"[11] "Yaksha" is also a story that bears significant relations to Todorov's concept of the fantastic, in which ambiguity and interpretative hesitance characterize the way the story is apprehended. In the end, it is impossible to say if the narrator's friend is insane, as proclaimed by a Western doctor, or if he has indeed encountered a female yaksha (or demon) while visiting the countryside. "Yaksha," as Zhang argues, also inheres a possibly misogynistic undertone in which assertive women are inscribed with threatening characteristics. This theme is also evident in Xu Xi's "The Stone Window," which, according to Amy Lai, activates a reverse fetishism whereby the Western gaze is revealed for its impotence and becomes objectified by the East instead (again, the East/West dichotomy is evident). In her essay, Lai considers the narrative's innovative deployment of the double motif that carries Asian and feminist overtones.

In both stories, Gothic motifs such as doubles and monsters feature prominently. Women become embodiments of the abject largely because they refuse to conform to Confucian notions of female submissiveness or Western/Orientalist construction of the hyperfeminine Asian woman. Although both stories do not fall into the New Wave category, what threads all these narratives is the foregrounding of retaliating bodies against attempts to circumscribe them within highly limited ideological confines. In fact, structurally, both stories — through conventions of the framed narrative and non-linear storytelling (which are, again, affiliated to the Gothic) — inscribe these ambiguous bodies *as texts* as well: their narrative forms defy easy reading, in as much as their contents resist definitive interpretations.

According to Henry Hughes, one of the oldest surviving literary work from Japan, and perhaps the first modern novel ever written — the Lady Murasaki Shikibu's monumental *The Tale of Genji* (possibly 1021) — is in certain respect an example of early Japanese Gothic.[12] Closer to our time is a host of Japanese writers who have either been directly termed Gothic (such as Ueda Akinari, 1734–1809; Izumi Kyōka, 1873–1939), or are obliquely so (Akutagawa Ryunosuke, 1892–1927; Mishima Yukio, 1925–70). But if the Gothic is a mode of expression that persistently delves into the darker forays of human complexities to unearth often unspeakable layers, then it may not be farfetched to argue that twentieth century Japanese literature is predominantly Gothic.[13] And with the more mass-oriented medium of the cinema, Japanese horror has not only captured the local, but the global imagination as well, with its unique brand of Gothic, spawning endless remakes in *other* national cinemas (for example, the overwhelmingly popular *Ringu* has been remade by the United States as *The Ring*, *Ju-On* as *The Grudge*, and *Honogurai mizu no soko kara* as *Dark Water*).

In a pioneering essay, Henry Hughes traces several important distinctions between Western and Japanese Gothic. One important difference is related to the notion of desire. According to Hughes, in Western Gothic, while desire is a means whereby the self seeks affirmation, and when denied, encounters a split (hence, the double motif), in Japanese Gothic, desire is to be expelled, or emptied, from the self so that the self may find "cosmic achievement," or *Mu*. He further argues that "in addition to the quest of the empty self, the Eastern Gothic more often depicts not a mission against some perceived evil but the discovery of an undivided world of good and evil" (Hughes 60). Evil, in other words, must be acknowledged as part of life, and accommodated rather than destroyed (84). Death, rather than something threatening, is viewed as a means of dissolving the physical self to hasten one's sublime union with *Mu* (which may explain why suicide is celebrated rather than feared). But because Hughes's analysis considers Japanese writers up to Mishima, it fails to explore some of the more recent developments in Japanese Gothic that have to do with the country's increasing Westernization which has disrupted traditional belief systems and which, in the process, has resulted in a new gesture of haunting in contemporary Japanese horror. Marilyn Ivy argues that Japanese-ness and Japanese traditions have to be constantly staged in the bid to resist total identification with Westernization, but as she also points out, the very fact that they have to be staged *already presupposes a loss* (Ivy 22). Its result: the split self. This dilemma, like the grotesquery of the

Chinese New Wave fiction is, I argue, again profoundly staged on the *site of the body*.

Shang-mei Ma's essay "Asian Cell and Horror" reveals an insidious way in which Westernization is negotiated in Japanese horror. By playing up the multi-dimensional meaning of the word "cell" (cellular phones, the human cell, confinement), Ma demonstrates how, in Japanese horror, Western technology is infused with traditional Asian spectres as a means by which the East/West, tradition/modernization dichotomies can be bridged, although with undercurrents of dark water perennially flowing. In this way, traditions in the form of religious beliefs and superstitions can reassert their presence through new mediums such as television, VHS players, cinema, the telephone and the cell phone, to reach a wider, more global audience. Rather than modernization relegating traditions to the margins, the latter has learned to manipulate modernity's innovative technologies to its own fearful, and sometimes vengeful, ends. Ma's essay also makes a considerably excursion into the realm of Korean horror. Analyzing three interrelated films by Korean director Park Chanwook, Ma reveals another consequence of the clash between modernization and tradition in an Asian country. According to theorist So-young Kim, "The fantastic mode of [Korean] cinema in its powerful conjuration of the obstinate past also provides a rich platform on which to think about non-synchronous synchronicity and the working of the premodern in modernity" (53), but Ma's essay seems to suggest that in some recent Korean horror narratives, so totally has modernity interpellated the contemporary subject that there is no possibility of recourse left to an "obstinate," premodern past from which to provide a critique. Technologies like the cell phone and the labyrinthine manufacturing factory (another "cell") have segregated people from each other so much so that the only way in which connectivity can be achieved is through extreme corporeal violence fuelled by anger, jealousy and hate — through the puncturing of the porous surface of the skin so that cells can be breached once again.

If there is one text that particularly exemplifies Glennis Byron's notion of Global Gothic in the broadest sense, it is the popular Japanese anime, *Vampire Hunter D*. A hybrid narrative that converges many genres (cowboy-western/horror/science fiction — just to name a few), it is an example of how a particular Western Gothic motif — the vampire — can transcend its cultural and geographical roots to become grafted with alternative signifiers and to do different cultural work. John Edgar Browning and Wayne Stein's essay, "The Western Eastern: De-Coding Hybridity and CyberZen Gothic in *Vampire Hunter D*" foregrounds precisely this argument. Drawing parallels to frontier Gothic, the Japanese post-moral genre, cyberpunk and Zen philosophy, the two essayists deliberate that *Vampire Hunter* D, while typifying, on the one hand, many conventional Western Gothic tropes and images, is also, on the other, critical of such Western "interventions" as well: as such, the text, although hybridized, also carries a sense of discomfit of its own liminal identity. The "marriage" between East and West is effectively staged in the text, but a sense of ambiguity continues to trouble this tie.

The last essay in this collection is perhaps more descriptive than the others, but its inclusion is important as it demonstrate how the concept of the Gothic can be amenable to a more global application. In her essay, "Grotesque and Gothic Comedy in Turkish Shadow Plays," Ayse Didem Uslu intimates that the Karagöz and Hacivat shadow plays, one of the oldest and most popular forms of entertainment in Turkey, provides a singular perspective on the multicultural usefulness of Gothic aesthetics that is carefully mediated by historical and cultural particularities. These plays, revolving around two Everyman-like characters, combine high comedy and extreme representations of violence and brutality to suggest a distinctive comic–Gothic experience. Like Bakhtin's notion of the carnivalesque, these plays celebrate the overturning of officialdom, the power of the grotesque, and the transgression of (gender, sexual, ideological) boundaries, among other things. The microcosm of these plays mirror the macrocosm that is the Ottoman empire, and are peopled by both humans and otherworldly beings. Uslu's essay traces the history of these plays, demonstrates their Gothic and grotesque proclivities, and makes vital comparisons between Turkish Gothic and the Gothic of the West.

It is hoped that this volume will extend the critical and aesthetical possibilities of the Gothic on a multicultural and comparative literary platform. Slavoj Žižek once articulated his fears about the notion of "multiculturalism" because, according to him, it promotes "the attitude which, from a kind of empty global position, treats each local culture the way the colonizer treats colonized people — as 'natives' whose mores are to be carefully studied and 'respected'" (44). Because the Gothic is primarily a Western aesthetics, to read non–Western writings *via* this perspective may seem like a realization of Žižek's warning. But what the reader will find in these essays is how the deployment of "Gothic aesthetics" as a framework for reading literatures outside the West and the Western canon precisely dislodges "the Gothic" from its Anglo-American centrism. The Gothic becomes, in the process, sharpened, broadened, and sometimes even reversed and resisted by the texts so much so that rather than an "imposition," it functions more as a mode of facilitating a literary experience that is always susceptible to adjustment, refinement, and transformation.

Notes

1. Moretti, "Dialectics of Fear," in his *Signs Taken for Wonders* (1983); Derrida, Specters of Marx (1994).

2. On history, see Andrew Smith, *Victorian Demons: Medicine, Masculinity and the Gothic at the Fin-de-siecle* (2004). On International Studies, see Devetak, "The Gothic Scene of International Relations" (2005).

3. For a more detailed discussion, see chapter one of my book, *Interrogating Interstices* (2007).

4. Recent works such as Howard Malchow's *Gothic Images of Race in Nineteenth-Century Britain* (1996) and many of the essays collected in *Empire and the Gothic* (eds. Andrew Smith and William Hughes, 2000) continue in the vein of interrogating British writings for its Orientalist-Gothic intimations.

5. The two most notable works are Ann Anlin Cheng's *The Melancholy of Race* (2002) and David L. Eng's *Racial Castration: Managing Masculinity in Asian America* (2000).

6. For example, much has been written about the many ghostly presences in Maxine Hong Kingston's *The Woman Warrior* (1976) such as Lee Ken-Fang, "Cultural Translation and the Exorcist: A Reading of Kingston's and Tan's Ghost Stories" (2004) and Patricia Chu, *Assimilating Asians* (2000).

7. It must be emphasized here that to read a text as Gothic does not entail that the text is Gothic. As argued earlier in the essay, I see the Gothic as more of an aesthetics (a way of thinking about and experiencing literature) than merely a mode of writing.

8. In her *Epistemology of the Closet* (1990).

9. This was a period when social-realist writings dominated the literary scene; and this was also a period which saw large-scale poverty, starvation and brutality — of which reality was suppressed by the Communist party. But as David Wang writes, "Fiction may be able to speak where history has fallen silent" (Wang 1), and what more fiction that foregrounds deeply disturbing images and themes.

10. Such narratives, as theorist Ban Wang notes, "[undermine] and [dislocate] the conventional narrative structure of socialist realism constructed on the presumed structuredness, coherence, and end-directed linearity that enable one to construct an event" (Ban Wang 239).

11. Popularized by the famous Chinese story-teller of the macabre, Pu Songlin (1640–1715).

12. See Hughes's essay, where he also discusses other early Japanese "Gothic" works such as *The Tale of Heike* (Hughes 64–66).

13. From sadomasochism and other forms of sexual perversions (Tanizaki Junichiro,1886–1965), to the corporeal and psychical deformities inherited from war (Kenzaburo Oē, b. 1935), from the heightened sense of anomie and becoming devoid due to increasing urbanization (Kobo Abe, 1924–1993), to the postmodern collision of culture that leaves the subject afloat and de-realized (Haruki Murakami, b. 1949), and from the violent resentment of contemporary Japanese youth towards socio-political manipulation (Ryu Murakami, b. 1952) to the fantastical indictment of patriarchal oppression (Yumiko Kurahashi, b. 1935), Japanese literature is rife with moments of profound horror that deploy the panoply of monstrosities and technologies of shock to drive their ideological messages.

Works Cited

Brantlinger, Patrick. 1988. *Rule of Darkness: British Literature and Imperialism, 1830–1914.* Ithaca/London: Cornell University Press.

Cavallaro, Dani. 2002. *The Gothic Vision: Three Centuries of Horror, Terror and Fear.* London/New York: Continuum

Cheng, Ann Anlin. 2002. *The Melancholy of Race: Psychoanalysis, Assimilation and Hidden Grief.* Oxford: Oxford University Press.

Chu, Patricia P. 2000. *Assimilating Asians: Gendered Strategies of Authorship in Asian America.* Durham/London: Duke University Press.

Cohen, Jeffrey Jerome. 1996. "Monster Culture (Seven Theses)." *Monster Theory: Reading Culture,* ed. Jeffrey J. Cohen. London/Minneapolis: University of Minnesota Press, 3–25.

Derrida, Jacques. 1994. *Spectres of Marx: The State of Debt, the Work of Mourning and the New International,* trans. Peggy Kamuf. London: Routledge.

Devetak, Richard. 2005. "The Gothic Scene of International Relations: Ghosts, Monsters, Terror and the Sublime after September 11." *Review of International Studies*, 31: 621–43.

Eng, David L. 1991. *Racial Castration: Managing Masculinity in Asian America*. Durham/London: Duke University Press.

Farber, Jerry. 2005. "What Is Literature? What Is Art? Integrating Essence and History." *Journal of Aesthetic Education*, 39. 3: 1–21.

Foucault, Michel. 1984. "What Is an Author," in *The Foucault Reader*, ed. Paul Rabinow. Harmondsworth: Penguin, 101–20.

Hughes, Howard J. 2000. "Familiarity of the Strange: Japan's Gothic Tradition." *Criticism*, 42. 1: 59–89.

Kilgour, Maggie. 1995. *The Rise of the Gothic Novel*. London: Routledge.

Kim, So-Young and Chris Berry. 2000. "'Suri Suri Masuri': The Magic of the Korean Horror Film: A Conversation." *Postcolonial Studies*, 3. 1: 53–60.

Lee, Ken-Fang. 2004. "Cultural Translation and the Exorcist: A Reading of Kingston's and Tan's Ghost Stories." *MELUS*, 29. 2: 105–27.

Lim, Bliss Cua. 2001. "Spectral Times: The Ghost Film as Historical Allegory." *Positions*, 9. 12: 287–329.

Ling, Jinqi. 1998. *Narrating Nationalisms: Ideology and Form in Asian American Literature*. Oxford: Oxford University Press.

Malchow, Howard L. 1996. *Gothic Images of Race in Nineteenth-Century Britain*. Stanford: Stanford University Press.

Moretti, Franco. 1983. *Signs Taken for Wonders: Essays in the Sociology of Literary Forms*, trans. Susan Fisher, David Miller and David Forgacs. London: Verso.

Newman, Judie. 1996. "Postcolonial Gothic: Ruth Prawer Jhabvala and the Sobhraj Case," in *The Modern Gothic: A Reader*, eds. Allan L. Smith and Victor Sage. Manchester: Manchester University Press, 171–187.

Ng, Andrew Hock Soon. 2007. *Interrogating Interstices: Gothic Aesthetics in Postcolonial Asian and Asian American Literature*. London/New York: Peter Lang.

Ng, Andrew Hock Soon. 2006. "Malaysian Gothic: The Motif of Haunting in K.S. Maniam's 'Haunting the Tiger' and Shirley Lim's 'Haunting,'" *Mosaic*, 39. 2:75–88.

Punter, David. 1998. *Gothic Pathologies: The Text, the Body and the Law*. Houndmills: Macmillan.

Sedgwick, Eve Kosofsky. 1990. *Epistemology of the Closet*. Berkeley/Los Angeles: University of California Press.

Smith, Andrew. 2004. *Victorian Demons: Medicine, Masculinity and the Gothic at the Fin-de-Siécle*. Manchester: Manchester University Press.

Smith, Andrew, and William Hughes. 2003. "Introduction: Enlightenment Gothic and Postcolonialism," in *Empire and the Gothic: The Politics of Genre*, eds. Andrew Smith and William Hughes. Basingstoke: Palgrave, 1–12.

Spivak, Gayatri. 1997. "Three Women's Text and the Critique of Imperialism" (1986), in *Postcolonial Criticism*, eds. Bart J. Moore-Gilbert, Gareth Stanton, William Maley, Willy Maley. London: Longman, 145–66.

Wallace, Diana. 2004. "Uncanny Stories: The Ghost Story as Female Gothic." *Gothic Studies*, 6. 1: 57–68.

Wang, Ban. 1997. *The Sublime Figure of History: Aesthetics and Politics in Twentieth-Century China*. Stanford: Stanford University Press.

Wang, David Der-Wei. 2004. *The Monster That Is History: History, Violence and Writing in Twentieth Century China*. Berkeley/Los Angeles: University of California Press.

Wong, Cynthia Sau-ling. 1993. *Reading Asian American Literature: From Necessity to Extravagance*. Princeton: Princeton University Press.

Žižek, Slavoj. 1997. "Multiculturalism, or, the Cultural Logic of Multinational Capitalism." *New Left Review*, 225: 28–51.

Part I

———∞∞∞———

*Postcolonial Asian
Gothic Literature*

1

Naipaul, "Muslims" and the Living Dead

Wendy O'Shea-Meddour

V.S. Naipaul's writing about the Muslim world has become increasingly influential in mainstream western culture. Since the publication of his travel narratives *Among the Believers: An Islamic Journey* (1981) and *Beyond Belief: Islamic Excursions Among the Converted Peoples* (1998), in which he offers an account of his travels in Indonesia, Iran, Pakistan and Malaysia, Naipaul has established himself as an authority on "Islam in action." With specific reference to his "Islamic journeys," critics have commended Naipaul for his "moral integrity" (Lukacs 70), "fearless truth-telling" (Nasta 4) and loyalty to the "proof of evidence" (Barnouw 55).[1] The favorable critical reception that *Among the Believers* and *Beyond Belief* elicited has given rise to the inclusion of Naipaul's work in books that promise "new levels of understanding about Islam."[2] Critical acclaim has been matched by official recognition; in 1990 Naipaul received a knighthood for his services to literature and, in 2001, was awarded the Nobel Prize. In contrast to this impressive résumé, other notable critics have referred to Naipaul as being a man "incapable of restraining his loathing for the Islamic world and its people" (Phillips 1, 4 & 13).[3] Concerns about Naipaul's hatred of Islam, as voiced by Eqbal Ahmad, Amin Malak, Caryl Phillips and even Salman Rushdie,[4] give the status that Naipaul enjoys in mainstream western culture a rather more sinister aspect.

The criticism or praise elicited by Naipaul's work tends to focus on "Naipaul-the man" but this is problematic when engaging with Naipaul's

*I would like to thank *The British Academy* for funding this research, Professor Catherine Belsey for her insightful comments and Dr. Cherif Meddour for his continual support.

travelogues. The idea that the "traveller's 'I'" in the text *is* "the traveller" out-side of the text is, of course, encouraged by the travel genre. Travelogues aim to convince the reader of their truth. But if we are too readily beguiled by the text, then our conflation of "Naipaul — the man" with "Naipaul — the narra-tor" will lead to the conflation of "characters in the text" with "real subjects." This will blind us to the complicated effects of both language and narration in the textual construction of "the real." It is important, therefore, to remem-ber that the Naipaul in *Beyond Belief* is a literary character and the "Muslim reality" presented is constituted in and out of skillfully crafted, though fre-quently disturbing, textual strategies. Disturbing because, unlike most travel narratives, *Beyond Belief* has gothic realism at its core. As the plot unfolds, we follow "Naipaul — the narrator" on his "Islamic Excursion" through lands inhabited by brainwashed subjects and haunted by unspeakable horrors.

Literary Conventions and Naipaul's Restricted Passages

Although literary critics overwhelmingly accept that there is an ambiva-lent relationship between travel writing and fiction,[5] travel writing is still largely referred to as *non-fictional* literature. This label is misleading as it detracts from the fact that travel writing is an established literary genre full of narrative conventions and fictional devices. Travel writing and fiction fre-quently overlap and intertwine and one of the main characteristics of the travel form is to convince the reader of its transparency: its ability to present us with a reliable account of an unfamiliar world. While critics continue to celebrate Naipaul for his "moral integrity" and "commitment to truth," it is not surprising that *Beyond Belief* continues to be read as if it were a factual text. Repeatedly, we are promised that Naipaul's travel writing will "enable" western readers to gain an "insight" into the life of Muslims and the text repeatedly encourages this sort of reading. In the prologue to *Beyond Belief,* the narrative voice assures us that "THIS is a book about people. It is not a book of opinions" (Naipaul 1998, 1). Following in the tradition of the travel narrator, the Naipaul that guides us through our narrative journey promises that "the truth" will be presented to us in an undistorted manner. Moreover, the sophisticated and highly educated narrator at the centre of *Beyond Belief* is sensitive to the ways in which obtrusiveness can undermine the authority of a "non-fictional" text, and therefore promises that the "writer will be less present, less of an inquirer." Instead, the voice of the Prologue informs us, he will be "in the background, trusting to his instinct" (2). Already, the narrator has split into a least two characters — the voice of the Prologue and the voice of the main narrative. Modeling himself on a figure esteemed by nineteenth century English romantics, the Naipaul of the Prologue claims to be a pure, natural and instinctive artist. In this manner, he assures us that we can rely on the later narrator's objectivity.

Victorian literary conventions not only influence the characterization of the text's narrator. In this literary period, the English novel as a genre had not yet found a narrative device that could provide the illusion that the reader could enter the mind of the character. Modernist conventions such as the "stream of consciousness" were yet to emerge. Consequently, the "internal" drama was displaced onto an excessively responsive physical body or environment. Nineteenth century literature twitches with hysterical characters prone to excessive blushing, hyperventilation, trembling and faints. For example, in Wilkie Collins' novel, *The Woman in White*, "womanish tears," shivering skin and severe bouts of "nervousness" besiege the main characters. All the doubts and concerns that the characters have are played out on the surface of the skin. Similarly, in a novel such as Charlotte Brontë's *Jane Eyre*, we know when the central character is angry or frustrated because, at these moments of crisis, a backdrop of scarlet colored soft furnishings and violent rainstorms suddenly appears. This technique of narrative displacement is repeatedly evident when the narrator encounters Muslims in *Beyond Belief*.

The symptoms that the narrator exhibits are not the typical shivers, faints or sweats of the Victorian hero or heroine. Instead, Naipaul's internal anxiety and, in some cases, clear disgust, manifests itself in a very specific manner. On encountering practicing Muslims, Naipaul begins to suffer from severe breathing restrictions and experiences an accompanying change in air quality. The first incident occurs when our narrator visits Imaduddin's office. Imaduddin lives in Indonesia and is referred to as an "unusual man" because he is "a man of science" and "a dedicated man of the faith." Naipaul is uncomfortable with this "contradiction" (despite their long and intertwined history, science and Islam are, in the narrator's view, incompatible). It is clear that Naipaul also regards Imaduddin to be a hypocrite: he takes exception to Imaduddin's wealth, preferring "his" Muslims to be pious and poor. Despite the kindness that Imaduddin shows his guest, his "Muslimness" causes Naipaul to experience unpleasant physical reactions. Naipaul enters the office and, loyal to nineteenth century realism, begins to make his inventory of the room:

> On one side of the laptop was a well-handled Koran; on the other side was a pile of shoddily produced paperback books, perhaps a foot high, of similar size and in electric blue covers, which had been published in Egypt and might have been a very long commentary on the Koran: no doubt like meat and drink to Imaduddin, [Naipaul 1988, 16].

Naipaul is safe while Imaduddin remains in the room, but when Imaduddin answers the adhan (call to prayer) and deserts Naipaul, the very presence of what Naipaul *suspects* to be a set of "Islamic books" (he cannot read Arabic and guesses the books' contents) is enough to provoke serious health implications for our guide. We are informed that "without the man himself [...] his missionary paraphernalia felt oppressive [...]. It was only someone like Imaduddin who could give point and life to the electric-blue Egyptian paperbacks on the glass-topped desk" (19–20). In his heightened state of anxiety, Naipaul transforms Imaduddin's private reading material into "dangerous missionary paraphernalia" with awesome powers. They are the "meat and drink," the life-blood upon which Imaduddin apparently survives. The "electric-blue" covers suggest that these books are made of hazardous, explosive materials and, being only "shoddily-produced," they are set in stark contrast to the laptop computer and glass-desk upon which they rest. Naipaul prefers not to ask Imaduddin about the content of these books, for this would deflate the tension of the passage. Naipaul reassures himself with the thought that this possible commentary on the Qur'an "is something that only a man like Imaduddin could give point and life to." However, mere proximity to these potentially "Muslim" books causes Naipaul to suffer from the "oppressive" atmosphere that they generate (19–20). This episode offers a foretaste of what is to come and Naipaul endures far more severe reactions when he is exposed to the material presence of Islamic literature in Pakistan.

The second change in atmospheric quality occurs when Naipaul visits Mohammed Akram Ranjha at a commune run by, in the narrator's words, "the most important of the fundamentalist groups: Jamaat-i-Islami." Imprisoned for kidnapping and possibly helping to murder his brother's wife (the narrator's choice of Muslim "interviewees" is not, as he earlier claims, quite "representative"), Mohammed shares a cell with a "political prisoner." This leads to his "jailhouse conversion." Eventually, a lawyer — who we are told is "crazed with religion"— helps Mohammed get into Law College. While practicing law, Mohammed becomes politically active on behalf of Jamaat-i-Islami. His son, a thirty-four year old senior customs officer called Saleem, agrees to drive Naipaul to the commune on the edge of Lahore. This is when Naipaul realizes that he has made his first major mistake: he failed to accept Saleem's "offer of air-conditioning." Naipaul refused the offer because he feared catching a "chill." He comes to regret this decision because the closer he gets to the commune, the more "choked" he becomes. Significantly, Naipaul's breathing restrictions once again coincide with the call to prayer. Like Imaduddin before him, Saleem deserts the afflicted Naipaul in order to worship (316). When Saleem returns, he takes Naipaul to his study and library. It is at this point in the journey that Naipaul encounters yet another set of "Islamic books": "Half the wall facing the door carried those Islamic sets in decorated binding [...]. I soon stopped looking at the books. I began to choke in the stale, enclosed air. I felt I was becoming ill" (317). The room of "Islamic learning" appears to be drained of oxygen. We are told that it is "entirely sealed." Naipaul tries to rectify this immediately and asks someone to open the window and switch the "air-cleaner" on. Sitting on the only chair in the room, one brought up at his specific request, he sits by the window, inhales some slightly less polluted air, and begins to recover. However, the relief he enjoys is short-lived.

Naipaul's breathing restriction reaches its peak during the following dialogue in which Saleem proudly introduces his young son:

> Saleem said, "He is going to learn the whole Koran by heart."
> "The whole Koran," the old man said, picking up the duet with his son.
> I asked, "How long will that take?"
> Saleem said, "Five or six years."
> I couldn't stay. My breathing had become very bad. Downstairs, the servants, thin and dark and dingy, behind the sacks with the split golden paddy. Outside, the fumes and grit of the Multan road. Saleem's driver drove me back to the hotel. Saleem didn't come with me [321].

So violent is Naipaul's reaction in the Akram household that he is unable to stay and hear Saleem's little boy recite a couple of verses. Instead, he is forced to flee back to the safety of his hotel in Lahore.

As one can see from these passages, the narrator's fear of Islamic literature, mosques, indeed, any form of Muslim worship, are clearly reflected in both his physical environment and personal ailments. Poor air-quality is an indicator of the presence of Islam and timely asthmatic responses reveal the narrator's irrepressible hostility towards Muslims. Fawzia Mustafa observes that Naipaul uses "physical discomfort [...] as a gauge for reading the functioning, or completeness, or societal health of the place in which he finds himself" (Mustafa 79). However, she curiously fails to mention that physical discomfort reaches its peak when Naipaul is in the presence of the "believers." Muslims of various persuasions, traditions and character, or simply their *possibly* Islamic artifacts, induce violent physical responses from this narrator of supposed "moral integrity." In *Beyond Belief*, the presence of practicing Muslims compels the narrator to rush out of "interviews," escape "oppressive" atmospheres, reach for "air-cleaners," and struggle to open windows in search of fresh air. Though it may well be true that Naipaul — the man — has a sensitive physical disposition, his commitment to this particular aspect of Victorian fiction helps to explain the persistence of faith-dependent air quality, the narrator's regular bouts of asthma, and their sudden onset in the presence of practicing Muslims.

The Gothic Novel

The presence of gothic realism in Naipaul's "Islamic travelogue" is multifaceted in its effects. Occasionally, the narrator is abandoned to the dictates of gothic realism so completely it produces rather humorous results. The typical plot of the gothic novel is that of the delicate but curious heroine who is lured into the ancestral home of a seemingly innocent but fearsomely dangerous count or aristocrat. Naipaul recycles this plot, placing his traveller's "I" at the centre. It goes like this. The inquisitive Naipaul visits Imaduddin's house in order to "hear a little more about his past — his ancestry" (41). But Naipaul arrives late and, to his disdain, is left to wait in an empty room. Once again, he fulfils the familiar role of "realist observer" and describes the objects surrounding him:

> On the pillars of the sitting room there were two or three decorative little flower pieces and, surprisingly, a picture of a sailing ship. About the sitting room were small mementoes of foreign travel, tourist souvenirs, showing a softer side of Imaduddin (or his wife), a side not connected with mental training, if indeed the house was theirs, and if their mementoes had truly tugged at their hearts (and did not, rather, preserve the memory of some pious giver) [Naipaul 1998, 42–43].

As the description develops, the language becomes increasingly gothic in style. On the surface, the room has the appearance of familiarity, even comfort, but there is the suggestion that this might just be a deceptive cover. In the narrator's view, Islamic education ("mental training") is simply not compatible with a love of travel, sentimentality, or a liking for nautical scenes. Therefore, the collection of "sentimental objects" become suspect and Naipaul doubts whether the house actually belongs to Imaduddin and his wife. The implication is that these comforting artifacts are being displayed in order to lure Naipaul into a false sense of security. The narrator's nerves get the better of him and he begins to experience a deep sense of panic: "how long [...] should I stay where I was, violating the house, and how when the time came [...] might I get away from the curious trap I had appeared to have fallen into" (43). This passage could have been lifted straight out of Jane Austen's *Northanger Abbey* or Brahm Stoker's *Dracula*. Naipaul, in his loyalty to the gothic narrative, has written his traveller's "I" into the role of a vulnerable, innocent heroine at the mercy of a dark lord. As if aware of the narrative trap that he has fallen foul of, and the weak narrative position that he has been accorded, the narrator attempts to recover narratorial authority with a well-used Naipaulian weapon: a toilet joke. Having discovered Imaduddin was engaging in nothing more menacing than having a massage, the narrator claims he had suspected Imaduddin's "bathroom problems" were the cause of his wait all along (43). However, the mark of the gothic genre in the text is usually more disturbing in its effects.

Gothic language is used to portray both Islam and Muslims throughout *Beyond Belief* and its powers of manipulation are alarming. In the section on Indonesia, Islam is described as having spread in a Dracula-like fashion: "Islam had come here not long before Europe. It had not been the towering force it had been in other converted places. [...] It had not completely possessed the souls of people" (24). According to the text, Indonesia only narrowly escaped this ghoulish fate. We need only glance at the description of Muslims (or "possessed souls") answering the adhan in order to see the importance of the gothic genre in Naipaul's narration.

> within the office, no doubt from the carpeted and rumpled open space at the end of the corridor, hesitant scraping sounds developed into a shy chant. [...] The chanting from the corridor became more confident. It couldn't be denied now. I could see that Imaduddin wanted to be out there, with the chanters and the prayers. The chanting now filled the corridor [...] he couldn't be held back [18–20].

This passage is infused with gothic tension: the "hesitant scraping sounds" and rising "chants" suggest the actions of a frightening and possibly sub-human sect rather than a group of Muslims at prayer. Muslims don't chant before beginning the main prayer. If a Muslim arrives early, he or she might do two rakats (bowing cycles), but this is always done in silence. It does not involve "hesitant scraping sounds." In Naipaul's view, by merely answering the call to prayer, Imaduddin reveals himself to be one of the walking dead, a mindless being seduced against his will. (Notably, those who are *not* Muslims in *Beyond Belief* are repeatedly referred to as being "their own men.") As in numerous instances in the text, the use of gothic imagery tells us more about the narrator's fears and prejudices than about "reality." This can also be seen in a later description of the character Saleem. When Saleem hears the adhan, he is described as responding in a spasmodic and zombie-like fashion: "in sudden haste" he "took off his tie and threw his jacket on the car seat and went to join in the prayers" (316). That Muslims are captured souls at the mercy of a mind numbing and unstoppable force is a persistent theme in Naipaul's text. According to the narrator, "cultural depression" causes "religious teaching and a knowledge of Islam" to flourish. Learning how to recite the Qu'ran, "how to have ablution" and "how to do the right prayers," we are told, involves an "isolating and beating down and stunning of the mind," a "kind of pain" (34). Once again, it is suggested that Muslims are like the living dead, their brains anaesthetized by pain and suffering. This theme is extended when Naipaul describes the theological school of Qom. Naipaul's translator, Mehrdad, informs him that "special night prayers involve a lot of bowing and rubbing of the forehead against the earth." Naipaul describes these "very pious people" as having "something like a scorch mark on their forehead; this was because they heated the cakes of earth for their prayers" (238). The underlying references have a powerful impact. Muslims, with their scorched foreheads, answer the call to prayer in zombie like fashion. The women who walk through the streets of this centre of learning are described in an equally sinister manner. Like enslaved creatures, they "held the chador over their face with their hands or bit an end of it between their teeth; they looked like people who were muzzling themselves" (217). Though it is traditional in a number of cultures for women (especially those of the older generation) to hold their headscarf between their teeth, the language infers that it proves these "subhuman" women have given up their souls and are suffering torturous consequences. The presence of the gothic genre in these passages reinforces the opinion that political Islam is "a complete form of control" that "deform[s] people's lives" (240).

The narrator fails to comment on the fact that, in the same areas in which he identifies this frightening "form of control," non–Islamic practices abound. For example, he encounters brothels, the caste system, local superstitions, fast-breakers, scantily clad women, military dictatorships and so on. Furthermore, and as Amin Malak remarks in response to Naipaul's earlier travelogue:

> two of the four countries — Pakistan and Indonesia — are under military dictatorships, the third (Iran) is undergoing a revolutionary process, and the fourth (Malaysia) is suffering from racial tension [...]. No wonder then that his search for Islamic institutions or Islamic law in practice becomes an exercise in futility, it would be hard to imagine stable and legitimate social structures existing, let alone functioning, in the political climates of the four countries visited [Malak 1984, 565].

Nevertheless, the narrator persists in his claim that all the ills of the people he meets have their origin in Islam. The text's message is clear: non–Arab Muslims are to be pitied because they have given away their souls.

It is no accident that *Beyond Belief* frequently reads like a gothic novel. The gothic genre is dominated by vulnerable characters who submit their will, often subconsciously, to a higher demonic force that feeds off their life blood and leaves them void. In the narrator's view, the men who are "unable to resist" the call to prayer and the women who "muzzle themselves" have signed such a contract of submission and have agreed to abolish "the self." Although I have warned against the unproblematised conflation of the "Naipaul — the narrator " with "Naipaul — the man," such conflations are clearly encouraged by Naipaul's public appearances. At a reading of his book *Half a Life* at Queen Elizabeth Hall in October 2001, Naipaul claimed that "Islam" demanded an "abolition of the self" that "was worse than the similar colonial abolition of identity [...] much, much worse in fact."[6] The narrator in *Beyond Belief* similarly asserts that "converted peoples have to strip themselves of their past; of converted peoples nothing is required but the purest faith (if such a thing can be arrived at), Islam, submission. It is the most uncompromising kind of imperialism" (Naipaul 1998, 72). Naipaul the narrator and Naipaul the man repeatedly assert that Islam demands that people annul their individuality. With regards to Pakistan, the narrator argues that "the fundamentalists wanted people to be transparent, pure, to be empty vessels for the faith. It was an impossibility: human beings could never be blanks in that way" (311). Yet, we are told, such people exist. Those who are "empty," those who are suffering from cultural depression and an ignorance about their past are identified as being those most "at risk" of conversion. In the narrator's view, certain people or cultures are more vulnerable to Islam than others. For example, in *Beyond Belief* the narrator states that Indonesians are susceptible to conversion because "they have no idea of themselves" (72). A vacuum of identity is stipulated as being the ideal environment in which Islam can prosper. Like the weak and vulnerable women that faint and submit to blood-sucking vampires in the gothic novel, Naipaul's text suggests that non–Arab Muslims, with their delicate mental constitutions, have inadvertently become the living dead.

Naipaul and Neurosis

Naipaul's evident concern with the mental health of Muslims constitutes another area of similarity between *Beyond Belief* and Victorian literature. Although not a genre as such, mental instability became a preoccupation in nineteenth century fiction, reaching its peak towards the latter part of the century. Instead of locking madness in the attic (such is the fate of Bertha Mason, the "madwoman" in *Jane Eyre*), *fin-de-siècle* novels brought madness downstairs to be "analysed." Central characters become increasingly "unstable" and even those marginal characters that are included in order to "cure" the afflicted begin to show signs of insanity. For example, one of the doctors of psychiatry in *Dracula* becomes slowly addicted to drugs while the other is prone to alarming bouts of hysteria. This ambiguous line between madness and sanity can also be seen in Joseph Conrad's *The Heart of Darkness* and Wilkie Collins' *The Woman in White*. The readiness to address the causes, symptoms and fluidity of madness in literature ran parallel to the increasingly influential academic discipline of psychiatry. During this period, the language of psychiatrists such as Andrew Wynter (*The Borderlands of Insanity*, 1875) and Henry Maudsley (*The Pathology of the* Mind, 1895), and later, Sigmund Freud, entered into popular discourse (Chamberlain and Gilman). Reflecting contemporary cultures' anxieties, characters in these novels regularly slip in and out of madness, experiencing hysteria, degeneration, insanity and other newly defined (or redefined) psychological states. In much *fin-de-siècle* literature, characters and narrators utilize the discourse of psychology in order to authoritatively "define" and explain the psychological states of others. Such "mental assessments" are not confined to those "qualified" to offer opinions. Madness is such a pervasive discourse that everyone, including the patients, is eager to practice amateur psychology. For example, in *Dracula*, Dr. Seward classifies the character Renfield as a "zoophagous patient" (explained by his penchant for eating flies) (Stoker 115). However, between fly eating episodes the "pet lunatic" Renfield asserts: "Since I myself have been an inmate of a lunatic asylum, I cannot help but notice that the sophistic tendencies of some of its inmates lean towards the errors of *non causæ* and *ignoration elenchi*" (233). In *fin-de-siècle* literature, authors eagerly experiment with this new authoritative discourse of the mind and narrators and characters alike define and classify the liberal spread of madness with "scientific" enthusiasm. Yet again, Naipaul does not fail in his allegiance to nineteenth century fiction. While traveling in the "Muslim world," his traveller's "I" regularly faces "irrational behaviour" and is quick to offer his diagnosis regarding the mental health of the "converted peoples":

> Islam is in its origins an Arab religion. Everyone not an Arab who is a Muslim is a convert. Islam is not simply a matter of conscience or private belief. It makes imperial demands. A convert's world view alters. His holy places are in Arab lands; his sacred language is Arabic. His idea of history alters. He rejects his own; he becomes, whether he likes it or not, a part of the Arab story. The convert has to turn away from everything that is his. The disturbance for societies is immense, and even after a thousand years can remain unresolved; the turning away has to be done again and again. People develop fantasies about who and what they are; and in the Islam of converted countries there is an element of neurosis and nihilism. These countries can be easily set on the boil [Naipaul 1998, 1].

Neuroris, a tendency towards nihilism, self-delusions, latent aggression and fantasy lives are, according to the narrator, characteristics of these simmering Muslims. Of Pakistan, we are told:

> The local people would hardly be there, in their own land, or would be there only as ciphers swept aside by the agents of the faith. It is a dreadful mangling of history. It is a convert's view; that is all that can be said for it. History has become a kind of neurosis. Too much has to be ignored or angled; there is too much fantasy. This fantasy isn't in the books alone; it affects people's lives [329].

Islam is found guilty of inducing mental illness on a national scale because it is an "Arab" religion with sacred places in Arab lands. According to this peculiar thesis, Arabs do not suffer from neurosis because they are not "converts." The narrator fails to mention that Arabs were generally polytheists at the time of the prophet Muhammad and in order to become Muslim necessarily "converted." Perhaps this point is dismissed because the narrator believes that the "sacred places" of Arabs are "in their own lands?" Assuming that this is the reasoning, it would follow that European and American Christians and Jews suffer from a similar "neurosis" because their "sacred places" are abroad. However, it is clear that in the narrator's opinion, Western Christians and Jews are mentally sound. The logic behind Naipaul's argument is impossible to follow. As Eqbal Ahmed asks,

> Who is not a convert? By Naipaul's definition, if Iranians are converted Muslims, then Americans are converted Christians, the Japanese are converted Buddhists, and the Chinese, large numbers of them, are converted Buddhists as well. Everybody is converted because at the beginning every religion had only a few followers. Christianity, Islam, Buddhism, Judaism, all prophetic religions developed through conversion. In that sense, his organising thesis should not exclude anyone [Ahmad 9–10].

Michael Gilsenan dismisses the argument that non–Arab Muslims suffer from "neurosis" with the accusation that this line of reasoning is made of "shallow stuff" (Gilsenan 1998). The narrator's attempts to identify and explain "the irrational energies of the faith" (Barnouw 61 & 63)[7] are poorly reasoned and his pains to assume the role of psychiatrist are less convincing than his literary predecessors.

Conclusion

In *Beyond Belief*, a variety of narrative techniques — more commonly found in the Victorian novel — combine to create a disturbing portrayal of the Muslim world. Literary conventions persuade us to "believe" in the transparency of the text, particularly in the character of the "honest narrator," with whose sufferings we are encouraged to sympathize. These sufferings are repeatedly provoked by mosques, the call to prayer, Islamic literature, Islamic dress and Muslim households. All generate an oppressive and suffocating atmosphere; one that results in choking fits, breathing restrictions and a compulsion to escape. Naipaul's use of this literary convention is rhetorically powerful and the reader cannot help but share the narrator's relief when windows are opened and the narrator able to breathe the clean air of non–Muslim space once more. Having manipulated the reader in this manner, the text becomes increasingly gothic in style. This genre is designed to terrify. As most readers are aware, gothic novels teem with demonic forces that clamor to possess the souls of the weak and vulnerable. Bloodthirsty vampires and immortal beasts take over the minds of their victims and threaten civilization, reason, modernity and sanity. By studying *Beyond Belief's* depiction of eerie Muslim households, threatening Islamic artifacts, and brainwashed Muslims at prayer, one can see how Naipaul's use of the gothic genre culminates in a powerful piece of propaganda. His "documentation" of "Islam in action" is expressed in the language of horror. Followers of Islam are repeatedly referred to as being violent and irrational, numbed by pain, and suffering from a nihilistic form of neurosis. Unsurprisingly, those who share both Naipaul — the man and Naipaul — the narrator's political views, regard *Beyond Belief* to be a "first-rate humanist study" of "contemporary Islamic converts" (Wallia). Unfortunately, the prestigious awards and critical acclaim that Naipaul has received suggests that this Islamophobic worldview is widespread, confirming Edward Said's fear that "malicious generalizations about Islam have become the last acceptable form of denigration of foreign culture in the West" (Said xii). In a time when Muslims and non–Muslims need to find grounds for mutual respect and understanding, it is essential that this gothic vision is not accepted as a transparent and worthy account of "the Muslim world."

Notes

1. Jason Cowley (2002) and Leon Gottfield (1984) also praise Naipaul for his loyalty to the truth.
2. For example, the editors of *Inside Islam* selected Naipaul to write a chapter on "Islam in Malaysia and Indonesia" (Miller and Kenedi 2002).
3. For a sophisticated analysis of Naipaul's writing and responses to his work, see Rob Nixon, *London Calling: Postcolonial Mandarin* (1992).
4. Eqbal Ahmed asserts that Naipaul is "a very sick man" whose writing is "irresponsible" and "scandalous" and concludes that "Islam" is one of the "imagined ghosts" that Naipaul continues "to

pursue" (Ahmad 10). Amin Malak criticizes Naipaul's "deplorable narrowness of vision" that, he argues, combined with a "lack of sound knowledge and understanding of Islam," compounds the "negative impact" of his first "Islamic Excursion" (Malak 561). Salman Rushdie accuses Naipaul of "aligning himself with the more dangerous and fascistic elements of Hindu nationalism." Salman Rushdie's comments are quoted by Susheila Nasta in her summary of "V.S. Naipaul," *British Council, http://www.contemporarywriters.com*

5. As Kabbani reminds us in *Europe's Myths of Orient: Devise and Rule,* writers of travelogues are still "writing *fiction,* the non-fiction genre of the travelogue is a creative convention only" (122, author's emphasis).

6. Quoted by Fiachra Gibbons in "V.S. Naipaul Launches Attack on Islam" (*The Guardian,* Oct. 4, 2001).

7. Barnouw praises Naipaul for following "reasoned evidence wherever it takes him" in order to help the reader understand the "irrational energies of faith." Though Barnouw's *Naipaul's Strangers* masquerades as literary criticism, it becomes clear that she is merely using Naipaul to express her own highly cultivated prejudices.

Works Cited

Ahmad, Eqbal. 1999. "Distorted Histories: An Interview with Eqbal Ahmad" by David Barsamian, *Himal, www.tni/org/history/ahmad/david1999.htm,* 1–13. (Accessed December 2003).
Barnouw, Dagmar. 2003. *Naipaul's Strangers.* Bloomington and Indianapolis: Indiana University Press.
Brontë, Charlotte. 2000. *Jane Eyre* (1847). Oxford: Oxford University Press.
Chamberlin, Edward J. and Gilman L. Sander. 1985. *Degeneration: The Dark Side of Progress.* New York: Columbia University Press.
Collins, Wilkie. 1996. *The Woman in White* [1860]. Oxford: Oxford University Press.
Cowley, Jason. 2002. "Don't give up the Day Job yet, Sir Vidia," September 22, 2002. *http://www.books.guardian.co.ukwww.contemporarywriters.com/authors/?p=author78&state=.* (Accessed January 2003).
Gibbons, Fiachra. 2001. "V.S. Naipaul Launches Attack on Islam." *The Guardian,* October. 4.
Gilsenan, Michael. 1998. "Manager of Stories." *London Review of Books,* 20:17.
Gottfried, Leon. 1984. "*Among the Believers: Two Views:* A Skeptical Pilgrimage," *Modern Fiction Studies,* 30. 3: 567–572.
Kabbani, Rana. 1988. *Europe's Myths of Orient: Devise and Rule* (1986). London: Pandora Press.
Malak, Amin.1984. "Among the Believers: Two Views: V.S. Naipaul and the Believers." *Modern Fiction Studies* 30, 3: 561–66.
Mustafa, Fawzia., 1995. *V.S. Naipaul.* Cambridge: Cambridge University Press.
Naipaul, V.S. 1981. *Among the Believers: An Islamic Journey.* New York: Vintage.
_____. 1998. *Beyond Belief: Islamic Excursions Among the Converted People.* London: Little, Brown and Company.
_____. 2002. "Islam in Malaysia and Indonesia" in *Inside Islam: The Faith, the People and the Conflicts of the World's Fastest Growing Religion,* eds. John Miller and Aaron Kenedi, Aaron. Washington: Marlowe and Co.
Nasta, Susheila. (2002). "Contemporary Writers: V.S. Naipaul." *The British Council, www.contemporarywriters.com/authors/?p=author78&state=* (Accessed February 2003).
Nixon, Rob. 1992. *London Calling: Postcolonial Mandarin.* Oxford: Oxford University Press.
O'Brien, Connor Cruise, Edward Said, and John Lukacs. 1986. "The Intellectual in the Post-Colonial World: Response and Discussion." *Salmagundi:* 70–71. 65–81.
Phillips, Caryl. 2000. "The Enigma of Denial." *The New Republic Online, http://www.TNR.com/052900/phillips052900.htm* (Accessed January 2003).
Said, Edward. 1997. *Covering Islam: How the Media and the Experts Determine How We See the Rest of The World* (1981). London: Vintage.
Stoker, Bram. 1996. *Dracula* (1897). Oxford: Oxford University Press.
Wallia, C.J.S. (no date). Book Review of *Beyond Belief, www.indiastar.com/wallia15.htm* (Accessed February 2003).

2

Where Meaning Collapses: Tunku Halim's *Dark Demon Rising* as Global Gothic

Glennis Byron

Monsters, as critics working in the field of Western gothic repeatedly stress, do cultural work: through difference, monsters police the boundaries of the human and consequently allow us to define the politics of the normal. And from the start, one of the main ways in which Western gothic has mobilized the monstrous is in the service of constructing and developing a sense of cultural and national identity. It is no coincidence that what is usually considered the founding text, Walpole's *Castle of Otranto* (1764), emerges at the precisely the moment when, through constructing an alternative Gothic past, Britain was engaged in the development of both a cultural and a political nationalism.[1] The gothic construction and development of national and cultural boundaries involve setting both internal limits — locating the monstrous in a barbaric past or present day rogue group — and external limits — locating the monstrous in the foreign. Whether barbaric past or alien other, difference allows for the construction and definition of a civilized rational world of the present.

Although critical attention has traditionally focused on the ways in which gothic participated in the construction of a British or American identity, the monstrous figures of gothic fictions, because of the ubiquitous binaries upon which they feed, easily lend themselves to the work of any nationalist agenda.

As the dominance of the British and American traditions has been challenged, an increasing number of critics world wide have begun to locate their own nationally specific forms of gothic. In *The Monster That Is History* (2004), for example, David Der-Wei Wang critiques conventional paradigms of modern Chinese literature and identifies a culturally specific gothic form through reinstating the local contexts of modern Chinese creativity. Similarly, Henry J. Hughes, in "Familiarity of the Strange: Japan's Gothic Tradition," emphasizes a uniquely Japanese gothic. As Hughes argues, "the term 'Gothic' does not specify those Japanese authors who were influenced by Western literature, but serves as a translation term for a similar tradition observable in both cultures"(Hughes 12).

Frequently, an identification of nationally specific gothic traditions is accompanied by an examination of the ways in which these traditions contribute to the production of national and cultural identities. This is particularly evident in the cases of so-called "new world" countries and countries moving towards a modern urban society and yet unable to exorcise completely a feudal and rural past. In New Zealand, for example, such critics as William Schafer have demonstrated the ways in which gothic enables the ideological work of transforming "colonization" into "settlement": "We move," Shafer observes, "from a sense of alienation and rootlessness — being separated and detached from the landscape around us — to a sense of being rooted in it, sprung from it, possessed and haunted by it" (Schafer 144).

But just as attempts to locate more nationally specific forms of gothic have begun to proliferate, the effects of globalization upon cultural production have also led to the literature and film of different countries feeding off each other to produce new cross-cultural monstrosities. Like the monsters it breeds, the gothic text has not only functioned to define the politics of the "normal," but also been a hybrid form that exceeds and disrupts those systems of classification through which we order experience. And as the idea of the state with clear geographical boundaries breaks down with the flow of cultural productions across boundaries, the systems increasingly disrupted are those of nation and culture. A new gothic form is emerging, a form marked by the increasing cross-cultural dynamics of the past century which might be identified as "global gothic." Analysis of this global gothic will have three main advantages. It will help identify what the gothic texts of different countries have in common. It will reveal the ways in which texts of one country are influenced by, and in turn influence, those of other countries. And most importantly, it should ultimately help us to assess more accurately what really *is* culturally specific about any particular gothic text.

This essay will take some exploratory steps towards considering these issues in the context of Southeast Asian gothic by focusing on a work of popular horror fiction with an overt interest in the effects of globalization: Tunku Halim's *Dark Demon Rising* (1997). Halim was born in Petaling Jaya, Malaysia, educated in Kuala Lumpur and in England, practiced as a lawyer in Kuala Lumpur, and now lives and works in Australia. He writes in English and has produced three collections of short stories and two novels.[2] *Dark Demon Rising*, his first novel, is the story of Shazral, a successful lawyer in Kuala Lumpur who has all the accessories of the brand name lifestyle: white Porsche, lunches in the fashionable Shangri-La restaurant and a beautiful fiancée called Minah. Shazral returns home to the *kampung* when his father, the village *bomoh* or shaman, is dying. He agrees to learn the *ilmu*, the knowledge of the shaman, and accepts his "inheritance"; that is, he acquires the familiar, the *hantu pusaka*, which is passed down from father to son and is the source of the shaman's power. The dark demon of the title, the *hantu jahat*, wants to destroy this spirit, but Shazral eventually conquers the demon and settles down in the village with his childhood sweetheart Roslyah.

There is no doubt that Halim is well plugged into the market and *Dark Demon Rising* self-consciously appropriates and exploits the rhetoric and conventions of popular Western gothic while basing itself in Malay folklore.[3] In particular, the ways in which monstrosity is defined and represented are full of cross-cultural resonances. The story begins with a framed narrative in which an Australian anthropologist comes to see Shazral, now an elderly man. "So you've come to hear of demons?" says Shazral, "And about vampires?"(9) and this is how the monster is labeled throughout: demon or vampire.

In fact, the monstrous figure has a much more specific basis in Malay folklore, combining elements of the various birth demons, in particular the langsuyar, the pontianak, and the penanggalan.[4] In "Fiction Writing in the Malay World," Halim suggests that his demon is "no Frankenstein monster, Dracula or werewolf of the western horror genre but rather a *hantu jahat* or evil spirit that comes in the form of a pontianak or vampire — one of the most feared creatures in Malay folklore" (Halim 2000).[5] Halim's demon, however, with its ability to detach its head from its body, would seem to owe as much, if no more, to the figure of the penanggalan.

Furthermore, the terms for the Malay birth demons are never used in the text, and the monster is instead infected by cross-cultural references. At the moment it first reveals its true nature, a rather notorious Western representation of the demonic is superimposed:

> She tossed her hair and flipped her head to the right. Her tongue fell, licking her lips, it seemed longer than it should have been. I gulped involuntarily as

her head, like a creaking doorknob, slowly turned — until it seemed at an impossible angle.

I couldn't believe it — my eyes were lying — but her head still continued turning[...]. The head continued its impossible revolution — creaking and ripping — until it faced me again, grinning from ear to ear. [...] The flesh was torn at her neck, the ligaments moist and shiny, the flesh raw, red — throbbing. The neck severed from her body! [...]

Its face — for it could not have been hers — formed zig zag lines, cracking like a broken egg — green slime bubbling, frothing, hotly out[...]. Its tongue, long and thin — like a snake's, flickered out and licked at it. Its grin widened, showing black, rotting teeth.

"Goodbye, my darling," it snarled and its head rose, lifting itself two feet above its shoulders. There was a dull ripping and snapping like flesh being strung apart, tendons and joints being broken [143].

The bubbling green slime, the flickering tongue, the creaking turning head — both the images and the language indicate that Halim is relying on his reader to have a certain genre competence and to recognize echoes of *The Exorcist*, in particular the second most notorious scene: when the possessed girl's head impossibly revolves, in Blatty's words, "with nightmare slowness," "turning, swiveling [...] creaking with the sound of some rusted mechanism" (Blatty 362).[6] The imposition of these overt references to the Western horror tradition at the very moment when the demon of folklore is revealed suggests that one of the new sites of horror in the global gothic may well be globalization itself.

What gives *The Exorcist* much of its significance in the history of horror is its challenge to an idea that dominates Western gothic in the last decades of the twentieth century: the movement, as Rosemary Jackson observes, towards an "apprehension of the demonic as mere absence, rather than as essentially diabolic" (Jackson 112). *The Exorcist* attempts to contest this movement through reclaiming metaphysical notions of good and evil. William Peter Blatty's book (1971) and to a lesser degree William Friedkin's film (1973), initially gesture towards the ambivalence associated with traditional Western gothic. They suggest psychological disturbance caused by the breakdown of family values may be the root cause of possession and promote a conservative moral agenda that aims to reinforce threatened values for middle America in much the same way as Stoker's *Dracula* once did for the Victorian middle class. Ultimately, however, *The Exorcist* works to re-establish good and evil as metaphysical, rather than psychic or social, categories. Father Karras, the Jesuit priest and psychiatrist who has lost his faith, yearns for some sign of the existence of God. Friedkin's film, even more emphatically than Blatty's book, takes on a single-minded crusade to provide Karras with just the evidence he requires. Possession is firmly established as the visible sign of the existence of the demonic and functions, through opposition, as the guarantee of the existence of some transcendent good, reinvesting the world with meaning.

There is a similar movement in *Dark Demon Rising*. The opening exchange between Shazral and the Professor problematizes questions of good and evil. "So you've come to hear of demons? [...] And about vampires?" Shazral asks. "Aren't they the same thing?" the Professor replies. "Mostly," Shazral concedes, "but then again what's a demon and what's a vampire? It all depends, you see ... We humans can be demons too ... and vampires" (9). The suggestion is that the dark demon of the title may well be what rises within the self and this would encourage a psychological reading. The novel ends, however, with an Epilogue that strives to eliminate all ambiguity and reinstate lost certainties. Like the doubting priest of *The Exorcist*, Shazral needs to believe in metaphysical notions of good and evil. As he says to the still skeptical professor, "The magic, the *ilmu*, the demons, they are all real, for otherwise my life would be meaningless" (226). Shazral's faith ultimately persuades even the professor: "I, for one," he affirms, "don't believe your life has been meaningless" (226). It is this threat of meaninglessness with which *Dark Demon Rising* primarily engages, and which it anxiously attempts to hold off.

From one perspective, it might seem that what Halim is doing by appropriating Western gothic rhetoric and motifs is staking his claim within a popular genre, moving towards the homogenizing of culture and commodifying local tradition for a Western audience. What I would argue instead is that Halim, although undeniably aiming for an international audience, is producing rather a new hybrid form which appropriates but also transforms Western gothic, merging it with a more local gothic tradition, for his own particular purposes. *Dark Demon Rising* attacks the workings of global culture: the false universalizing of the Western, and the silencing of other discourses through the imposition of its own "authorized" truths. This is a global Gothic text that mobilizes hybrid monstrosity to attack a value system associated with globalization. Through this hybrid form Halim stages a confrontation between the competing discourses of the rural and the urban, the local and the global, the traditional Malay *kampung* and the multicultural modern world of Kuala Lumpur. He locates globalization as the new site of monstrosity, global discourse as that which works to drain "reality" out of the local and render it meaningless. Consequently, while *Dark Demon Rising* shares with such Western texts as *The Exorcist* a fear of the meaninglessness of life produced by an "apprehension of the demonic as mere absence," it sites the source of the threat in culturally specific terms.

As Shazral begins his story, he locates the origins of the modern city in an outpost over a hundred years ago of Chinese miners in "runty shacks, gambling dens, gangs and cold nightly murders" (15). "Here it began" (15), he says, and within two paragraphs he has whisked us through the British with their cricket clubs, war and "heads mounted on tall Japanese poles," independence and the subsequent frenzied move towards industrialization, and deposited us in Ziggy's Zag, the hottest nightclub in Kuala Lumpur. This is a flashy world of glossy surfaces and constant sensual stimulation: flashing lights, belching smoke machines, blasting, thumping music, and voices shouting over it all, unheard, ignored. It may be different superficially from that old mining outpost, but remains connected to history by the same "eager glimmer" in the people's eyes (15). There are still "cold nightly murders" as social and humanitarian obligations are replaced by the consuming desire for profit. Kuala Lumpur is produced as a textbook case of the increasing difficulty of producing a homogenous sense of community, of national identity, in the global city with its racial, religious and linguistic diversity. There is no sense of a cultural identity here, no knowledge of, or interest in, national or local traditions.

The news that his father is dying forces Shazral to return to the *kampung*, and as he begins to recall the events that led to his departure, the traditional Malay village is set in opposition to this modern global city. As Shazral looks back to his childhood, the coherence of this culture is already shown to be under threat. To some degree, the village shows signs of resistance; the products of the city are transformed as the villagers appropriate them for their own purposes. The Imam, for example, is the proud owner of a new Rediffusion speaker, but uses it to blast out the five daily calls to prayer. The Western world has infiltrated in the form of Coke, Fanta, and 7-Up, but the children roll the strings they attach to the homemade boats they race around the empty cans. Nevertheless, the values and practices of the city begin to invade along with its products and evil is then made manifest. Shazral's uncle, Pak Khamis, misuses the *ilmu* for material gain — to increase production in his orchard — and he breaks the law of proximity that forbids unmarried men and women being alone together. The young Shazral observes his uncle's illicit affairs and, determined to beat his friend Zak when they race their boats on the river, bribes Pak Khamis to put a spell on his boat. Self-interest is put above communal values and the *ilmu* fails to work: another friend, Affendi, wins the race and the disruption of local values and beliefs accelerates. Shazral had believed in Pak Khamis's magic but when misused its power is usurped. Once the convictions of the culture are corrupted, once social identity breaks down, another virus, the demon, assumes power and can enter in. And this now leads to a number of deaths. Affendi, the first victim, falls into the river and, despite Shazral's attempts to hold on to him, is swept away to his death. That night Shazral, full of guilt, sees in a dream a tall dark shape of a woman with glowing red eyes and glinting white fangs across the bank of the river, a woman who gloatingly affirms the connection between Shazral's cheating and his friend's death: "Your fault, Shazral!" (81). The subsequent murder of Shazral's mother by this dark figure intensifies his guilt and increases the already existent rift with his father. Dismissive of his father and his *bomoh* "paraphernalia" (29), Shazral eventually rejects his inheritance and leaves for the city. The betrayal of local values leads to the breakdown of community.

Once in the city, Shazral accepts its values and its perspectives. He believes his father's work has "no relevance in the modern world. We have trained and qualified doctors," he argues: "We don't need this traditional medicine anymore" (113). When he returns to the village, he still sees partly with the city's eyes: the village seems dirty and primitive; his old home squats "eagerly on its stilts like some savage beast, ready to swallow [him] whole" (46). Nevertheless, the authorized truths of the city that would silence other discourses also begin to break down on his return and no longer speak to him so insistently, a moment effectively signaled by the breakdown of his mobile phone.

The deception, greed and spiritual emptiness that are associated with the city are most notably embodied in Minah, Shazral's fiancée. A vacuous giggling dolt who is, everyone agrees, "one hell of a girl" (180), Minah appears as the perfect product of that most insidious form of globalization: advertising. "A wonderful night, darling," she tells Shazral as they drive home from Ziggy's Zag, "Great fun, great drinks, good people." As Shazral thinks at the time, she sounds like "an ad for rum on ice with tanned bodies running on a tropical island" (20). Minah's house, however, set in a wealthy suburb, is a monument to capitalism of which Shazral thoroughly approves. Only one thing bothers him: the replica gas lamp on a black post that sits outside. "Something about the way the electricity burned fiercely within its glass casement never failed to draw my attention," Shazral observes, "something it said — which was always beyond my grasp" (22). What it says is deceit, illusion, and what it also says, referencing the famous shot of Father Merrin's arrival at the McNeil house in *The Exorcist*, is here be monsters. Further emphasizing the infection and corruption of the local by the global, the demon or vampire of folklore turns out to be taking the form of the material girl Minah.

The only way to beat the demon, the text suggests, is to attack the authorized truths of the global culture, to effect a change in perception in order to recognize that nothing lies behind those supposed truths but a concern with the material. Only then can the realities of the local and the meaningful truths of the spiritual be reclaimed. As Shazral becomes the shaman he recognizes Minah for what she is — flashy surface that cracks open to reveal monstrous materiality — and he turns to Roslyah, his childhood sweetheart. Minah retaliates by beheading Shazral's uncle Pak Khamis (a long delayed punishment for those earlier transgressions which have left him vulnerable to attack) and Shazral returns to the city to confront the demon. Now he also sees her house for what it is: an abandoned decrepit building with broken windows and peeling paint, rooms empty save for a couple of bent spoons, syringes and, buried in the dust, "scores of needles, broken with age and rust" (169). Here is the underbelly of globalization. What lie behind the glossy surfaces of the city are empty meaningless lives, people in search of nothing more than a "few hours of numbing peace" (169). Minah's house is a corrupt and empty shell.

The need to reject the false universalizing perspective of the global and reclaim one's own vision is implicit in the way Shazral, as shaman, can counter the effects of the demon upon its victims. With the movement towards a recuperation of the local, the horror begins to throw off its Western associations and turns back to the Malay. When the demon enters the body of its victims, its presence is signaled by black thorns that surround the *semangat*, the "soul itself, present in all things" (156), and feed upon its essence. The traditional Malay shaman treats the symptoms of spirit attack by "counteracting the spirits' hot breath with his own, made cool by an incantation" (Laderman 44). Similarly, Shazral sends his breath into the victim's body to dissolve the thorns — a much gentler penetrative cure than the violent stakes which dispatch those unfortunates infected by Western vampires — and the result is a change in perception. The victim's eyes open and "a different person look[s] out"; there is a "glow" in the eyes that speaks "of someone who had been lost and had returned home" (200).

An adjustment of vision is similarly evident in the way Shazral is relieved of his guilt. There is one other thing in Minah's house apart from the numerous needles and the spotty youths. Where a painting of a young girl resembling Minah in a white dress used to hang, there is now another portrait:

> Filling up that wall was a painting of it with its decaying ugly head, still hideously, yet impossibly, resembling Minah. Hair spilling down among bits of worms and insects. A fat and bloody intestinal tract worming its way out of the head, like the remains of a freshly gutted animal. Its crimson eyes still bore in my head, the words "Kiss me" spilling out of its hungry evil grin. Lying at the bottom near what looked like its tail was a decapitated head, the

blood pouring from the severed neck, tongue lolling out of his wide open mouth. The resemblance was unmistakable. It was Pak Khamis [170].

As Shazral sprawls tied on the floor with this hideous image grinning behind him, his mind nevertheless fills with memories of making love to Minah in this very bedroom. "Oh Roslyah," he thinks, "How my mind has betrayed you," and he is hit by a wave of nausea. "The sordid feelings, the awful pleasure made me want to retch" (192).

While this is clearly a scene of some psychological complexity, on one level the text works to reject any ambiguity in favor of clear-cut metaphysical notions of good and evil. There is no betrayal, no guilt, no repressed desire, his father tells Shazral in a vision: "the demon is playing tricks with your mind" (197). Even Shazral's earlier cheating is now dismissed as a cause of evil. "It was not my fault!" he yells at the demon. "I was young and didn't know better. My cheating had nothing to do with their deaths. You did it!" (217). Unlike Western psychoanalysts, Malay healers locate the affected person's problem outside of that person: the shaman projects the problem on to a culturally accepted external entity. This is precisely what happens here. Rather than finding or constructing a myth or story that illuminates the inner workings of the psyche, the shaman looks outward to the demons that are seen to exist on a more conscious and "real" level (Laderman 85).

Dark Demon Rising, therefore, can be said to contest a demonized global culture that would silence the local partly through the reinstatement of traditional customs and beliefs. As Shazral tells the professor, the *ilmu* and the demons must be real, "otherwise my life would be meaningless" (226). In this respect, the text supports Khoo Gaik Cheng's contention that in 1990s Malaysian film and literature modernity facilitates the recuperation of *adat*: "the local customs or customary laws that existed before the advent of Islam" (Khoo 5).[7] Concepts of custom, tradition and "inheritance," of course, tend to be deployed by patriarchies, and rural ethnic identities in *Dark Demon Rising* resist the homogenizing effects of globalization not only through a return to animistic beliefs and traditional methods of healing, but also, since modern urban living threatens traditional values of social and family unity, by reinstating more rigid roles for men and women. Bodies, sexualities and gender roles consequently function as equally crucial sites of struggle within the social and cultural transformations the text rehearses.

Pak Khamis is "emasculated" because he fails to uphold the Malay value system; Shazral succeeds because he accepts his "inheritance," moves from self-interest to social responsibility, and ultimately conforms to the male dominant role. It is, however, the female body that becomes the primary performance site on which anxieties about modernity and tradition are enacted. Minah and Roslyah conform to the opposing stereotypes of *racun dan penawar*, poison and antidote, identified as the dominant female images in Malay cinema of the 1950s and which such critics as Khoo see as continuing in the film and literature of the 1990s: the independent and sexualized and/or materialistic woman and the dependent, sweet, supportive and patient love interest or wife (Khoo 113).

Although still firmly patriarchal, Aithwa Ong notes, traditional "Malay society is often cited as an example of a Muslim society that permitted relatively egalitarian relations between the sexes" (Ong 163). This is suggested in the village depicted in *Dark Demon Rising* where the women, including Shazral's mother, have a certain economic independence—although it may be significant that she is killed by the demon when she goes on one of her twice-weekly trips to sell traditional Malay cakes to travelers on the main road out of the village. Gender differentiation in the Malay village, Ong notes, was expressed primarily in terms of morality: a man was the guardian of the virtue of his wife, sister, and daughters, and by extension, all village men were responsible for the virtue of all village women (Ong 165). Again, this is a repeated focus of concern in *Dark Demon Rising*. Like Pak Khamis, Shazral's childhood friend Zak is guilty of breaking the laws of religious proximity. But Zak is discovered and driven out of the *kampung* by the other villagers. The refusal to uphold the laws and customs allows the demon in once more, and Zak dies of a "mystery" illness the modern doctors cannot explain.

One of the factors that undermined the *adat* emphasis on bi-laterality and which made the regulation of female sexuality increasingly difficult was the New Economic Policy (1971–90). With the production of an increasingly female industrial force through the migration of *kampung* girls to the city, the regulation of female sexuality became problematic. In this context, Minah's name becomes particularly suggestive. While it links her to the mynah bird with its imitative skills, suggesting the demon's ability to mimic the human, and perhaps to Mina of Stoker's *Dracula*, relating her to the wider world of vampires, more importantly in the local context it recalls Minah Karan (literally Electric Minah), the name given to the women workers in the electronic industry during the 1980s, girls from the *kampung* who served as cheap labor in the cities and were dangerously sexualized, seen as a threat to traditional culture in their independence (Khoo 126; Ong 171–4). The modern global world, therefore, is not just embodied within Minah: it is what produces women like Minah, and the rejection of the values of the material global city involves not only the recuperation of the *ilmu*, but also the demonization of the transgressive feminine and the reinstatement of more rigid gender demarcations within the Malay community.

Minah becomes, in Julia Kristeva's terms, the site of the abject, "what disturbs identity, system, order. What does not respect borders, positions, rules" (Kristeva, 1982: 4). As her head detaches from her body, monstrous materiality breaks out of its containment: "ligaments moist and shiny, the flesh raw, red — throbbing," the "glistening heart pulsating," and spilling out the bloody "worm-like" entrails "moist and slimy" (143), "fat and bloody ... like the remains of a freshly gutted animal" (170). Exploding the fantasy of the stable body constructed by and within the symbolic, Minah as both the embodiment and product of globalization becomes the site which "draws me toward the place where meaning collapses" (Kristeva 2).

Minah must be replaced by Roslyah, the girl who upholds the customs and laws of the *kampung* and reinforces the patriarchal order. Associated mainly with coconut cakes and clucking chickens, loyal to her community and supportive of its values, Roslyah offers a striking contrast to Minah in moral terms. While Minah, challenging, beckoning, first picks Shazral up in the nightclub parking lot and sleeps with him that very evening, Roslyah, loving him from the start and yet never forward enough to speak, waits patiently for him all those years.

In the context of the physical, however, attempts to distinguish the two are less successful. With Minah, the text repeatedly returns to the body, not only the monstrous materiality of the demonic form, but also the highly sexualized human form; in particular there is an emphasis on sensuous, voluptuous curves, long hair billowing, cascading (17, 136), and the "heady, musky perfume" (22, 37, 136) she exudes. Roslyah, in contrast to the insistent materiality of Minah, sometimes appears a rather shadowy figure. When Shazral first sees her on the bus which returns him to the village, he notes that her "face formed a soft, glimmering image on the glass which remained out of focus like a distant ghost that dared not form" (41). When Roslyah is described physically, it is primarily in terms of innocence and freshness, most notably through the short curly hair that bounces lightly upon her shoulders (41, 104, 120, 151) and smells of apples and pears (152, 153). But while city girl is thereby distinguished from *kampung* girl, it is also Roslyah's traditional associations that allow her to be suggestively sexualized, with the sarong that clings gently to her curves (151) and her legs (104), and while some physical descriptions aim to distinguish the two women, others threaten to dissolve difference.

And indeed, for all the attempts to segregate *racun* from *penawar*, Minah and Roslyah nevertheless literally merge in two telling moments. First, at the very moment when Minah is otherwise occupied tearing Pak Khamis's head from his body, Shazral dreams of Roslyah running towards him in a white cotton dress — the non-traditional garb is a signal. As he watches, a dark stain appears on her cheek and spreads: "Black blotches sprouted on her face like a rush of bruises"; the face begins to melt into "a mask of featureless darkness" and out of that features re-emerge, leaving the "perfect" face of Minah (160).

The second merging occurs when Shazral has defeated the demon and returns to the village; this time it is no dream. On his way to Roslyah's house, a vision of Minah's decaying head springs into his mind. He begins to run, and reaching the house he looks up to see "a dark figure with cascading hair, standing with the bright sun behind her.... Such a figure had once stood outside my window" (222). And then she speaks: "Maybe you couldn't wait for more coconut cakes" (222) and with these reassuring words, the figure is reconstructed as Roslyah: "Short hair bounced just above her shoulders" (223).

Throwing new light on the early description of Roslyah's image being "out of focus like a distant ghost that dared not form" (41), there is an uneasy sense in these two passages that both women are somehow linked to "featureless darkness." It is not specifically Minah, but what the feminine represents more generally, that exposes the constructedness of, and threatens, the "reality" produced by and within the symbolic, and in such moments as this, Roslyah too edges dangerously close to the monstrous.

In this context, the ending of Shazral's narrative becomes particularly interesting. The rejection of both the global and the transgressive feminine seems to necessitate stepping out of horror and, as signaled by the language, leaping into an idyllic rural fantasy, into a world that is emphatically a construction. Shazral and Roslyah walk down to the bank of the river where the children once raced their boats and where evil first became manifest. A bird sings a simple melody among the lush trees, the once treacherous river seems smaller, flowing calmly, lapping and gurgling at the bank; a gentle breeze kisses their faces, and on the opposite bank, where once a dark threatening figure stood, blooms a large flower in the royal yellow of Malaysia. The text has evoked a lost world and identified the source of that world's corruption. But with the self-conscious piling up of clichés in the idyllic ending of *Dark Demon Rising*, there appears to be an admission that this world can never be reclaimed, perhaps, as Halim himself suggests elsewhere, "never even existed," and that the construction of this world in fantasy is nothing more than a rejection of the equally illusory, but spiritually barren, world of the "real," the expression of a yearning, "a desire for something simpler, deeper and, perhaps, more meaningful" (Halim 2000).

Notes

1. On the connection between English Gothic and the emergence of nationalist ideologies see Schmitt (1998).

2. *The Rape of Martha Teoh and Other Chilling Stories* (1997), *Dark Demon Rising* (1997), *Bloodhaze: Fifteen Chilling Tales* (1999), *Vermilion Eye* (2000) and *The Woman Who Grew Horns and Other Works* (2001).

3. Even the source of the folklore positions the text as global. Halim has observed the inspiration for this novel came from K.M. Endicott's *An Analysis of Malay Magic* (http://www.users.bigpond. com/hradin/article.html). When I emailed Professor Endicott, an American anthropologist at Dartmouth, he was to say the least surprised to learn that a Malaysian horror writer had been inspired by his work.

4. There are numerous versions of these birth demons in South Asian folklore and they overlap in many ways, most notably in their predilection for the blood of new born babies, children and pregnant women. Roughly speaking, the langsuyar is the spirit of a woman who died in childbirth; she has a hole in the back of her neck through which she drinks blood and is said to be able to take the form of an owl. The pontianak is the child of a langsuyar and like its mother flies through the night and can be heard wailing in the trees. The pennangalan, known in the west through the cult film *Mystics in Bali* (1981), takes the form of a trunkless head with the intestines still attached which flies about seeking for the opportunity to suck blood.

5. To name the demon as pontianak at this point may well have been a marketing decision. The pontianak had become a popular figure in South Asian horror, with the series of pontianak films produced in Singapore between 1956 and 1965, but these were Malay language films and had little impact in the West. The pontianak would not have been a widely recognisable creature when *Dark Demon Rising* was published in 1997. By the time Halim wrote this article in 2000, however, the release of the Singapore English language production of *Voodoo Nightmare/Return to Pontianak* (2000) a film that built on the popularity of the American cult film *The Blair Witch Project* (1999), meant that a wider audience had become familiar with the figure of the pontianak. Certainly, in a subsequent short story, "Night of the Pontianak," published in *The Woman Who Grew Horns and Other Works* in 2001, Halim had no hesitation in naming his monster.

6. Other references to *The Exorcist* include Shazral's Captain Curly who seems to echo Regan's Captain Howdy.

7. In the works Khoo studies, this reclamation of *adat* is "simultaneously a postcolonial or anti-imperialist strategy and a subversion of more restrictive notions of Islamic discourse that emerged since the 1980s" (Khoo 4). Both Westernization and resurgent Islam are equally equated with modernity and globalization. While Halim does not seem to engage directly with resurgent Islam as a modernizing force, the text makes some interesting visual connections between Islam and the West, such as the moment Shazral, returning to the city by plane, sees the city below him "with its minarets piled high-interspersed by skeletal towers and cranes, each one eagerly trying to climb over the other" (165).

Works Cited

Blatty, William Peter. 1971. *The Exorcist*. London: Corgi.
Cheng, Khoo Gaik. 2006. *Reclaiming Adat: Contemporary Malaysian Film and Literature*. Vancouver: University of British Columbia Press.
Endicott, K.M. 1970. *An Analysis of Malay Magic*. London: Oxford University Press.
Halim, Tunku. 1997. *Dark Demon Rising*. Petaling Jaya: Pelanduk.
_____. 2000. "Fiction Writing in the Malay World," http://www.users.bigpond.com/hradin/article. html. (Accessed 2 Feb. 2007).
Hughes, Henry J. 2000. "Familiarity of the Strange: Japan's Gothic Tradition," *Criticism* http://www. findarticles.com/cf_0/m2220/1_42/63819091 (accessed 10 Dec. 2006).
Jackson, Rosemary. 1981. *Fantasy: The Literature of Subversion*. London: Methuen.
Kristeva, Julia. 1982. *Powers of Horror: An Essay on Abjection* (1980), trans. Leon S. Roudiez. New York: Columbia University Press.
Laderman, Carol. 1991. *Taming the Wind of Desire: Psychology, Medicine, and Aesthetics in Malay Shamanistic Performance*. Berkley: University of California Press.

Ong, Aihwa. 1995. "State Versus Islam: Malay Families, Women's Bodies, and the Body Politic in Malaysia," in *Bewitching Women, Pious Men: Gender and Body Politics in Southeast Asia.* Berkeley: University of California Press: 159–94.

Schafer, William J. 1998, *Mapping the Godzone: A Primer on New Zealand Literature and Culture.* Honolulu: University of Hawai'i Press.

Schmitt, Cannon. 1997. *Alien Nation: Nineteenth-Century Gothic Fictions and English Nationality.* Philadelphia: University of Pennsylvania Press.

Wang, David Der-Wei. 2004. *The Monster That Is History: History, Violence and Fictional Writing in Twentieth-Century China.* Berkeley: University of California Press.

3

Ghosts of a Demolished Cityscape: Gothic Experiments in Singaporean Fiction

Tamara S. Wagner

Increasingly in Singaporean fiction, haunted government housing-estates or offices rival relocated cemeteries, forgotten shrines, or the liminal spaces left by demolished mansions, traditional shop-houses, and colonial bungalows, as sites of preternatural occurrences. They combine in charting a Gothic aesthetics that encompasses a condition of constant flux, mobility, and instability in the densely populated, continuously expanding city-state. Integrating divergent literary or cultural traditions of the ghostly, the mystic, or the paranormal in the mundane spaces of the city, Gothic experiments in recent fictional representations of Singapore indeed fascinatingly play in particular with the confines, the extendable constrictions, of the urban ghost story. This narrative form significantly constitutes a colonial importation. As such, it at once captures, and yet also complicates, the haunting presence of literary legacies in contemporary Singaporean fiction at large. In taking a close look at Singaporean ghost stories, I seek to cast new light on their adaptation of social, cultural, and specifically literary conventions. The traditional short supernatural tale set in urban spaces, as introduced during Britain's colonial presence in the region, and as it quickly became institutionalised as a model for ghostly tales in English-language writing, has always been used to encapsulate a prevalent unease with the emergence and rapid development of modernity. From its beginnings in the nineteenth century, it has been permeated, engendered even, by a dread/fascination with a sense of defamiliarization that is specifically linked to the liminal locations of changing cityscapes. When its tropes — especially its identification of the mystic, or ghostly, with the exotic — are transposed into diverse cultural contexts, the ruptures or breakages that their transformations generate at the same time create opportunities for a self-referential and often specifically self-ironic reworking. It is this engagement with different fictional conventions of negotiating an urban preternatural that renders the contemporary Singaporean urban ghost story so intriguing as well as revealing as a cultural phenomenon.

If the legacies of Victorian fiction haunt Singapore's post–Independence writing in more ways than one, moreover, its urban Gothic importantly helps to untangle such flows of influence. It unearths the anxieties of a society at once repulsed and fascinated by the growing speed of its own change. Hence, the fictional representations of the haunted sites of exhumed graves, bulldozed shrines, and the high-rise block in all its anonymous sterility, present revealing attempts to engender distinctly Singaporean Gothic tropes that reflect local preoccupations with development-projects, with submerged or newly conceptualised heritage, and most pointedly, with suppressed aspects of turbulent histories, both on a national and an individual level. The ghosts that materialise in short-stories and novels of post–Independence Singapore simultaneously signify a form of repression and a deliberate stirring up of the past that can become just as threatening. As more and more self-ironically exoticized versions of urban Gothic serve as the backdrop and a leading metaphor of new cultural fictions of the furiously globalising island-state, they thus increasingly translate the cityscape's ongoing renegotiation of a drive for modernisation into unique Gothic scenarios that play out the underlying struggle for a distinctly Singaporean literature.

While drawing on various examples, I shall focus particularly on those texts that critically reflect on or creatively transform the tropes on which they capitalise as part of a larger literary and cultural reformulation. Thus, they take up the by now traditional spookiness of liminal spaces of a fast-moving city and, with markedly self-ironic twists, simultaneously endeavour to fill them in with an often deliberately indeterminate rendition of the "exotic." Their redeployment of such neo-orientalist tropes, we shall see, proves particularly insightful in the contexts of the Singaporean ghost story's remaking of the urban preternatural. Catherine Lim's pointedly titled short-story "Alien" in her collection of ghost stories, *The Howling Silence: Tales of the Dead & Their Return* (1999), evokes Chinese legends and traditional "superstitions" that are shown to resurface in order at once to alienate and to redefine meeting-points of various immigrant cultures. What is most revealing, however, is the self-ironic representation of an imported "Western" or "Westernised" stance that attempts to frame the experience, yet which instead frequently ends up ruptured by it. To an extent, this reinforces the self-consciously neo-orientalist framework. At the same time however, it also casts a different light on the transformation of both the Gothic and the exotic in Singaporean fiction. Gopal Baratham's "Ghost," recently reprinted in *The City of Forgetting* (2001), is perhaps even more poignantly about hybridisation and multiculturalism: the pitfalls of suppressed bigotry become manifest in the ghost of a woman driven to suicide by ethnic barriers. Before exploring in more detail the ways in which these narratives resist and transform the boundaries of urban Gothic, I first seek to clarify both the traditions of the urban ghost story and its ambiguous role in the development of Singaporean literature.

Self-Irony and the Preternatural: Defamiliarizing the City-State

English-language fiction of post–Independence Singapore is, it has widely been acknowledged, firmly rooted in the traditions of the British novel. Philip Holden (2000) writes of the making of the "discipline of English literature" that formed part and parcel of, from the late nineteenth century onwards, the homogenising processes of an intrinsically multiethnic colonial Malaya and Singapore, now the nation-states Malaysia and Singapore. Ismail Talib (2002) and Ann Pakir (1992) have gone further to highlight the impact of post–Independence language policies on literary developments in Britain's former colonies in Southeast Asia. The official bilingualism endorsed as a government policy in Singapore after its split from Malaysia in 1965 unfortunately made the use of English part of an ongoing debate on "Asian values."[1] While English came to be considered a "neutral" language in that it was not explicitly associated with any of the country's neatly stratified ethnic groups (Chinese-Malay-Indian-Other, or CMIO), this also denoted it as a value-free and hence, it has even been suggested, a "value-less" language. In addition, it was still associated with the culture of a former coloniser as well as increasingly with neo-imperialist commercialism.[2] Pakir refers to fears of "Pseudo-Westernisation" or "De-Asianization" that were seen to be turning Singapore into "an extremely soft-shelled community" (247). For English-language writing, grown as it has out of nineteenth-century British (including colonial) fiction, and which moreover importantly dates back to the primarily English-speaking "Straits Chinese" in the region, these discourses expectedly proved extremely damaging. The Queen's (or King's) Chinese of the British Straits Settlements may have published short fiction from the late-nineteenth century onwards, yet this literary legacy came to be seen in conflict with what is now often pointedly reconceptualised as Singapore's stake in postcolonial writing — at least in the context of general discussions of Southeast Asia's contribution to the New Literatures in English.[3]

Local criticism has directed much attention to the problematics of Singapore's long-standing English-language tradition and its connection to colonial modernity. This has nonetheless become complicated by the very pervasiveness of English writing in Singapore itself as well as by the popularity of imported books and genres. Especially, it is important to note, the immensely versatile adaptations of the ghost story that have flooded the local book-market over nearly three decades are more than simply a symptom. They have proved a crucial catalyst for an integration and extension of literary traditions and generic boundaries. This is of central significance especially for the markedly ambiguous function of language itself as both potential gap-bridger and possible hindrance to understanding. In 1984, Kirpal Singh still firmly maintained that "the Singaporean novel" would take a long time coming and that its achievement was doubtful after the hiatus of World War II and postcolonial Singapore's temporary merger with Malaysia (Singh 1984, 11). By contrast, in his introduction to the volume on fiction in the series *Interlogue: Studies in Singaporean Literature*, published in 1998, he criticised the apparently automatic dismissal of local novels such as Z.Y. Moo's *The Weird Diary of Walter Woo* (1990) as suitable texts to teach Gothic literature at high school or undergraduate level, while nevertheless deploring the popularity of ghost stories at the Singaporean book-market (Singh 1998, xiv).

After the undoubtedly popular success of *The Almost Complete Collection of True Singapore Ghost-Stories* (1989) by Russell Lee, the ghost story collection as a genre, in fact, seemed to be the only form of local writing that was widely read throughout the nineties.[4] Similar works quickly traded on the indeed no less than astonishing marketability of short sensational fiction set in urban Singapore. They tellingly ranged from *Death Rites: Tales from a Wake* (1990) by the playwright and academic K.K. Seet to F.J. George's *Teenagers' Ghost-Stories* (1991) or Goh Sin Tub's *Ghosts of Singapore!* (1990), *More Ghosts of Singapore* (1991), *Mass Possession* (1994), or *The Campus Spirit and Other Stories* (1998), in the nineties alone. Catherine Lim had significantly been writing supernatural tales since the early 1980s such as *Or Else the Lightening God and Other Stories* (1980) and *They Do Return* (1983), yet they had primarily been grounded in Chinese folklore and beliefs. The immense popularity of urban ghost stories set in contemporary cityscapes, by contrast, exhibits an emphatically urban spookiness, divorced from any regional tales and only tangentially related to often oddly framed imported traditions from pre-modern China.

This very popularity, moreover, has ironically in itself been seen as problematic with reference to the emergence of a Singaporean English-language canon and therefore in the contexts of literary tradition and value at large. Kirpal Singh early on in the debate voiced his doubts about the value of the ghost story's contribution to Singapore literature: "In reading some of the recent fiction published I am not assured that the direction we are taking is altogether wholesome or qualitatively better" (Singh 1993/94, 21). Thus, he repeatedly referred to "the famous/infamous Ghost Stories" that had "hit on the right formula" to appeal to a mass readership (Singh 1998, xiv). In 1999, in volume ten of his "true ghost stories" series, Russell Lee significantly countered with a snide remark on this love-hate relationship that critics still had with the country's popular writing: "It shouldn't surprise us that there are some Singaporeans who, like Dr Kirpal writes, 'cringe' at what most of us like to read" (Lee 1999, "Author's Note"). This made it particularly significant that two of Singapore's by then already canonical writers both of short tales and some of the country's first novels began to work the supernatural into their novels. While capitalising on a popular trend, partly giving new impetus and credence to it, they made the representation of the supernatural part of the Singaporean canon. In their later writing, moreover, they drew specifically on an urban Gothic.

Catherine Lim and Gopal Baratham had both made their mark primarily with realist short-stories from the seventies or eighties onwards. Their first novels centred on specific points of social criticism that addressed Singapore's political structure, its one-party system, its preoccupation with material success and the emphasis on its display, and more generally, a prevailing pragmatism and materialism. Both Lim's *The Serpent's Tooth* (1982) and Baratham's *A Candle or the Sun* (1991) appeared abroad, published first by Serpent's Tail, while Baratham's was furthermore reprinted by Penguin a year after its initial publication. Specifically the latter was controversial for various reasons. Not only did it reference dissatisfaction with the government, but it was also overtly satirical in its representation of "Asian Values," an issue that was considered a touchy one at best throughout the eighties and nineties. There is of course a double irony in nearly all discourses on the subject, although in particular with reference to its representation in English language-fiction, in that these "values" were Victorian in origin and were then filtered through the English-educated Straits Chinese (Mauzy and Milne 57). Nevertheless, testifying perhaps to the sustained erasure of this legacy, even in Baratham's

controversial novel, the focus of criticism remains on their present-day commodification: in yet another ironic twist that additionally underscores the
complexities of Singapore's early social fiction, this particularly satirical
moment revolves around the manufacture of fake heritage, of the fabricated
relicts of a sanitised history. A sales-manager suggests that they "install traditional Asian values" by selling remade "antique" furniture instead of "Western" products:

> "We must flung [*sic*] out false Western values leading to moral decay, unem-
> ployment and social welfare. No more imitating falsity. Right here in furni-
> ture department," he waved his arm expansively, "we install traditional Asian
> values. Soon we sell antique Chinese furniture — [...]. We manufacture
> cheap," he said. "You mean imitation antique furniture," I suggested. "Mod-
> ern Chinese antiques," he snapped. "Singaporean-manufactured, by skilled
> carpenters" [Baratham 1991, 45].

The passage is of course chiefly comical in its play with the defamiliarization
of marketable pasts that was later to become central to the Singaporean
Gothic. Yet it is important to recognize that this had been an acknowledged
cliché in Singaporean fiction, a cliché that could then form the basis of a
mundane that harboured the supernatural. What is more, in its identification
of materialism and "more than a simple sinophilia [as] modernisation, capit-
ulation to the mass market" (Baratham 1991, 46), *A Candle or the Sun* res-
onated well with the popular image of Singapore abroad when it was published
in the early nineties. Much has consequently been made of its significance as
a mouthpiece of social criticism. Peter Wicks has called it a "political fable
of conspiracy and intrigue [that] attracted considerable public comment"—
an apt description of much of Singapore's early postcolonial fiction (75–76).
Leong Liew Geok has similarly stressed the extent to which such writing has
been "forcibly redirected in its course by politics" to give rise to self-consciously dissenting voices (2000, 285).[5] The confines of purely social-realist
and material-historical readings of postcolonial literature can, however, be
limiting to a reading of texts that do not necessarily fall within any specific
(nationalist, postcolonial) agenda. As Andrew Ng (2007) has highlighted in
his recent work on Gothic aesthetics, it is vital to move away from these paradigms. A reassessment of the Gothic and its adaptations can crucially facilitate a critical apparatus to read postcolonial literature anew to discover
neglected aspects that have ironically been obfuscated by strategies aimed to
bring it to critical attention in the first place.

What is more, while Baratham and likewise Lim, from her tellingly titled
short-story collection *Little Ironies: Stories of Singapore* of 1978 onwards, have
always been effective in invoking considerable irony, their later works have

expanded social analysis to engage more extensively with the fissures not only of widely promoted value-systems, but of counter-ideological thrusts as well. The defamiliarization produced by a sudden introduction of the supernatural or mythological within the confines of a realist narrative brings this out the most forcefully. Hence, Baratham and Lim both introduced preternatural elements into their second novels, respectively *Moonrise, Sunset* and *The Bondmaid* (both 1995). Lim moreover straddled the romance genre in a colonial setting. In its invocation of "a little dilapidated shrine in the way of a three-hundred-million dollar industrial development project" (Lim 1995, n.p.), the framestory of *The Bondmaid* thus outlines the eponymous heroine's transformation into popular legend. It throws up an exoticized past that is physically erased from the cityscape: "Today, a huge petrochemical complex stands where once the strange goddess with eyes and ears dispensed miracles" (Lim 1995, n.p.). Where there once was a multiplicity of temples, shrines, or traditional mansions, there is now only a generic urban landscape characterised by government housing, office-blocks, mega-malls, and industrial sites. Yet even as the evoked nostalgia implies a tentative critique of neo-imperialism and the government policies that help to promote it, such an emotional investment in retrospect remains curiously muted. There is almost a sense of relief that the legacies of past tragedies are thus curtailed, even though it may be a loss to the country's heritage. The preternatural is safely contained by the sanitisation of inner-city space.[6]

It is in revealing contrast that *The Serpent's Tooth* has symptomatically little to say on the spaces of the past. A realist novel that aims to criticise the society of the time (the 1980s), it pays into a dismissal of "superstitions" even while it satirises the forward-looking attitudes that have caused such cultural amnesia in the first place: "that the blocks near Ghim Moh were built over a hilly Hakka [a Chinese dialect group] burial site" is easily and all too quickly reduced to urban legend: "But soon, the unusual story that the bricks of the estate were set on vacated tombs would only be legend" (Lim 1982, 33). It is, however, precisely such submerged histories that later sparked off a new, disconcertingly neo-orientalist, curiosity. Lim's *The Bondmaid, The Teardrop-Story Woman* (1998), and *The Song of Silver Frond* (2003) are historical romances that trade on buried mysteries. In the latter, the exhumation of the heroine's grave in "an ongoing exercise of the government to reclaim land for residential and industrial use, [...] valuable land, marked for the development of a Science and Technology Park," negotiates just such revived interest: in a list of a descendant's failed literary enterprises, she has become "the subject of some short-stories, a poem and even a play" with the "play (which never made it to the stage)" revolving on "three generations of women, in a country somewhere in Asia" (Lim 2003, 327 and 325).

It is noteworthy that Lim's novel that touches most centrally on present-day concerns gives most credit to supernatural elements. They are articulated by an old servant's visions of her homeless, nameless god: Lim's tellingly titled *Following the Wrong God Home* (2001) takes the relocation of a "god-with-no-home" as the guiding-motif itself. But if the razing down of a "tiny bit of useless land, tucked away in some obscure part of the island, covered with *lallang* grass" (Lim 2001, 65), yet which comes to stand in the way of building-projects, once again literalises the breaking in of modernisation and pragmatism into the dwindling spaces of the traditional and the supernatural, it is nevertheless somewhat disconcerting that a beautiful Chinese woman's poetry on her servant's god primarily serves to attract the attention of a foreign exchange-lecturer. The titular motif threatens to fragment into an "East-West-conflict" articulated through a convergence of adultery and the adulteration of literature. Most importantly, like Lim's colonial romances, it becomes couched in a "Western" interrogative framework. Just such framing has been diagnosed as the exploration of "a traditional, ethnically grounded female consciousness and sensibility, female identity [...] in relation to a network of cross-cultural, international sites" (Leong 2002, 241). Yet it intriguingly puts a different spin on representations of Singapore's ghosts as well. They form embodiments of different traditions, manifestations of family anecdotes and the dread of the housing-estate's anonymity. In the density of the high-rise apartment-blocks, you may inherit the ghosts of any stranger's past. In order to understand better the amalgamation of traditions that become a subject of interest in fiction itself, it is therefore important to consider first the urban ghost story's literary legacies as well as the significance of their transformation.

Framing Local Gothic

In his recent study of urban Gothic in nineteenth-century literature, Julian Wolfreys has convincingly argued that the spectre of modernity manifests itself in apparitions of an "uncontrollable spectral economy," a "spectralisation of the gothic": "Exorcised from its haunted houses, the spectral-gothic takes on its most *unheimlich* aspects," as its "recirculation" manifests itself "in ever stranger articulations of revenant alterity" (Wolfreys 7–11). In Victorian representations of such unhomely city-spaces, this urban Gothic indeed became registered as a new development, tied up with the emergence of modernity. The slippage between the urban and a domestic realm defined against an "outside world"—what Ruskin so poignantly termed, in his in *Sesame and Lilies* (1865), "that outer life" that was seen to penetrate "the true nature of home" (1905, 122) — engendered the juxtaposition of the domestic and the disconcertingly unfamiliar, what came to be conceptualised as the "unhomely" or "uncanny." In her study of narratives of residential areas and the apartment block in nineteenth-century Paris and London, Sharon Marcus similarly speaks of spectral eruptions that accompany domestic disruption as they broadcast the urban deformation of the domestic ideal (122).[7] The trope of the haunted house functions as an epitome of urban modernity.[8]

Recent Singaporean representations of the haunted housing-estate constitute a unique engagement with the Gothic poetics (as outlined by Wolfreys and Marcus) in their reflections on the encroachment of architectural modernity, they articulate the same concerns as the Victorian variants do, but when it comes to the location of an often indeterminately defined "exotic" space, the reworking becomes additionally significant. The necessary inversion of the alignment between the exotic and "the other," including specifically the preternatural or monstrous, suggests that local preoccupations form the subject of the authors' explorations of the preternatural. Its framing by a "Western," or "Westernised," gaze therein often functions as a double exploration of the traditional paradigms (Gothic included) of English-language fiction in the region and their neo-orientalist repackaging.

The opening story of Lim's *Howling Silence*, "Great-grandfather with Teeth," perhaps most explicitly turns on the "Westernised" first person narrator's speculation on the neo-orientalist exotic with which he wishes to impress a significantly imagined rapt American audience. Even before the encounter with his ancestor's ghost in a condemned shop-house, a relic symptomatically "soon to be torn down to make way for a gleaming shopping complex" (Lim 1999, 7), he indulges in anticipations of being able to export an authentic tale of a twofold exotic: insight into the tropical and the spooky at the same time. On holidays from his studies abroad, he suddenly exhibits an eager interest in the dilapidated, now deserted, family home. It is made clear that it is an interest developed abroad. His motivation is presented with marked self-irony; the expected narrative already mapped out neatly in italics before the event:

> I relished the prospect when back in the States after my vacation, of tantalising my college mates, especially my room-mate, Bryan Roberts, a dry, cynical Business Studies student, with a cool, detailed description of "My Adventures in the Haunted Ancestral Home."
>
> *I spent a night with the spirits of my forbearors, apologising sincerely, on behalf of the Singapore Urban Redevelopment Authority, for the rude expulsion from their home, and promising to help them, in whatever way I could, in their*

resettlement in a new home. On behalf of the government, I offered at least a
million dollars in compensation, burning ten stacks of ghost money until every-
thing was properly reduced to ashes [8–9, author's emphasis].

This passage suggests a mixture of the encitingly, vaguely defined, exotic and
the neo-orientalist cliché of the expanding Asian city. The narrator relishes
the retelling of what he identifies as "authenticity of detail" to be appreciated,
if not verified, by his "Western friends": "Indeed, I was elated at the thought
of having a real supernatural experience, one actually independent of my
imagination, that I could later narrate to my Western friends in every authenticity of detail" (10). Yet, as the story unfolds, this self-orientalization ultimately collapses into a rethinking of family histories. The appearance of his
grandfather's toothless ghost changes his image of the tyrannical patriarch as
a threat to subsequent generations to a more ambiguous attitude towards the
complexities of family history. The brief glimpse of the ghost proves a much
cited family anecdote of a much feared grandfather polishing his impressive
teeth to be biased, if not completely untrue. While this effectively exorcises
the ghost, the narrative is curiously open-ended. The visitor from "the West"
remains at a loss as to what to do with his experience. What is clear, however, is that it has failed to serve as the anticipated exotic tale.

The stories collected in *Howling Silence*, in fact, play with the framework of the marketable exotic, sensational, tale that is then refused or replaced.
In "Song of Mina," a prostitute's apparition is dismissed as an eccentric tale
of no publishable value, rejected by a newspaper's editor in favour of a possible piece on the overgrown, aged, female pimp who relates it, an ex-pros-
titute who would nicely feature as part of "a frank series of articles on 'the
other side' of Singapore. I'll keep my Mina story for myself" (27). It is not
at all that the sensational "other side" of streamlined Singapore that is erased
by the editor, but the search is for the sordid side of present-day shadiness,
not for an exoticization of an ethereal prostitute with a "red flower in her hair"
(28). It is similarly significant that the ghost appears in what is described, with
a parodic evocation of excessive hyphenation, as "an old, crumbling, two-
storeyed hotel-brothel" (25), exhibiting a double function in luring in the
sojourner in search of the exotic. The reporter himself, "always on the prowl
for interesting stories" (26), is intrigued. The end of the story sees him con-
templating a visit to the ghostly prostitute; the pimp having the final word
of warning: "'I wouldn't, if I were you,' says Bunga Mas with a shudder"
(30).

Most of the narratives in the collection indeed shuttle between various
traditions of the supernatural by filtering the revisiting of marginalised spaces
through a "Western" lens. Lim's "Alien," however, does something significantly

different. In a multiplication of alterities that explodes any neat dichotomies of the "Western" and the "local," the gaze of "the other" that defamiliarizes representations of the seemingly mundane is that of "an engineer from Madras, India, with the status of Permanent Resident in Singapore" (78). The congratulatory stance of the opening sentence is already suspect in its emphasis on orderliness, which does not bode well in the context of a ghost story's promise of the disorderliness of ruptured realms: the eponymous "alien" settles in Singapore "enticed [by] the city-state's cleanliness, orderliness and ambitious commitment to the goal of front position among the world's most technologically advanced, successful, prosperous and gracious societies in the twenty-first century" (78). Yet it is thanks to prevailing superstitions that he, "an alien, can afford to own an apartment in this unique country" (78). Such uniqueness clearly is not meant as a positive trait. The flat turns out to be the site of "the most systematically carried out murder-cum-suicide, planned to the last detail and meticulously recorded, in advance" (80). It is the result of an excess of the methodological: a father has systematically killed his three sons, his wife, and then himself; with even the customary tribute to the dead arranged in advance. Chinese tradition is delineated as part of an official report read by a recent immigrant, who is moreover most puzzled by the "scrupulous preparations" preceding this unscrupulous act:

> There was an altar on which stood a framed formal picture of the family, with offerings of candles, tea and oranges set neatly before it. According to the report, the candles were still burning when the bodies were discovered. The Jek family massacre was probably the only instance in the annals of suicide in Singapore where scrupulous preparations had included paying advance respect to one's own dead self [81].

It is not merely that meticulous planning is taken to its logical conclusion, but that it also turns out to have been faulty. In a general complacency of arranging even for the afterlife, something has been forgotten, and hence the haunting commences. In an additional spin, the apparitions of the three murdered children are Chinese and therefore their customs are alien to the narrator: "The ghosts of the Jek family were becoming a problem. An Indian would know nothing about appeasing Chinese ghosts" (83). It is a pointed, almost parodic, manifestation of Singapore's multiethnic legacies and the need for cross-cultural communication: "I wanted to do whatever Chinese people do to get rid of the ghosts from their houses" (84). Ultimately, he discovers the murdered sons' dried umbilical cords left behind in a drawer. They had been kept by the children's parents according to Chinese tradition, and in an endorsement of the beliefs attached to this custom, they need to be burnt to be reunited with the dead in the afterlife. This exorcism ends with an embrace of the relics of a different culture.[9] The engineer from Madras decides to keep the piece of furniture that held the umbilical cords, preserving the memory of the dead children. What is particularly significant in this context is that where the consulted traditional temple mediums fail, the Indian's decision "to appeal to the ghosts directly"—in English—provides a suitable conduit:

> I spoke aloud, in English which I hoped they would understand; after all, it is the working language in Singapore and the language of communication among its diverse ethnic groups. Besides, communication between ghosts and humans supposedly transcends language and culture. So I, an Indian, spoke in English to three little Chinese ghosts [86].

This invocation of English as a working language, a language of communication that transcends boundaries, approaches the comical. Yet after this appeal, the overlooked piece of furniture is suddenly rendered visible. The haunting of the flat and its exorcism through the use of English, however parodic the release itself may be, achieve a bridging of gaps. In other words, "Alien" addresses the presence of "the other" in an importantly different and hence particularly revealing way. Nevertheless, while such an engagement with the meeting of traditions is a common feature in Singaporean Gothic, this happy solution stands out. Baratham's "Ghost," in marked contrast, evinces the reverse narrative of just such a neatly solved problem of communication. Finding their plans of a "mixed marriage" denounced as simply "not a practical proposition today," the descendants of Indian and Chinese immigrants to Singapore face the hypocrisy of a markedly superficial concept of multiracialism premised on the separateness of ethnic groups and their retention of difference (Baratham 2001, 320). The universality that has so far informed the young couple's discussions is exploded in the face of familial conflict. Tolerance stops at home: "We face a tight personal problem. One to which we are so close that we will never be able to generalise on the experience we gain from it" (324). The merely instrumental use of English as a language detached from ethnically (or linguistically) defined values itself renders it ineffective in countering bigotry:

> "You say that you and Cheng are Singaporeans?"
> "Yes," Leela answered with eyes downcast.
> "Do his parents speak to each other in English or in Chinese?"
> "They speak in their dialect, Hokkien."
> "And Cheng speaks to them...?"
> "Sometimes in English. Sometimes in Hokkien."
> "Just as mother and I always talk to each other in Tamil and you occasionally speak to us in Tamil. [...] And you still don't see the difference between your marrying a Tamil and ... a non–Tamil?" [319–20].

Their separation, eventually effected by Cheng's pragmatic choice of further studies abroad — an admitted bribe by his equally bigoted father — causes Leela's death. Her suicide involves sucking off the sugary coating of the bitter pills that epitomise the realities of such severance. Sleeping pills clearly are not alone in being sugar-coated or outwardly colourful in a society that practices a "boutique multiculturalism" targeted at the tourist industry, but which at the same time ensures that intermarriage remains problematic. Leela's suicide is moreover the only scene that is confined to a private space within the high-rise apartment-block in Singapore. It is the single moment of individual retreat in a story that is otherwise heavily structured by dialogue, and especially dialogue that is invoked as representative of prevailing social prejudices. Consuming colourful poison suggests the allure of escape from grey reality through death. But it is also an individual's deliberate action in a repressive society: "Leela placed the sleeping tablets on the table beside her bed. They made a rather eye-catching collection: pale blues, gentle pinks, tiny sinister sugarcoated affairs and a variety of rather grandiose bicoloured capsules" (316). The haunting of the lover reflects this one bright moment — it is an aesthetically pleasing, instead of frightening, experience. A mysterious bright light casts a spell on the mundane: "A long golden light flooded the school playground. The prancing of the schoolboys on the playground acquired the quality of a ballet" (326). Cheng, alone and depressed abroad, is enchanted: "their prancing in the golden light produced in him a surprising and totally inexplicable sense of happiness" (326). Life is momentarily lit up, and yet this remains just another camouflage, another sugar-coating that masks nausea.

The result is an urban Gothic of the nauseatingly mundane, of death-in-life literalized in the concealed spaces of anonymous apartment-blocks, divorced from the mysteries of neo-orientalist searches for personal heritage. The contemporary Singaporean ghost story, in fact, strives to integrate urban spookiness into broader social critiques by focusing on different forms of the liminal: on in-between spaces that throw up ruptures in the seemingly so neatly stratified cityscape. Most importantly, in its renegotiation of traditional urban Gothic, its Singaporean reworking at the same time pays tribute to (and plays with) anxieties of influence and the strictures of self-consciously "re-presenting" the multiethnic nation-state as well as the globalising island-city. The micropolitics of the family that had already set up the domestic Gothic in nineteenth-century narratives are made to incorporate the escalating movements and spins of an all too flexible, mobile, social body. The endorsement of mobility, in other words, is not quite digestible. It generates a wealth of nightmares that, in turn, offers opportunities for a new, specific Gothic.

Notes

1. In 1959 Singapore became a self-governing colony; in 1965 it achieved independence after two years in the Federation of Malaysia.

2. This ethnic stratification, a colonial legacy in itself, has received much criticism for artificially enhancing divisiveness and practicing a neo-orientalism targeted primarily at the tourist industry (Chua 28–50; PuruShotam 207).

3. The Straits Chinese form a culture unique to the region, which originated in intermarriages between Chinese merchants and Malay or Burmese women in colonial Southeast Asia over the centuries. Their cultural and political importance ensured their central significance to the development of English-language fiction (Wagner ch. 1).

4. It was a "runaway bestseller of the Singapore book fair '89," as the description on the book cover now proudly announces. It has spawned an entire series, all published under the pseudonym of Russell Lee. Published locally, these chiefly anecdotal narratives proclaim to be true accounts of preternatural sightings or occurrences in Singapore. Compare also Wagner (308–311). Clery's discussion of the rise of literacy and the problematic status of the supernatural tale in eighteenth-century Britain (7 and ch. 6) similarly sheds light on current ambivalent attitudes towards the popularity of ghost stories in Singapore.

5. Such social-problems-novels of the nineties notably include numerous first novels such as Baratham's *A Candle or the Sun* and Philip Jeyaretnam's highly political *Abraham's Promise* (1995), yet Leong also focuses on Suchen Christine Lim's *Fistful of Colours* (1993), the first Singapore Literature Prize Winner, which extends the social critique of Lim's *Rice Bowl* (1984).

6. Spanning Singapore's history as a colonial port-city and its occupation by the Japanese in World War II, *The Bondmaid* ultimately shows the past effectively exorcised. As I have shown in detail elsewhere, *Moonrise, Sunset*, by contrast, is a comic thriller, a detective story with a local setting (Wagner 2005). Its ghost has more affinities with the kindly spectres of recent Hollywood comedy than with either local or imported traditions of supernatural tales.

7. Drawing on Freud's conceptualisation of the uncanny, Anthony Vidler similarly investigates an important "slippage between what seems homely and what is definitively unhomely" (ix-x). The uncanny, Vidler argues, links the "unstable nature of 'house and home' [to] questions of social and individual estrangement, alienation, exile, and homelessness" (ix). Freud seminally linked the *heimlich* [homely] to the *unheimlich* [uncanny] in his essay on "The Uncanny": "there is a doubling, dividing and interchanging of the self" in uncanny experiences, pointing to the displacement of the *heimlich*, the origin, the lost first home of the womb (234). However, as colonial as well as domestic writing of the nineteenth century undoubtedly played with the "exotic" potentials of the Gothic uncanny, precisely the simultaneity of the *heimlich* and the *unheimlich* gave rise to new potentials for postcolonial inversion that then ruptured national as well as (or commonly instead of) the customary domestic alignments. As Homi Bhabha reminds us in his introduction to *Nation and Narration*, "the *heimlich* pleasures of the hearth" and "the *unheimlich* terror of the space or race of the Other" are complementary sides of the same coin, making clear the one-sidedness of "imagined communities" (2).

8. Imperialist and orientalist metaphors indeed form part and parcel of Victorian representations of the supernatural. Brantlinger (1988) conceptualizes imperialist Gothic as a specific development. Especially the suburban Gothic, it has recently been argued, shares central preoccupations as well as metaphorical linkages with colonial writing (Cunningham 431; Kuchta 173). But it is the orientalist references in domestic and urban Gothic that I am concerned with here.

9. In a similar vein, one of the most gruesome stories in Lim's collection, "Temple of the Little Ghosts," features the ghost of an aborted fetus. A stereotyping of a more licentious "West" and its engagement with "pro-life" agenda are interwoven with ancient Chinese beliefs in the ghosts of the unborn.

Works Cited

Baratham, Gopal. 1991. *A Candle or the Sun*. London/New York: Serpent's Tail.

———. 1996. *Moonrise, Sunset*. London/New York: Serpent's Tail.

———. 2001. *The City of Forgetting: The Collected Stories of Gopal Baratham*. Singapore: Times Books International.

Bhabha, Homi, ed. 1990. *Nation and Narration*. London/New York: Routledge.

Brantlinger, Patrick. 1988. *Rule of Darkness: British Literature and Imperialism, 1830–1914.* Ithaca: Cornell University Press.

Chua, Beng Huat. 1998. "Racial-Singaporeans: Absence after the Hyphen," in *Southeast Asian Identities: Culture and the Politics of Representation in Indonesia, Malaysia, Singapore, and Thailand,* ed. Joel S. Khan. London: IB Tauris, 28–50.

Clery, E.J. 1995. *The Rise of Supernatural Fiction, 1762–1800.* Cambridge: Cambridge University Press.

Cunningham, Gail, 2004. "Houses in Between: Navigating Suburbia in Late Victorian Writing," *Victorian Literature and Culture,* 32. 2: 421–34.

Freud, Sigmund. 1995. *Works.* Edited by James Strachey and Anna Freud, et al. London: Hogarth.

Holden, Philip. 1996. *Orienting Masculinity, Orienting Nation: W. Somerset Maugham's Exotic Fiction.* Westport: Greenwood.

Kuchta, Todd. 2005. "Semi-Detached Empire: Suburbia and Imperial Discourse in Victorian and Edwardian Britain." *Nineteenth-Century Prose,* 32, no. 2: 163–98.

Lee, Russell. 1989. *The Almost Complete Collection of True Singapore Ghost-Stories.* Singapore: Flame of the Forest Pte Ltd.

_____. 1999. *The Almost Complete Collection of True Singapore Ghost-Stories. Book 10.* Singapore: Angsana Books.

Leong, Liew Geok. 2000. "Dissenting Voices: Political Engagements in the Singaporean Novel in English," *World Literature Today: A Literary Quarterly of the University of Oklahoma,* 74. 2: 285–92.

_____. 2002. "Situating Gender, Evolving Identities: Women in Four Novels by Catherine Lim and Christine Lim," in *Singaporean Literature in English: A Critical Reader,* eds. M.A. Quayum and Peter Wicks, 241–251.

Lim, Catherine. 1982. *The Serpent's Tooth.* Singapore: Times Books International.

_____. 1995. *The Bondmaid.* London: Orion.

_____. 1999. *The Howling Silence: Tales of the Dead & Their Return.* Singapore: Horizon Books.

_____. 2001. *Following the Wrong God Home.* London: Orion.

_____. 2003. *The Song of Silver Frond.* London: Orion.

Marcus, Susan. 1999. *Apartment Stories: City and Home in Nineteenth-Century Paris and London.* Berkeley: University of California Press.

Mauzy, D.K, and R.S. Milne. 2002. *Singapore Politics Under the People's Action Party.* London/New York: Routledge.

Ng, Andrew. 2007. *Interrogating Interstices: Gothic Aesthetics in Postcolonial Asian and Asian American Literature.* New York/London: Peter Lang.

Pakir, Anne. 1992. "English-Knowing Bilingualism in Singapore," in *Imagining Singapore.* Edited by Ban Kah Choon. Singapore: Times Academic Press, pp. 234–249.

PuruShotam, Nirmala Srirekam. 1998. *Negotiating Language, Constructing Race: Disciplining Difference in Singapore.* Berlin: Mouton de Gruyter.

Quayum, Mohammad A. and Peter Wicks. 2002. *Singaporean Literature in English: A Critical Reader.* Serdang: Universiti Putra Malaysia.

Ruskin, John. 1905. *Works.* Edited by E.T. Cook and Alexander Wedderburn. London: George Allen.

Singh, Kirpal. 1984. "An Approach to Singapore Writing in English," *Ariel,* 15.2: 5–24.

_____. 1993/94. "Singapore Fiction in English: Some Reflections." *Singapore Book World,* 23: 21–23.

_____. 1998. "Introduction," in *Interlogue: Studies in Singaporean Literature, Volume 1: Fiction.* Edited by Kirpal Singh. Singapore: Ethos Books, xi–xv.

Talib, Ismail. 2002. "The Development of Singaporean Literature in English," in *Singaporean Literature in English: A Critical Reader,* eds. M.A. Quayum and Peter Wicks, 1–11.

Vidler, Anthony. 1992. *The Architectural Uncanny: Essays in the Modern Unhomely.* Cambridge, MA: MIT Press.

Wagner, Tamara S. 2005. *Occidentalism in Novels of Malaysia and Singapore, 1819–2004: Colonial and Postcolonial Financial Straits and Literary Style.* Lewiston, NY: Edwin Mellen.

Wicks, Peter. 2002. "Singapore, Literature and Identity," in *Singaporean Literature in English: A Critical Reader.* Edited by M.A. Quayum and Peter Wicks, 73–80.

Wolfreys, Julian. 2002. *Victorian Hauntings: Spectrality, Gothic, the Uncanny and Literature.* Basingstoke: Palgrave.

4

Seeing Through the Evil Eye: Meiling Jin's Caribbean Counter-Gothic in *Gifts from My Grandmother*

Paula K. Sato

Meiling Jin was born in British Guiana in 1956; however, she moved to England with her family at the age of eight. Her autobiographical poem "Strangers in a hostile landscape," from her 1986 collection *Gifts from My Grandmother,* briefly recounts the history of the Chinese in the British colony on the Caribbean coast of South America. Her poetic "I" speaks of her Chinese grandfather who traveled to the Caribbean on "the ship Red-riding Hood" (18, ll. 28–29), recalling a boat christened *Red Riding Hood* that sailed to the enclave from Canton with three hundred and eleven Chinese in 1860, three hundred and ten in 1861, and three hundred and twenty-four in 1862 (Sue-A-Quan 1). Approximately 13,500 Chinese, mainly contract laborers, arrived in the British colony from 1853 to 1879 following the abolition of slavery in the British West Indies in 1838 (Look Lai 1–20).[1] In 1964, Jin and her family moved to England to escape the social and political unrest in their soon-to-be-independent West Indian country (Jin 8, 19).[2] The barbed and unsettling reception she received in England and her ensuing loss of personhood are reflected in her poem and are constant themes throughout her collection, a testimony to the hardships faced by

61

England's Caribbean immigrants of color in the latter half of the twentieth century.[3]

For Jin's poetic "I" the loss of personhood, which she refers to as "soul loss" (71), occurs when she gazes into a mirror only to find that her reflection is missing in one instance and that it is frighteningly distorted in another. The mirror is English literature. The poet's quest to recover her lost soul takes her to roads already explored by African American and Caribbean writers who offer a counterpoint to Gothic conventions through various strategies of "haunting back." The trope is one that Joseph Bodziock uses in 2004 to refer to the way Frederick Douglass, in his autobiography *My Bondage and My Freedom* (1855), locates the source of Gothic horror in the dominant white culture rather than in his own demonized, racialized body (Bodziock 255–256). Bodziock borrows the term from Teresa Goddu who uses it in 1997 in reference to Harriet Jacobs' refusal in her slave narrative *Incidents in the Life of a Slave Girl* (1861) to remain slavery's silent victim.[4] In addition to haunting back in a fashion analogous to Douglass and Jacobs by locating white England as the source of her horror and by bearing witness to that horror, Jin also does so in a manner that situates her within an emerging body of Caribbean writers. These writers simultaneously embrace the stereotypes that the West attaches to their bodies — stereotypes that demonize them as the monstrous Other — and transform those stereotypes into the very evidence of their humanity. In a similar manner, Jin transforms the monstrous Otherness of her poet persona into the concomitant site of emergence of the Sino-Caribbean-British subject.

Haunting Back

In the final poem of *Gifts from My Grandmother* titled "Grandmother Ho," there is a nostalgic recollection of an irrecoverable past as the poet mourns the absence of her grandmother's many memories from the books that she (the poet) has read: "I wish I had paid attention then, / to her memories [...] / Instead of filling my head with books, / And she never was in any book" (79, ll. 16–20). The sad recognition of her grandmother's non-presence in English literature is coupled with the poet's identification with that lacuna and with her recognition of it as the legacy passed down to her from her grandmother through her mother: "I see her in my mother sometimes, / I see her now in me" (79, ll. 24–25). Paradoxically, what the poet sees is absence. In her introduction to the collection, Jin speaks of another such nonappearance as she underscores the necessity of fighting to speak; otherwise, others —

white sociologists, anthropologists, historians, ideologists, and poets — will speak for her and will occlude her point of view with theirs (7). The void about which she speaks is one she assigns herself the task of filling through the insertion of her voice into English literature. However, her path is fraught with obstacles: "It's as if, I am hurling myself against an enormous concrete wall," she writes; "the only dent being to my head" (7). This is because the English language, in which she finds the equation of whiteness with the pure, and darkness with the foreboding, the color schema found in conventional Gothic literature, is a "straight jacket" that hinders her self-expression (10). Nevertheless, as we shall see, similar to the authors of African American slave narratives and autobiography, Jin will find a way to subvert Gothic connotations of color in order to reflect her experience in a manner that is more historically accurate than it otherwise would have been.

When Jin's persona in "Strangers in a hostile landscape" travels from the Caribbean to dangerous white England, her text both counters and echoes Joseph Conrad's tale of horror *Heart of Darkness* in which Marlow travels from England into the dark heart of the African jungle (Conrad 60–62; Jin, "Strangers in a hostile landscape" 17–20, ll. 3, 80, 93 and "One of Many" 31, ll. 15–17). Even as she moves in the opposite direction (south to north) from Conrad's narrator/protagonist, she draws inspiration from Marlow's inversion of the conventional civilized north and barbarous south in his account of the perilous journey of the first-century A.D. Romans who entered the utter "darkness" of the untamed territory known today as England — that "mysterious wilderness" of what was stirring "in the hearts of wild men" (19–21). Jin's poem "No more fighting" parallels Marlow's discourse when ashen Britain in the north becomes the haunter and its people of color from the south the haunted as "Gwei lo [white ghost]" comes to take their children away (35, ll. 5–13). The evil British apparition that threatens the immigrant Chinese British "We" is also an arresting reversal of the haunting invasion of good England by a demonic Eastern presence that forms the basic plot of both Bram Stoker's *Dracula* and Sax Rohmer's *The Insidious Dr. Fu-Manchu*. In a similar inversion of conventional notions of East and West, in the poem "Mani in the asylum," Mani's face is "contorted by fear" because he has been brutalized in England. However, the poet "dreams" that his face gazes "peacefully out" at the "Eastern Hills[...]. Watching and waiting / For the Hills to move" (53, ll. 1–5, 29–30), countering the illustration of the yellow peril commissioned by Kaiser Wilhelm II and printed in London's *Morning Post* on November 11, 1895. As the drawing's accompanying description explains, the nations of civilized Christian Europe, allegorized as women dressed in warrior's mails, look over their "peaceful landscapes" to the East from whence the "threatening" figure of a Buddha approaches, the Asian "idol" who sits in ominous "clouds of calamity" that are "twisting," like Mani's own visage, "into the form of hellish distorted faces" (in Hindle 195–196, 228). However, Mani is the *victim* of panic; whereas the yellow peril and its fomenting, mountainous clouds threaten to spawn insanity.[5] In her subversion of the Kaiser's imagined yellow peril, Jin reveals England to be the author of Mani's horror and madness, and the Eastern Hills to be the source of his peace.

In the poem "Soul loss," Jin's persona is haunted by another "demon" which she takes to "aping" (71, l. 16), her action of imitation recalling both a line from the collection's Introduction, in which Jin refers to the Wordsworthian expression that haunts her own, and to the poem "I get around," in which Jin's persona parrots back a British woman's stereotypes of the Chinese. Both mimetic instances lead me to interpret the demon that the poet imitates as English literature and the English imagination. Together the latter steal the poet's soul, causing her personhood and voice to disappear from their pages, leaving only the empty outline of her body: "When i was a child / a demon came / and stole my soul / all he left was an empty shell" (71, ll. 5–8). The rest of the poem is the poet's quest to recover her lost soul: "i wandered around," no doubt lonely as cloud, "looking for the demon / looking for my soul" (71, ll. 9–12).[6] When the poet finally locates and springs on the demon literature/imagination, he swallows her soul, metaphorically swallowing her perspective into his own. Nevertheless, in the poem's final verse, the poet reverses the action, ingesting the demon in turn, thus swallowing his perspective into her own: "i teetered on the brink / of despair / and ate him" (72, ll. 34–36). Her final action is a metaphor of her ultimate recuperation of her lost voice on the pages of the English literature that had once denied her expression. As we shall see, her insertion of her voice into that literature will be counterintuitively coupled with her embracing of the role of the Gothic Other through her appropriation of the Gothic evil eye.

Caribbean Counterpoint

There is hardly a Gothic tale in which some form of the evil eye does not appear. In Conrad's *Heart of Darkness* the recurring memory of an eerie suspicion troubles the embedded English narrator — the impression that a mysterious, brooding African jungle "looked at [him] with a vengeful aspect" (49). The African jungle's otherworldly, enigmatic gaze haunts the reader as well, as the latter instinctively identifies with Marlow who recounts in the first person, "I felt often its mysterious stillness watching me" (50). Similarly,

Englishman Jonathan Harker, in his journal dated 30 June, writes that Dracula's glowing red orbs "fell full upon me, with all their blaze of basilisk horror"— another haunting first-person narration of the Gothic evil eye (Stoker 43, 54). However, reversing the roles of haunted speaker and haunting gaze, the persona in Jin's "Strangers in a hostile landscape" vows, also in the first person, to haunt white England with her vengeful regard after her death: "and when I die[...]. / Only my eyes will remain / to watch and to haunt, / and to turn your dreams / to chaos" (20, ll. 109, 112–115). As a child, Jin memorized parts of Samuel Taylor Coleridge's "The Rime of the Ancient Mariner," in which corpses lie about sinisterly, a spine-chilling curse in their eye, as they direct an avenging glare at the seaman whose murder of the albatross provoked their untimely death (Jin 10; Coleridge 31, ll. 249–252). Thus, Coleridge's Gothic poem was a likely inspiration for the posthumous, havoc-wreaking gaze of Jin's persona. However, her haunting eyes have also another literary antecedent in Rohmer's *The Insidious Dr. Fu-Manchu*, in part because the Chinese fiend's *oculi* emanate a "reptilian gaze [...] which must haunt" the English narrator's "dreams forever"; but also because their "certain filminess," similar to "the *membrane nictitans* in a bird," a grotesque magnification or extension of the epicanthic fold, makes them hyperbolically Asian (72, 168). Among these texts, Jin's remains exceptional in that in it the speaker is the subject, rather than the object, of the evil eye's threatening gaze; and her poem is unusual in that its poet speaks from the position of the Gothic Other.

In Ruth Bienstock Anolik's definition, the Gothic Other is the dark, mysterious, and fearful unknown that Gothic literature represents as the inhuman, supernatural, uncontrollable, incomprehensible, and monstrous (1–2). Although uncommon in English Gothic literature, Jin's vision of the world, refracted through the lens of the monstrous evil eye, resonates with a number of textual identifications by an emerging body of canonical Caribbean writers. Focalizing her third-person narration in her abolitionist novel *Sab* from the perspective of a mulatto slave and social pariah, Cuban novelist Gertrudis Gómez de Avellaneda (1841) concomitantly models that eponymous hero after the monstrous creature in Mary Shelley's classic *Frankenstein*. I see the middle section of Shelley's novel, written in the voice of the Monster who paints himself in a human light, as a precursor to the Caribbean's self-representations as the monstrous Other (see Shelley, 92–128 [Chapters XI–XVI]). Similarly, Gabriel García Márquez, who qualifies his northern Colombian culture as Caribbean on numerous pages of his autobiography *Vivir para contarla* (2002), also writes from the point of view of traditional objects of Gothic horror— the living corpse, the buried alive, and the ghost — in his Kafkaesque marvelous realist third-person short stories "La tercera resignación (1947),

"La otra costilla de la muerta" (1948), and "Eva está dentro de su gato" (1948), respectively. As a final example in this non-exhaustive list, in the marvelous realist novel *Moi, Tutuba, Sorcière... Noire de Salem*, by Guadeloupean writer Maryse Condé (1986), the narrative voice belongs to the ghost of a black slave who was tried as a witch during the infamous Salem trials.

Lizabeth Paravisini-Gebert (23, 254–255) reasons that the Caribbean's appropriations and reinventions of the Gothic Other are the consequence of its having learned "to read 'itself' in literature [...] as the frightful other, the defeated, the eerie, the disappeared, the dead," first in travelogues that depicted the region "as the site of the mysterious and uncanny," and then "in histories that underscored the violent process that led to its colonization." In a more recent example of the Caribbean's brush with its Gothic Otherness, the Caribbean Creole Jean Rhys (1890–1979) first encountered the Caribbean-born Bertha Mason, in Charlotte Brontë's *Jane Eyre*, "upon arriving in England from Dominica at the age of sixteen" (Rody 135). It was her shock at seeing the demonization of Bertha in the nineteenth-century romance — Brontë constructs her as a "demon" and "monster" gamboling at "the mouth of hell" (Brontë 251, 264) — that was the catalyst for Rhys's writing of her counternarrative *Wide Sargasso Sea* in 1966. As Rhys (235) explains in an interview: "I thought, why should she think Creole women are lunatics and all that? What a shame to make Rochester's first wife, Bertha, the awful mad-woman[...]. She seemed such a poor ghost. I thought I'd try to write her a life" (235).

However, Frantz Fanon explains that during Aimé Césaire's generation of writers the monstrous Other that French Antilleans encountered in literature was not their own image but that of the African *nègre* (Fanon 1952, 119; 1961/1969, 24–25).[7] And it was with the monstrous *nègre* of the European imagination that Césaire identified in 1939 in his long poem and affirmation of negritude "Cahier d'un retour au pays natal" (see Fanon 1961/1969, 26–28). Jin's creation of a persona who assumes the role of the Gothic evil eye places her within this corpus of Caribbean writers who identify with the monstrous Other in their works. She is also exemplary of these writers in that similar to them she transforms her persona's monstrous Otherness into a profound representation of humanity.

Invisibility, Visibility, and the Gothic Asian Eye

Homi Bhabha (1994/2001) describes the eyes of Jin's persona in "Strangers in a hostile landscape" as "the eerie, avengeful [sic] disembodied [...] evil eye

[...] implicated in the petrifying, unblinking gaze that falls Medusa-like on its victims," echoing Conrad, Stoker, and Coleridge's haunting imagery of the Gothic evil eye (50, 52, 56). However, as he links that eye to the magical wraith-like quality that the poet assumes in the following lines of the same poem, "One day I learnt / a secret art, / Invisible-Ness, it was called" (20, ll. 101–106), he concludes that her secret art allows her eyes to wreak revenge "by circulating, *without being seen*" (55, emphasis in the original). Thus, he sees her representation of subjectivity, spoken from the site of a disintegrating body that the eye cannot contemplate, as making her eyes invisible as well. It is in this disavowal of the body that Bhabha finds Jin's poem, and those of other postcolonial poets, most subversive of conventional Western conceptions of identity — "a tradition of representation that conceives of" the "identity" of "the Self (or Other) [...] as the satisfaction of a totalizing, plenitudinous object of vision" (46–47). By thwarting his "desire to see, to fix cultural difference in a containable, *visible* object," Jin confounds the white Westerner's inscription of Orientalist stereotypes on the body of the Other (45–46, 50, emphasis in the original). Thus, according to Bhabha's interpretation, Jin's construction of her persona's body in a state of phantom-like dematerialization frustrates the Westerner's ability to demonize her.

While Bhabha's theory is provocative in that it implies that the postcolonial poet can counter the dehumanizing effects of stereotypes by her self-representation as a pure disembodied subjectivity or ghost, it fails to take into account an important detail — the evil eye of Jin's persona that is explicitly marked as Chinese and that curses her with a lamentable hyper-visibility. By supplementing Bhabha's suppositions with Traise Yamamoto's commentary on the Asian and Asian American eye, we can begin to understand the concomitant visibility and invisibility that plagues Jin's persona, and we can clarify how Jin uses the Gothic evil eye to reinstate her persona's humanity. Yamamoto maintains that "[o]f all Asian features, the 'Oriental eye' is the most likely to be identified as what differentiates Asians from everyone else" (Yamamoto 94). And what is particularly problematic for Asians and Asian Americans is that their eyes "must circulate in a field of meaning where whiteness and white features have normative value" (94). Because of the white Westerner's ensuing inability to read the Asian eye, he blanks it and writes on it the script of his own "racist projections" (94). Therefore, "the contradictory nature of the economy of racial visibility [...] results in the Asian American [and Asian] as an invisible subject who is nevertheless highly visible as a racially marked object" (67). Similar to Bhabha in his observations on the postcolonial poet, Yamamoto further remarks that because of the stereotypes attached to her body, the Asian American woman writer often disavows that body "in an attempt to reclaim subjectivity" (81). Moreover, she suggests that when many Asians and Asian Americans, in an analogous disavowal, undergo eye surgery to rid themselves of the epicanthic fold (that gives the impression of their having slit, sneaky eyes), they do so not in order to look Caucasian but to reverse the loss of subjectivity that Western cultures impute to them because of the facial feature (95–99). In fabricating a persona with a disintegrating body, Jin seems to construct subjectivity through a disavowal similar to that of Asian American women writers. We must note, however, that her persona does retain possession of her eye: the one physical feature that identifies her as Asian; that, therefore, does not allow her to pass as "white"—the equivalent of human, in the Western imagination (Fanon 1952, 79); and, to borrow Yamamoto's words, that "precludes recognition of the subject beneath or within" (93).

Jin attests in the poem "One of Many" to the hindrance that the eyes of the Chinese pose to their passing as white in Britain. Although they go about their lives trying to make themselves "thin enough" or "transparent enough / to go unnoticed," some of them "are deeply wounded" by the "malice" they are subjected to; this is because their "eyes betrayed" them "and the spikes stuck" (31). In a similar lament, the poet focuses on her own Chinese eyes in the poem titled "A long over-due poem to my eyes." Here, she shows how her eyes also prohibit her from passing: "but for you, I would be, / Totally invisible" (70, ll. 3–4). They also render her a social pariah in England: "When children teased, / It was because of you / They hated me" (70, ll. 9–10). In addition, she underscores the way English storybooks construct their heroine's soulful eyes — "In story books, / Her big blue eyes opened wide" (70, ll. 11–12) — in opposition to her own eyes that narrow into "[h]ard brown slit eyes" reflecting the world's most deep-seated and oft-repressed fear, that of its own death: "Echos [sic] of the pain / You mirror back the world, / And I can see them all, / Drowning there" (70, ll. 14–18). As Jin articulates this encounter in "story books" with her own Gothic Otherness, her construction of the Asian eye as a hard reflective surface in which the world sees its own repressed fears, rather than as a flexible organ of communication expressive of an inner soul, reveals how the Western imagination robs that eye of humanity, leaving only a frightening shell. As Jean Khalfa (drawing on the theories of Maurice Merleau-Ponty) explains, to be human one must be perceived as someone or something that stares back at the world: "seeing the body of a human being is not seeing a thing, it is seeing the evidence of another perspective, another world" (47).[8] The racist gaze dehumanizes the racial subject by suppressing the perception of the latter as the source of a point of view, which has the effect of reducing that subject to a flat surface:

To the racist gaze, the opacity which is essential to the perception of the body of the Other as an Alter Ego (*Autrui*), as the irreducibly unpredictable source of possible worlds, has simply vanished. What is left is a surface. [...]. [W]hen abruptly faced with the reality of the racist gaze, [the] body [is] flattened to a veil, an insignificant but vaguely threatening thing in the world [44, 47].

Jin, however, does not fix her persona's eyes in the state of threatening *thingness* imputed to them in storybooks. Instead, she counters those storybooks' flattening dehumanization and demonization of her persona's eyes with an inscription of their human depth. As she writes in the poem's closing lines: "Soft brown slit eyes / "Windows of the Soul / I can see you staring back / Frank, open, lovely" (70, ll. 19–22). In this final stanza, she does not rid her persona of her Chinese "brown slit eyes"; instead, she performs a sort of semantic eye surgery, countering the connotation of their Gothic Otherness found in English literature by endowing them with a gaze that stares back at the world, giving evidence of a soul behind or within. Here, we see a concrete example of how the poet, in order to recover her stolen soul, dissolves the perspective of the demon of English literature in her own — the final metaphor in her poem "Soul loss."

Coda

Although Jin's poetic journey relates specifically to her unique experience as an Asian in the West, she acknowledges Toni Morrison's influence on her writing (Jin 10), who has taken her own inspiration from African American slave narratives (Morrison 1976, 229). The writers of these slave autobiographies partially paint their narratives with a counter–Gothic palette when they color evil villains white and innocent maidens black, in correspondence to the actual color relations in slavery's history in the Americas.[9] As Jin transforms white England (the *Gwei lo*) into the haunter, and England's immigrants of color into the haunted, she subverts the Gothic's connotations of color in a similar manner. And by using the word "lovely" to refer to the particular body part that inspires Western hatred, the inscrutable Asian eye, she actually anticipates by a year Baby Suggs's exhortation in Morrison's *Beloved* (1987/1988, 88), to ex-slaves and descendants of slaves, to "love your flesh [...] eyes [...] skin [...] hands [...] mouth[...]," because "yonder" they despise them. Her poems further resonate with African American literature when she constructs a persona who is the victim of terror, but who nevertheless resists victimization by haunting back — by swallowing the demon that swallows her soul — and by writing back — infusing the demon of English literature with the perspective it sought to occlude. Finally, she belongs to a growing corpus of Caribbean writers who embrace and transform the role of the Gothic monster. Jin does so when she creates a persona whose vanishing body only partially disappears, leaving her most monstrous body part, her Asian eyes. Therein lies her genius. For the same eyes that fix her persona as a threatening thing in the Western imagination become the very evidence of her subjectivity as her human gaze emerges out of the disintegrating memory of their Gothic Otherness.

Notes

1. For more on the history of the Chinese in the Caribbean, see *The Cuba Commission Report, A Hidden History of the Chinese in Cuba* (1993), *Idéologie et ethnicité: Les Chinois Macao à Cuba* (Helly, 1979), *From the Middle Kingdom to the New World: Aspects of the Chinese Experience in Migration to British Guiana* (Kirkpatrick, 1993), *The Chinese in Trinidad* (Millet, 1993) and *Indentured Labor, Caribbean Sugar: Chinese and Indian Migrants to the British West Indies, 1838–1918* (Look Lai, 1993).

2. The race riots of 1964, two years before Guyana's independence (formerly British Guiana), led to over one hundred fifty deaths and the immigration of thousands of Guyanese to Britain and the United States. It is now believed that the United States Central Intelligence Agency incited the riots in order to ensure the defeat of the Marxist incumbent Cheddi Jagan and the election of the U.S.–backed Forbes Burnham in the 1964 Guyanese presidential election (*Cable News Network* [6 March, 1997], "Guyanese President Cheddi Jagan dies," http://www.cnn.com/WORLD/9703/06/guyana.pres/index.html?eref=sitesearch-10k).

3. James Hampshire (19–43) further attests to the difficulties that Caribbean immigrants of color encountered in England, noting that a number of conflicting citizenship and immigration laws passed between the years 1948 and 1981, whereby the British government sought to retain the sphere of influence that it enjoyed under its empire while maintaining Great Britain's identity as white, rendered life in England precarious for non–white citizens of Britain's former colonies. For a poem dealing with shifting citizenship and immigration laws and the effects of that instability on England's Caribbean immigrants, see Jin, "The Knock" (1986, 27).

4. Goddu titles Chapter Six of her study *Gothic America,* "Haunting Back: Harriet Jacobs, African-American Narrative, and the Gothic" (1997). In it she maintains that although for Jacobs "spectres seemed to rise up on [American] shores" (Jacobs's phrase from [1861/2001], *Incidents in the Life of a Slave Girl,* Dover, New York, 151), "she is able to haunt back by writing her narrative and by speaking the unspeakable about slavery," exposing the damning abuses on which the slave masters prohibited commentary: "Haunted by the shadows of her past and the continued oppression of her present, Jacobs cannot completely exorcise the demons of slavery; yet in bearing witness to them she haunts back" (151–152).

5. We could extend to the Kaiser's commissioned lithograph Karen Kingsbury's (108) apt assessment of the depiction in Rohmer's Fu Manchu novels of a "complete inversion of actual power relations between East Asia and the West," which provides "the justification for incessant vilification of the Chinese."

6. In her Introduction Jin writes: "There is a certain Wordsworth way of expression (*I wandered lonely as a cloud...*) that seeps into my writing and determines how I express myself [...] I write because I want to. Because I have to. And even after this, there lurks the white ghost of Wordsworth somewhere" (1986, 10).

7. Clayton Eshelman and Annette Smith (eds.) (1983) translate *nègre* as "nigger" in *The Collected Poetry of Aimé Césaire,* University of California Press, Berkeley; whereas Emile Snyders (ed.) (1968) translates the term as "Negro" in the bilingual edition of Césaire's *Cahier d'un retour au pays natal,* Présence Africaine, Paris. However, both translations are inadequate to connote the concomitant phobia-generating monster and victim of trauma that Césaire associates with the word *nègre*. Therefore, I leave it in the original French.

8. See Merleau-Ponty, *Parcours deux, 1951–1961* (39).

9. See Douglass, *Narrative of the Life of Frederick Douglass* (46); and Goddu *Gothic America* (137).

Works Cited

Anolik, Ruth Bienstock. 2004. "Introduction: The Dark Unknown," in *The Gothic Other: Racial and Social Constructions in the Literary Imagination,* eds. Ruth Bienstock Anolik and Douglas L. Howard. Jefferson, N.C.: McFarland, 1–14.
Bhabha, Homi K. 2001. *The Location of Culture* (1994). London/New York: Routledge.
Bodziock, Joseph. 2004. "The Cage of Obscene Birds: The Myth of the Southern Garden in Frederick Douglass's *My Bondage and My Freedom,*" in *The Gothic Other: Racial and Social Constructions in the Literary Imagination,* 251–263.
Brontë, Charlotte. 2001. *Jane Eyre* (1847). New York: Norton Critical Edition.
Cable News Network. 6 March, 1997. "Guyanese President Cheddi Jagan dies," *http://www.cnn.com/WORLD/9703/06/guyana.pres/index.html?eref=sitesearch* (Accessed at 11 March 2007)
Césaire, Aimé. 1939. "Cahier d'un retour au pays natal," *Volontés,* 20: 23–51.
Césaire, Aimé. 1968. *Cahier d'un retour au pays natal,* trans. Emile Snyders. Paris: Présence Africaine.
Césaire, Aimé. 1983, *The Collected Poetry of Aimé Césaire,* eds. and trans. Clayton Eshelman and Annette Smith. Berkeley: University of California Press.
Coleridge, Samuel Taylor. 2002. "The Rime of the Ancient Mariner (1798)," in *William Wordsworth and Samuel Taylor Coleridge: Lyrical Ballads and Related Writings,* eds. William Richey and Daniel Robinson. New York: Houghton Mifflin, 23–43.
Condé, Maryse. 1986. *Moi, Tituba, Sorcière ... Noire de Salem.* Paris : Mercure de France.
Conrad, Joseph. 1996. *Heart of Darkness* (1899). New York: Bedford/St. Martin's Press.
The Cuba Commission Report, A Hidden History of the Chinese in Cuba. Baltimore/London: Johns Hopkins University Press, 1993.
Douglass, Frederick. 1969. *My Bondage and My Freedom* (1855). New York: Dover.
Douglass, Frederick. 2003. *Narrative of the Life of Frederick Douglass, an American Slave, Written by Himself* (1845), ed. David W. Blight. New York: Bedford/St. Martin's Press.
Fanon, Frantz. 1952. *Peau Noire, Masques Blancs.* Paris: Seuil.
Fanon, Frantz. 1969. *Pour la révolution africaine* (1961). Paris: Maspero.
García Márquez, Gabriel. 1986. *Todos los cuentos* (1948). Bogota: Oveja Negra.
García Márquez, Gabriel. 2002. *Vivir para contarla.* Bogota: Norma.
Goddu, Teresa. 1997. *Gothic America: Narrative, History, and Nation.* New York: Columbia University Press.
Gómez de Avellaneda y Arteaga, Gertrudis. 1993. *Sab* and *Autobiography* (1841), ed. and trans. Nina M. Scott. Austin: University of Texas Press.
Hampshire, James. 2005. *Citizenship and Belonging: Immigration and the Politics of Demographic Governance in Postwar Britain.* Basingstoke: Palgrave.
Helly, Denise. 1979. *Idéologie et ethnicité: Les Chinois Macao à Cuba.* Montreal: Presses de l'Université de Montréal.
Hindle, Wilfrid. 1974. *The Morning Post 1772–1937: Portrait of a Newspaper* (1937). New York: Greenwood Press.
Jacobs, Harriet A. (Linda Brent, pseud.). 2001. *Incidents in the Life of a Slave Girl* (1861). Dover: New York.
Jin, Meiling. 1986. *Gifts from My Grandmother.* London: Sheba.
Khalfa, Jean. 2005. "My Body, This Skin, This Fire: Fanon on Flesh," *Frantz Fanon,* special issue of *Wasafiri,* 44: 42–50.
Kingsbury, Karen. 2004. "Yellow Peril, Dark Hero: Fu Manchu and the 'Gothic Bedevilment' of Racist Intent," in *The Gothic Other: Racial and Social Constructions in the Literary Imagination,* 104–119.
Look Lai, Walton. 1998. *The Chinese in the West Indies: A Documentary History, 1806–1995.* Kingston, Jamaica: The Press University of the West Indies.
Merleau-Ponty, Maurice. 2000. *Parcours deux, 1951–1961,* ed. Jacques Prunair. Paris : Verdier.
Millet, Trevor. 1993. *The Chinese in Trinidad.* Port of Spain: Inprint Caribbean Ltd.
Morrison, Toni. 1979. "Intimate Things in Place: A Conversation with Toni Morrison," Robert B. Stepto (interviewer), in *Chant of Saints,* eds. Michael S. Harper and Robert B. Stepto. Urbana: University of Illinois Press, 213–229.
Morrison, Toni. 1988. *Beloved.* New York: Plume-Penguin.
Paravisini-Gebert, Lizabeth. 2002. "Colonial and Postcolonial Gothic: The Caribbean," in *The Cambridge Companion to Gothic Fiction,* ed. Jerrold E. Hogle. Cambridge: Cambridge University Press, 229–257.
Rhys, Jean. 1979. "Jean Rhys: The Art of Fiction LXIV," Elizabeth Vreelad (interviewer). *Paris Review,* 76: 218–237.

Rhys, Jean 1982. *Wide Sargasso Sea* (1966). New York: Norton.
Rody, Caroline. 2001. *The Daughter's Return: African-American and Caribbean Women's Fictions of History.* New York: Oxford University Press.
Rohmer, Sax (pseud. of Arthur Sarsfield Ward). 1913. *The Insidious Dr. Fu-Manchu: Being a Somewhat Detailed Account of the Amazing Adventures of Nayland Smith in His Trailing the Sinister Chinaman.* New York: McBride, Nast and Company.
Shelley, Mary. 2003. *Frankenstein* (1818). New York: Barnes & Noble.
Stoker, Bram. 1997. *Dracula* (1897). New York: Norton.
Sue-A-Quan, Trevelyan. 2004. "Passengers," in *Chinese in Guyana: Their Roots. http://www.rootsweb. com/-guycigtr/* (Accessed at 11 March 2007)
Yamamoto, Traise. 1999. *Masking Selves, Making Subjects: Japanese American Women, Identity, and the Body.* Berkeley: University of California Press.

5

Encrypted Ancestries: Kazuo Ishiguro's *The Remains of the Day* and Its Uncanny Inheritances

Hilary Thompson

Monstrous Aging

Why do people applaud the coming of artificial light? This is the riddle Stevens the butler turns on himself in the closing pages of Kazuo Ishiguro's *The Remains of the Day*. Seated alone at Weymouth Pier, Stevens notes that the setting sun affords enough daylight. Yet the gathered people cheer when the pier lights come on, as though they want night to happen. The answer must have been, he muses, in the words of the stranger he has just spoken to as they sat on the bench. It must have been just as he said, "that for a great many people, the evening was the best part of the day, the part they most looked forward to" (240). Why else applaud the flicking of a switch? The riddle and the answer seem to form a tight circuit in Stevens's characteristically circular turns of thought: the strangeness of the phenomenon might be explained by the stranger's strange assertion because truly the phenomenon is strange. And yet for Stevens and for Ishiguro's readers, something more than a moment of cerebral circularity has happened here.

In this moment that is both signaled by the novel's title and that marks the close of the text, we feel a day in its fullest synecdochic sense ending. We feel a world's aging. While drawing attention to the end of an era at the end of a novel may seem traditional, even a "textbook" move for the genre, Stevens's perplexity asks us to wait and ponder a moment longer. *The Remains of the Day* does not end with a naturally descending twilight, but rather a precipitous flash of electric light, as though we are not simply watching an end, but willing a world to age faster, before it has to. And while this closing might seem to have canonical Western precursors, it has another partly Eastern parallel, as well as a mysterious, equally international forebear. To pursue the meanings that flash simultaneously in this burst of light as well as the intricate paths of Ishiguro's inheritances, we ourselves have to play a part in reconstructing a narrative at once Gothic, modern, and global in scope, a narrative that at its fulfillment lets us catch a glimpse of the estate that through Ishiguro's text devolves to us.

Stevens describes the twilight, saying, "the sky over the sea has turned a pale red," and this pale sky might recall Ishiguro's first novel *A Pale View of Hills* in which a remarkably similar description occurs but in which the novel's ominously repeated word "pale" is coupled with "purple" and used to describe the summer light of a post–Bomb Nagasaki (120). This recollection, if it occurs to a reader, would link these two Ishiguro novels through the force of chance association or involuntary memory, and it is the great artist of involuntary memory, Proust, whom Ishiguro reports having read and been changed by in between writing his first and subsequent novels. Although he says he did not at that time read more than sixty of his pages, for Ishiguro, Proust becomes one of many uncanny strangers with answers he can insert into his spiraling musings. Proust's answer is involuntary memory, or as Ishiguro says, "the fluidity of the mind, particularly when it's remembering," and this becomes useful as a nonlinear way of ordering narrative, a way a text can move through leaps, loops, gaps, and offshoots just as acts of recollection do (Shaikh). But involuntary memory has more than individual importance for both Proust and Ishiguro. As Walter Benjamin explains, it is Proust who presides over, even performs, the world's aging in an instant of artificial light.

Proust's involuntary memory, Benjamin claims, is "much closer to forgetting" than to ordinary memory, and it suggests an intriguing relationship of night to day:

> When we awake each morning, we hold in our hands, usually weakly and loosely, but a few fringes of the carpet of existence, as woven into us by forgetting. However, with our purposeful activity and, even more, our purposive remembering, each day unravels the web, the ornaments of forgetting. This is why Proust finally turned his days into nights, devoting all his hours to undisturbed work in his darkened room with artificial illumination, so that none of those arabesques might escape him [238].

Forgetting may weave into beautiful tapestries the remnants of memory, but how much more sublime the artistry of involuntary recollection, the shock that opens up a rapturous eternity. This eternity in Proust is not "platonic" or "utopian," but rather, Benjamin specifies, "The eternity which Proust opens to view is intertwined time, not boundless time." And we experience this intertwining time in life "in remembrance within and aging without." Involuntary memory in the midst of aging brings home the fact of lived time and becomes, Benjamin claims, a force of rejuvenation. Describing a climactic moment of such recollection in Proust, when the discovery of an "intermingling of roads" brings a long-familiar landscape into surprisingly fresh view, when, echoing Baudelaire, the world seems both big in the light of lamps and small in the eyes of memory, Benjamin announces, "Proust has brought off the monstrous feat of letting the whole world age a lifetime in an instant" (244). Alone on the pier, Benjamin is applauding.

Ishiguro is explicit that a technique of nonlinear time comes to him directly from Proust, and Benjamin helps us see the use of intertwining time as compatible with a desire to track the world's aging, even to take hold of it in a reflective lived instant, and these connections in turn suggest answers to a reader's riddle of why it is, in a significant closing scene of Ishiguro's third novel, that what remains of natural daylight is cut short by the lighting of the lamps. But in Ishiguro's time an even wider "whole world" has aged beyond the alterations Proust and Benjamin recognized, raising new questions. What if the "monstrous feat" of Proust's and Benjamin's world aging a lifetime in an instant has come to seem small in the light of new lamps? What if the world aged several lifetimes at a stroke? If Ishiguro captures this instant, what other inheritances does he intertwine and can such an intermingling still take a moment of involuntary memory as its aesthetic model?

Ruins and Dragons

European literature furnishes Ishiguro with a ready-made genre of monstrosity, hybridity, anachronism, and cataclysm. The Gothic is often cited as the genre of remnants, ruins, and unsettled as well as unsettling inheritances. Mario Praz gives a helpful inventory of the Gothic's stock figures and motifs:

> An introductory story in order to produce an old manuscript where the happenings are written down, a Gothic castle forming a gloomy background with its secret corridors and labyrinthine network of subterranean passages, a mysterious crime frequently connected with illicit or incestuous love, and perpetrated by a person in holy orders, a villain (as a rule an Italian or a

Spaniard) who has pledged himself to the devil, who finally hurls him into the abyss; ghosts, witches and sorcerers, nature conspiring to effects of terror and wonder, portraits endowed with a mysterious life, statues which are suddenly seen to bleed [33].

And to this list we could add other features Praz notes in passing: doppelgangers or doubles and "the innocent accused and tried for a crime he has not committed, and incapable of proving his innocence" (7). The genre's founding English text is acknowledged to be Horace Walpole's 1764 work *The Castle of Otranto* in which the motifs of inheritance and wrongful accusation merge into the question of whether the sins of the father, in this case, Manfred, the wrongful usurper of Otranto, are more likely to be visited on his offspring, as though nonlinearly skipping generational order. If Walpole's text is prototypical, we could say that the Gothic is the genre in which the unresolved demands of one time come to call on another, or in Fred Botting's words, there is a "disturbing return of pasts upon presents," one that yields "emotions of terror and laughter" (1). In *Otranto*, the would-have-been rightful heir Alfonso haunts the castle as an out-of-proportion apparition. Although an enormous helmet from Alfonso's statue grotesquely crushes Manfred's own heir, the feeble Conrad, at the romance's outset, a more straightforwardly farcical element later emerges in the work as domestic servants sight gigantic fragments of Alfonso's figure and armor. The appearance of these out-of-place (but rightfully entitled to the place) fragments forms a metaphor for the Gothic genre itself, which, as Botting explains, many have seen as marked by archaic anxieties persisting in the age of Enlightenment ideals, haunting memories of "a feudal past associated with barbarity, superstition and fear" (3). The Gothic seems the perfect genre for a world aging ahead of its time.

But a less discussed feature of the Gothic fascination with excess turns out to be crucial. Zhang Longxi tells us, "In the eighteenth century [...] those who grew tired of the vogue of chinoiserie often mention the Gothic and the Chinese in tandem as equally grotesque and extravagant," and he quotes as evidence a satirical poem from 1757, Robert Lloyd's *Cit's Country Box*:

> Now bricklay'rs, carpenters and joiners
> With Chinese artists and designers,
> Produce their schemes of alteration,
> To work this wondrous reformation.
> The trav'ler with amazement sees
> A temple, Gothic or Chinese,
> With many a bell, and tawdry rag on,
> And crested with a sprawling dragon [qtd. in Zhang 115].

Among the amazing features of this example are that the poem's date precedes the appearance of the first English Gothic novel by seven years, as though fatigue with chinoiserie formed part of Gothic literature's prehistory, and that in the poem the ends of tacky architecture are fulfilled equally by Gothic ornaments and signs of the orient. We have the suggestion that from quite early on for Gothic texts as well as buildings, a dragon could be a viable substitute for a ruin and a ruin for a dragon.

We know that Ishiguro, too, is fascinated with stock figures and cultural storehouses of images. Asked whether he feels challenged as a writer by the contemporary "proliferation of popular media and images which tend to make the examination of the interior lives more difficult," he replies that, on the contrary, he finds these images and stereotypes a resource: "I feel that when I'm writing a novel, I'm actually tapping into this, what in the pejorative sense people might call the garbage and ephemera in people's heads." And his two examples are the "international myth of the English butler" he used to create Stevens in *The Remains of the Day* and the stereotype conjured up by the words "old Shanghai," one you can see "evoked over and over again" if "you walk around the Chinatowns on the West Coast, in San Francisco and Vancouver" (qtd. in Shaikh), the Shanghai that forms the setting of Ishiguro's fifth novel *When We Were Orphans*. Here Ishiguro, like Robert Lloyd before him, puts English relics and repeated Chinese motifs into equation. But we might think, too, of the role Japanese popular media played in Ishiguro's early years. When as a child he came to England with his family, they thought the move was temporary. To ease his eventual return and help him stay in touch with the childhood his Japanese peers would have been experiencing, Ishiguro's grandfather sent him monthly parcels filled with Japanese children's books, magazines, and comics (Mackenzie). For Ishiguro, stock figures, whether relics, recreations, or remembrances, offer access to cultures through their assumptions and shorthands, their idle, if not always ideal, caricatures and doodles.

In what senses, then, might *The Remains of the Day*, a novel of a catastrophic global aging, also be usefully seen as Gothic? If the Gothic is the genre of cultures' age-old anxieties and epochal uncertainties, if in its repeated use of an inventory it seems to be forever trying to take stock, how does it meet Ishiguro, a writer who seeks to raid the larder, to open up histories to each other, not through a conveying of necessarily accurate information, but through an interchanging of repertoires, the mingling of motifs Robert Lloyd found so fatiguing?

The Gothographic

Intriguingly, *Remains* can be made to fit much of Praz's Gothic cata-logue, all the while maintaining its putative claims to realism. The opening move to produce the manuscript is Stevens's address to us, his readers, and his signaling that he is about to make and detail to us a motor trip from his workplace Darlington Hall to the West Country. We correctly infer we are about to receive a traveler's diary. The gloomy castle with its endless corri-dors is, of course, Darlington Hall, and Stevens's labyrinthine digressions into memories of his employment there in the pre–World War II years are filled with melancholy. The crime and the illicit love connected with a holy per-son are found both in Stevens's ill-advised devotion to his Lord, Lord Dar-lington, and Lord Darlington's Nazi sympathies and unofficial lobbying for appeasement policies with Germany. While incest is not present as such (although Lord Darlington is a father figure Stevens exalts above his own father, to the point at times of seeing himself as his helpmeet), forbidden loves are hinted at, since the strictly ascetic and male-centered atmosphere of the manor makes for a climate distinctly unfriendly to heterosexual attraction (the male and female servants' falling in love with each other becomes a trans-gression in itself) and strongly favoring homosocial and even homoerotic bonds. Lord Darlington attributes his commitment to Germany to his post–World War I friendship with former enemy but fellow gentleman Herr Bremann, and this strong attachment is one of the few close friendships we know Lord Darlington to have. While no villainous Italian or Spaniard plagues the manor, the evil Mediterranean figure comes to call in the character of M. Dupont, the suspicious and rather obnoxious French diplomat ever dogging Stevens's footsteps as he complains of his own dire foot pain. And most intriguing of all, is the way doubling and uncannily animated beings appear.

After the manor's previous housekeeper and under-butler commit the barely forgivable sin of eloping, Stevens brings into the house as replacements two people on whom the shame of these sins will be visited: Miss Kenton, who will become the object of Stevens's disavowed desires, and Mr. Stevens Sr., his enfeebled father, from whom he inherits the mission to always man his station, and whom he consequently emotionally neglects. The doubling occurs when Stevens insists to Miss Kenton that although his father as under-butler is her subordinate, she must nevertheless refer to him as she refers to Stevens himself, by surname. Underscoring his point, Stevens argues that if Miss Kenton were more observant, she would see that Mr. Stevens is more than he appears to be, that though his title of under-butler is lowly, his example might teach her a "wealth of things" (54) such as, for example, the ability to know immediately items' proper identities and positions. The notion of the lowly character whose manner indicates a secret wealth or nobility, a true identity, is part of the Gothic repertoire established in *Otranto*, with a handsome young peasant, Theodore, emerging at a climactic moment as the castle's true heir's descendant. In *Remains*, Stevens the elder allows the Gothic to enter the text in multiple, often innovative, ways: he is a father upon whom shame not his own is visited, he is the feeble bearer of a family lineage, he becomes a double in name for our narrator, and he introduces the motif of observation of signs, one that returns to haunt Stevens the younger.

In *The Castle of Otranto* foretold signs such as the appearance of bits of a giant's body emerge to confirm the prophecy that the castle's current owner will lose his title and house when its true owner has grown too big to inhabit it. The domestics cower and scamper whenever they see an enormous hand or foot in a corridor, and they unsuccessfully try to get others to notice. Comic as this plotline is, it becomes more so when an equivalent for it is seen in Ishiguro's narrative in Miss Kenton's determination that Stevens note, not a piece of armor in a corridor, but a dust-pan on a polished floor, one his father has absent-mindedly abandoned. This blot on the escutcheon is followed by a further tarnish to the family reputation: the "practically black" end to an incompletely polished silver fork (56). Worse still, Miss Kenton announces, "I have noticed your father's nose" and explains this body part was remarkable for the drop suspended from it as its bearer, Stevens Sr., carried bowls of soup. Although Stevens wishes to see these instances as the "most trivial of errors," Miss Kenton insists on their "larger significance," that Stevens's father is "entrusted" with too much. Prophesying doom, she exhorts Stevens that these are signs that his father's "powers are now greatly diminished" and that if he does not "heed them," his father will commit "an error of major proportions" (59–60). Incapable of upholding a tradition and seen through telling fragments of enormous significance, Stevens Sr. does more than double duty as he condenses into one figure Manfred the usurper, Conrad his feeble heir, and Alfonso's out-of-proportion gigantic apparition.

Among the figures Stevens Sr.'s appearance signals, one other is peculiarly noteworthy: the Chinaman. No stranger to chinoiserie, Lord Darlington seems to have several decorative porcelain figures of Chinese men, and during Stevens Sr.'s tenure as under-butler, they become ominously misarranged. Whereas in *Otranto*, uppity servant Bianca, terrified by a giant hand in armor, may cry to unheeding Manfred, "Go to the foot of the great stairs yourself—As I live I saw it" (136), Miss Kenton's pleas reach their crescendo when she demands to Stevens, "I would ask you, Mr Stevens, to turn around and look at that Chinaman" (58). Because Stevens has accused her earlier of not immediately discerning items' true identities, she throws in his face his father's errors (suggesting they are his true heirs), the misplaced Chinamen she calls "incorrect." Stevens may plead for her to keep it down, asking, "What would employees below think to hear us shouting at the top of our voices about what is and is not the correct Chinaman?" But Miss Kenton will have none of this appeal to stable vertical order, and her critical campaign culminates with the declaration, "The fact is, Mr Stevens, all the Chinamen in this house have been dirty for some time! And now, they are in incorrect positions!" (59). One of the few appearances of Asia in the novel, these incorrect Chinamen seem to come to life in Miss Kenton's and Stevens's animated altercation, as though they themselves have been intentionally lowering hygienic house standards and demanding new positions to boot. Persuasive as it is to read this satirically subversive representation of the ethnic other in light of late eighties English race riots, contestations of Margaret Thatcher's conservative cultural politics and popular culture's wave of Anglophilic nostalgia for a time when Britain was "great,"[1] another interpretation suggests itself as well.

In an interview with Cynthia F. Wong, Ishiguro explains his motivation to write *Remains* came partly from his frustration with critics who read his first two novels, both set chiefly in post–World War II Japan, "in terms of their Japanese-ness," as though their main value lay in what they could reveal to others about Japanese culture and people. He concluded that these earlier works' "Japanese setting was to some extent limiting the response and slightly leading to a misreading of my intentions" (318). We could say that these early readings put Asianness, the author's and the texts,' in an incorrect position, the position of making Ishiguro the native informant and the books ethnography. The out-of-place Chinamen in Ishiguro's stereotypically English novel might become, then, an ever-expanding joke and a paradox like the self-proclaiming perpetually lying Cretan's, as though we can hear in the Chinese figurines the author's voice saying, "If you think I'm here, you've got me all wrong."

We can begin to take stock, then, of the Gothic's role in the novel by observing that this from the start melodramatic and farcical genre is one of the many "cartoons" Ishiguro pulls from his storehouse of stereotypical images of cultures, and he even includes the chinoiserie with which the Gothic was once viewed in tandem. And this outlandish equivalent allows the author to poke fun at the then current politics, former overly author-based critics, and those who would rely on caricatures of cultures unthinkingly — the ethnographic readers. It is this sketchy use of the Gothic with all its orientalizing trappings that I call "gothographic."

The gothographic element of Ishiguro's third novel is related to what critics have viewed as its irony, and this irony has become a bone of contention.

Bo G. Ekelund, for example, has seen the way *Remains* might be read as a postmodern (or postcolonial and postimperial) novel and thus deemed "almost by definition 'subversive' of the literary tradition to which it self-consciously belongs." Contesting the "postmodern commonplace that the undermining of genre is a structural function of any incorporation of other genres" (70), Ekelund advances an argument that runs nearly counter, "that the themes introduced explicitly in Stevens's narration are reinforced by the genres manipulated by Ishiguro, which carry sets of meanings in themselves" and that "these meanings are not easily controlled or automatically subverted by a strategy of generalized irony" (72). Pointing to the novel's borrowings (both in its digressive narrative structure and its narrator's regressive political sentiments) from such former appeasers' self-exculpating political memoirs as Lord Halifax's *Fulness of Days*, Ekelund finds room for suspicion. The novel's links to Halifax and even the unwitting traitor Wodehouse, ever marked by his ill-advised radio broadcasts for Germany while its captive, become evidence not of subversive multiplicity but of insidious complicity. But James M. Lang argues, by contrast, that the novel's focus on past private memory and its divergence from later public sentiment works as a caution against the dangers of "backshadowing," viewing the course of particular historical events as inevitable and holding past actors accountable for what we now know was to unfold (152–153). Ishiguro's handling of genres becomes crucially part of a historiographic strategy that is either party to progressive trends or indiscriminate in the company it keeps.

We might legitimately wonder where our sympathies should lie. Are critics reenacting the Gothic theme of wrongful accusation by conflating Ishiguro the author with his narrative sources or narrator? Or is there something strange about a writer who displays a desire to rehearse, seemingly with a straight face, all the tricks and tropes of those who later wanted sympathy for engaging in unofficial diplomacy with the Nazis? How much weight should we give the judgments of history, how much free rein to the forces of empathy? If Ishiguro's novel asks us to feel for Lord Darlington, and in turn Stevens, even in their most unethical moments because of something they feel, with whatever degree of atrocious judgment, if it asks us to take on these feelings while suppressing thoughts of the truths borne out by history, as though simply siding with the facts that won out were a banality in itself, is the novel suggesting that we suspend moral urges towards the end of some other ethics or is the novel asking us to engage in an unsavory appeasement? How do we determine the "correct position"?

It is worth observing that the extreme poles of this debate share a certain theoretical predisposition: they end up attributing to genres themselves ideological positions. Although Ekelund usefully illuminates Ishiguro's intertexts, inventories several of the genres the novel incorporates, and scrutinizes reckless critical uses of Linda Hutcheon's concept of historiographic metafiction, still one wonders about the effect of a certain absence: this analysis of "complicitous genres" leaves out what is arguably the genre of complicity — the Gothic. If this genre, not as inherent premise but more as questionably inherited property, has always been fascinated with the issue of whom guilt and shame should visit and has never felt the need to keep to direct lines of descent, then is not merely noting Ishiguro's novel's proximity to the complicit beside the point? We need to go further. We might widen our scope as we pursue the question of correctness by considering the figure of the Asian other, the chinoiserie that so often comes with the Gothic manor, and the position, not just of the author, but of the reader.

The Remains of the Day can be read as desiring to make its readers chinoiserie, items that can become animatedly aware of their habitual positions or of being placed out of them. The Chinaman was the point at which readers could say, "There's a figure of the Asian," and then castigate themselves at the ludicrousness of seeing an English Japanese writer as "the incorrect Chinaman." Chinoiserie, like autobiography, the genre notorious for never getting the person writing and the person written about to be either distinct or identical, would be the mark of where someone is and is not.[2] The genre of autobiography and the question of its relation to Ishiguro, particularly in his third novel, have been crucially important in his critical reception. Many have wanted, for example, to bring Japaneseness into discussions of the novel, claiming as Meera Tamaya does at the close of her convincing demonstration of Stevens's similarity to a colonized subject that his tragedy is outlined "with the delicate economy of a sketch by Hokusai" (54), or as Suzie Mackenzie does in an insightful discussion of Ishiguro's life and work that his "novels set in Japan [...] are the least about Japan" whereas *The Remains of the Day* she "cannot read without thinking about Japan." And these comparisons and reflections need not be read as orientalizing or exoticizing impulses, though Ishiguro has been victim to these tendencies, too. Tomo Hattori has analyzed sharply "the racial incredulity over Ishiguro's talent as a writer of the English language" even quoting one interviewer who while talking with the author "studied his face with its broad Oriental planes" and found his British accent "a startling juxtaposition" (220 n. 4). Nonetheless, Hattori still sees Asianness as relevant to *Remains*, interpreting Stevens's character as a critique of the model minority stereotype so often foisted upon Asians. Even Ishiguro himself says that after he often appeared reticent when asked to speak as an authority on Japan, people in the media got the hint and even went to the other extreme, becoming "very apologetic if they brought it up. It was sort of, 'Whatever you do, don't talk about Japan.' Which is not true at all." We need not conclude, then, that Asianness in general or Japan more specifically is irrelevant to *Remains*, but our discussions of these topics may often feel added on, as though we have to draw out an extra dimension to the text, something that is and is not there, and this extra effort may make us feel a little shaky about our own positions. Through a paradoxical play with ethnography, Ishiguro would put the reader in the impossible position of the writer of memoir or autobiography. If this is true, Asianness would become exemplary for a way Ishiguro's text's politics cannot be analyzed without taking into account a burden placed on the reader. In this paradigmatic instance, Ishiguro would have taken his plight of being incorrectly recognized as author, seen principally as Japanese and even as a Japanese authority rather than one of many possible versions of being Japanese, and transposed it onto his readers, making them turn to look, if they heed the cue, at their own arrangements. To focus, then, on generic complicity without the play of chinoiserie would be to miss one half (or hemisphere) in the gothographic equation.

The Many Possible

It might seem a novelty to see one's identity, all components included, as one of many possible versions of that identity, but it is equally an archaism. On the one hand, in Ishiguro's most recent novel, *Never Let Me Go*, set in a parallel England where human cloning became institutionalized, young clones give themselves paradoxical priority by calling the people who may have been their originals their "possibles." On the other hand, Jorge Luis Borges reminds us in his essay "From Allegories to Novels" that though the allegory, the idea that a form is supposed to have *another* content or more than one content at once, came to seem erroneous and even monstrous to later periods, for the Middle Ages, an era that privileged the idea, nothing of the sort was the case. Allegory could make perfect sense when "reality was not men but humanity, not the individuals but mankind, not the species but the genus, not the genera but God" (166). Both clones and creators allow us to see behind identities a play of multiple moveable figures and possibilities, a notion most concretely brought to life in another Borges text, one that also makes peculiar and perhaps inheritable use of chinoiserie, "The Garden of Forking Paths."

This World War I story is the account, really a deposition, of Yu Tsun, a Chinese man working undercover in England as a spy for Germany, a nation he tells us he hates. This hatred, he explains, inspires him to overachieve for their cause, to prove "a yellow man [can save their] armies" (21). When a colleague is apprehended by archenemy Captain Richard Madden, an Irishman working equally ambivalently — Yu Tsun assumes — as a spy for the English, Yu Tsun realizes his time is short. Madden will similarly close in on and arrest him. Before that happens, Yu Tsun wants to convey a secret to his chief in Germany: the name of a hidden artillery camp that the Germans must bomb. To get his message out, Yu Tsun plans to find and murder a man with the same name as the city where the camp is located. When this murder makes the headlines, his chief will link Yu Tsun's name with his victim's, infer the artillery camp's location, and order the city's bombing. Yu Tsun's and Richard Madden's race to beat ethnic stereotypes, each other, and the clock, forms the story's background.

What then unfolds is unexpected and partly unrelated to this wartime espionage backdrop. Although we may imagine we hear a bomb's clock ticking throughout the action, Yu Tsun actually accomplishes his task smoothly. He locates a man with the appropriate name, Stephen Albert, and he catches a train to Albert's town just as Madden reaches the platform and is forced to take a train leaving forty minutes later. These forty minutes added to the time it takes to walk from the station to Albert's home create a crucial near hour's lag time. This near hour becomes a spot of time that will stand out from the constant ticking's sound. At its end, Albert will be shot, and a captured Yu Tsun will dictate his account as he awaits execution, knowing his message found his chief, that the city was bombed. There is no glitch in the plan.

But there is a glitch in consciousness since Stephen Albert is not the man Yu Tsun anticipates. Instead, this Sinologist is coincidentally the keeper of one of Yu Tsun's ancestral treasures, the eponymous garden of forking paths. And, as befits the eponymy, this garden is both a space and a book. Yu Tsun's ancestor Ts'ui Pen allegedly retired from political life to compose a novel and create a labyrinth no one could navigate. The labyrinth turns out to be a spatial metaphor for the manuscript now in Albert's hands, a fragmentary novel in which time is infinite, characters simultaneously choose all alternatives before them, plotlines contradict each other, and parallel universes diverge, converge, and proliferate. The book, Albert explains, is the embodiment of Ts'ui Pen's philosophy of time as a network of infinite parallels. As Albert elaborates on this infinitely and simultaneously ramified time to Yu Tsun, it becomes clear that, following a logic similar to an ontological argument's, this time, if it exists, cannot be separate from the time of their conversation, and if it does not exist and remains hypothetical, is not truly the time Ts'ui Pen conceived. As Yu Tsun moves closer to realizing his own plan, he feels a "swarming sensation," as if "the humid garden that surrounded the house was infinitely saturated with invisible persons," other versions of himself and Albert, "secret, busy, and multiform in other dimensions of time" (28). And at the moment he assassinates the random man named Albert, Yu Tsun realizes the surrounding garden has virtually become Ts'ui Pen's and its guardian his ancestor. He redeems his race, he believes, in the eyes of Germany by completing his task, he regains his lost ancestral treasure, and he sees rehabilitated the reputation of his eccentric ancestor, but all at the cost of killing the man who stands for and opens up these possibilities. In several senses, Yu Tsun executes his mission.

But, in keeping with nonlinearity, it is before the garden both opens to embrace all happenings and has its revelatory appearance extinguished by its guardian's assassination, that the story's most epiphanic moment occurs. Before Yu Tsun and Albert ever meet, when Yu Tsun is approaching Albert's house, he muses that the directions the boys at the train station have given him (always turn left) are similar to those used to navigate mazes. He then recalls his ancestor, Ts'ui Pen, and ponders how he was allegedly killed by "the hand of a stranger," how "his novel was incoherent," and how "no one found [his] labyrinth." As his musings intensify, he reports:

> Beneath English trees I meditated on that lost maze: I imagined it inviolate and perfect at the secret crest of a mountain; I imagined it infinite, no longer composed of octagonal kiosks and returning paths, but of rivers and provinces and kingdoms[...] I thought of a labyrinth of labyrinths, of one sinuous spreading labyrinth that would encompass the past and the future and in some way involve the stars. Absorbed in these illusory images, I forgot my destiny of one pursued. I felt myself to be, for an unknown period of time, an abstract perceiver of the world. The vague, living countryside, the moon, the remains of the day worked on me, as well as the slope of the road which eliminated any possibility of weariness. The afternoon was intimate, infinite [22–23].

His epiphany reaches a further height when he tells us, "I thought that a man can be the enemy of other men, but not of a country: not of fireflies, words, gardens, streams, of water, sunsets (23). Yu Tsun has gotten the point of his rendezvous with Albert and with his ancestral destiny before he ever reaches them. The remains of the day work on him before daylight's final hour and he immeasurably ages before his time.

When Stevens sits on Weymouth Pier, he imagines "that all these people who have been gathering on this pier for the past half-hour are now willing night to fall" (240). But for Etsuko, narrator of *A Pale View of Hills,* this would be very uncharacteristic English behavior. In the midst of describing her Nagasaki sunset, she informs us, "In Japanese cities, much more so than in England, the restaurant owners, the teahouse proprietors, the shopkeepers all seem to will the darkness to fall; long before the daylight has faded, lanterns appear in windows, lighted signs above doorways" (120). Beneath their pale skies, Yu Tsun, Etsuko, and Stevens play out remains of fates in parallel, whether living out the penitent destiny of being an unwilling enemy, the extended aftermath and fall-out of being an atrociously defeated enemy, or the belated shame of newly recognized complicity. Playing out the logic of another kind of parallel, Ishiguro observes that had he been born a mere decade earlier, "I would have been alive when the bomb was dropped." And then recalling a conversation he had when his work began being published, he adds, "I remember my mother saying, 'You are in the public realm now, you have some power. There are certain memories that should not die with me'" (qtd. in Mackenzie). He reports that she passed on to him memories and descriptions of Nagasaki and of those who died in its bombing. Such intimations, whether individual and hypothetical or ancestral and historical, go well beyond involuntary memory and make one entertain the realm of macro-memory Borges uses an old Chinese manuscript to symbolize. Yet while Yu Tsun's destiny may be to discover why it is impossible to be an enemy of another country or of the sun's falling, and in this accommodating manner he may become one of the Gothic's model items of chinoiserie, for Ishiguro, influential, even inheritable, as this model may be, left as it is, it may not seem fully correct. In a further twist, perhaps, he intertwines along with Yu Tsun's legacy history that in his own age must also be brought to light the history of others who, whether they turn out to see it or not, were willing night to fall.

Notes

1. Both John Su and Meera Tamaya discuss *The Remains of the Day* in this light.
2. Paul Veyret analyzes Ishiguro's *The Remains of the Day* and *When We Were Orphans* as dramatizing the famous split between the enunciating and the enunciated "I," particularly of autobiography, and he, too, sees the figure of the Chinese man as a recurrent, if oblique, sign of displacement in memory. I dwell more specifically on the connotations of chinoiserie and their consequences for readers' acts of recognition.

Works Cited

Benjamin, Walter. 1934. "On the Image of Proust," in *Walter Benjamin, Selected Writings Vol. 2 1927–1934*. Trans. Rodney Livingstone et al., ed. Michael W. Jennings, Howard Eiland, & Gary Smith. Cambridge, MA: Harvard University Press, 1999: 237–247.
Borges, Jorge L. 1949. "From Allegories to Novels," in *Other Inquisitions 1937–1952*, 1966, trans. Ruth L.C. Simmons. New York: Washington Square Press, 163–166.
_____. "The Garden of Forking Paths," trans. Donald A. Yates, in *Labyrinths, Selected Stories & Other Writings*. Ed. Donald A. Yates & James E. Irby. New York: New Directions, 1962: 19–29.
Botting, Fred. 1996. *Gothic*. New York: Routledge.

Ekelund, Bo G. 2005. "Misrecognizing History: Complicitous Genres in Kazuo Ishiguro's *The Remains of the Day.*" *International Fiction Review* 31, 1–2: 70–91.

Hattori, Tomo. 1998. "China Man Autoeroticism and the Remains of Asian America." *Novel: A Forum on Fiction* 31, 2: 215–236.

Ishiguro, Kazuo. 1982. *A Pale View of Hills.* New York: Vintage.

_____. 1989. *The Remains of the Day.* New York: Vintage.

Praz, Mario. 1968. "Introduction," in *Three Gothic Novels.* Ed. Peter Fairclough. New York: Penguin, 7–34.

Lang, James M. 2000. "Public Memory, Private History: Kazuo Ishiguro's *The Remains of the Day,*" *Clio: A Journal of Literature, History and the Philosophy of History* 29, 2: 143–65.

Mackenzie, Suzie. 2000. "Between Two Worlds." *Guardian*, March 25.

Shaikh, Nermeen. Copyright 2007. "Q & A, AsiaSource Interview with Kazuo Ishiguro." *http://www. asiasource.org/news/special_reports/ishiguro.cfm* (Accessed 14/03/07).

Su, John J. 2002. "Refiguring National Character: The Remains of the British Estate Novel." *Modern Fiction Studies* 48, 3: 552–580.

Tamaya, Meera. 1992."Ishiguro's *Remains of the Day*: The Empire Strikes Back." *Modern Language Studies* 22, 2: 45–56.

Veyret, Paul. 2005. "The Strange Case of the Disappearing Chinamen: Memory and Desire in Kazuo Ishiguro's *The Remains of the Day* and *When We Were Orphans.*" *Etudes britanniques contemporaines: revue de la Societe d'etudes anglaises contemporaines* 29: 159–172.

Walpole, Horace. 1764. *The Castle of Otranto, A Story*, in *Three Gothic Novels.* 1968. Ed. Peter Fairclough, New York: Penguin, 1968.

Wong, Cynthia F. 2001. "Like Idealism is to Intellect: An Interview with Kazuo Ishiguro," *Clio: A Journal of Literature, History and the Philosophy of History* 30, 3: 309–325.

Zhang, Longxi. 1988. "The Myth of the Other: China in the Eyes of the West," *Critical Inquiry* 15, 1: 108–131.

Part II

---⊗⊗⊗---

*Asian American
Gothic Literature*

6

Sky Lee's *Disappearing Moon Cafe*: A Testimony of Incorporation

Nieves Pascual Soler

Deliberately, like Maxine Hong Kingston, Amy Tan, Fae Myenne Ng, Wayson Choy, Paul Yee, Judy Fong Bates, and Denise Chong, Chinese Canadian writer Sky Lee complicates the idea of generic integrity in *Disappearing Moon Cafe* (1991), her first novel. Partly fictitious, the text is also bound by the real, where places and events are recognizable, as Alison Calder notes. In "Paper Families and Blonde Demonesses: The Haunting of History in Sky Lee's *Disappearing Moon Cafe*," she examines the historical, geographic, political, and cultural details in the novel, to conclude that the 1923 Canadian law against Chinese immigration, the emergence of racist associations, the rebellion against immigrant labour in Vancouver during the years 1887 and 1907, the Janet Smith Bill for the protection of working white women, and the racial violence hidden in the legal discourses of the period, are at the base of the novel.

Although haunted by the local specificities of history, Lee ensures that they are comprehensible in other circumstances by careful explanations and the use of popular and transhistorical forms which, in Ann Barr Snitow's opinion, "appeal to the depth structures in all our minds" (246), with a "language mainlining into areas of our conscious and subconscious selves by routes that by-pass many of the things we know or believe about the real world of our daily experience" (252). In this understanding, Graham Huggan examines Lee's novel as part of the genealogical romance, "a tradition in which romantic adventures are assimilated to identitary fable, and the generational conflicts of an extended family are contained within a redemptive structure of collective — 'group' — endeavour" (35–36). Redemptive insofar as Lee's narrator learns to overcome the colonial stigma associated with hybridism by parodying TV melodrama, and combining its structures with certain organizing principles in Cantonese opera. Through parody Sky Lee — Huggan claims — deconstructs the myths of racial purity and superiority that obsess the characters, destroys the fiction of patriarchal lineage, and builds up the need for solidarity among women.

But the reality presented by Sky Lee is also mediated by Gothic conventions. "Gothic plots are family plots," writes Anne Williams in *Art of Darkness* (22), and Lee's text is the plot of the life-and-death struggles of the Wong family in Canada through four generations, till its final disintegration in 1987. The castle, "a central term of the Gothic in the early days" (22) is substituted by a restaurant that houses the feelings and desires of the narrator's ancestors, and a dream, which Williams describes as the Gothic grammar (71), opens the text and sets the story's tone (Lee 2). Finally, "that quintessentially Gothic issue — legitimate descent and rightful inheritance" (Williams 239) mobilizes the actions of the characters. Apart from that, Gothic tropes (ghosts, crypts, secrets, lies, incest, guilt, shame, tombs, traumas and forbidden desires) abound in Lee's novel as well.

The aesthetics of the Gothic provide an interesting perspective from which Confucian rules of ancestor worship and filial piety can be construed. In adhering to these values, Lee simultaneously reinforces and reverses the Gothic imperative to disclose and dispel. Traditional Gothic narratives often serve as a testimony of relinquishment that allows solace to the writers through an expurgation of memories. By way of writing, the ghosts of ancestors are revived to be exorcised. A different mechanism, however, seems at work in Lee's novel. Although Lee's narrator, Kae Ying Woo, also revives her ancestors through writing, it is to *maintain their presence*. Writing enables these ghosts to return and to "stay" with and in her. Using the psychoanalytical theories on mourning (introjection) and melancholia (incorporation) propounded by Freud, and then refined further by Nicholas Abraham and Maria Torok, I argue that whereas traditional Gothic discourse "introjects" the dead to expel them from memory, Lee's narrative "incorporates" them to comply with their demand for remembrance and attention, as Confucius dictates. This analysis also provides an insight into the divergent ways in which different cultures perform respect for the dead, and more importantly, how these differences have direct ideological impacts. A brief outline of Confucianism and the virtue of filial piety is also provided to frame this reading of Lee's novel. A comparison of Western and Chinese ways of mourning demonstrates that against the western diagnosis of incorporation as a pathological condition that impoverishes the self, the Chinese manner of incorporating the dead permits the reconstitution of a healthy racialized body.

The Gothic and Its Dead Other: Mourning and Melancholia

Consistently, says Fred Botting, the Gothic "has depicted the transgression of moral laws, aesthetic rules and social taboos," creating uncertainty about the perimeters of the nation and the self (1). Anne Williams corroborates this point further when she writes that the "Gothic is so pervasively organized around anxieties about boundaries (and boundary transgression) that the border between self and other might indeed characterize the 'essential situation'" (16). In light of these views, and if, as Hayden White argues, narrative events determine the kind of story to be told (40), the Gothic seems an appropriate venue for dramatizing ethnic identities torn between assimilation (read as threat to boundaries) and exclusion (as maintenance of one's own cultural integrity). Inevitably, what Williams calls the "essential [Gothic] situation" also organizes the works of psychoanalysis, which is invariably structured around relationships between "what's inside, what's outside, and what separates them" (Sedgwick 12).[1] For Williams, this "essential situation" that features so prominently in the Gothic is the Freudian unconscious. The "unconscious" in psychoanalysis is of course, a multilayered configuration, but one of the ways in which it manifests itself is through the mechanism of melancholia of which its symptoms, according to Williams, "coincide with conventional Gothic paraphernalia" (63).

A brief outline of Freud's views on mourning and melancholia, and their later modification by Abraham and Torok, is useful at this juncture. According to Freud, a mourner undergoes three stages: identification with/introversion of the loss object (the dearly departed), decathexis (whereby all libido is withdrawn from its attachments to that object), and finally, forgetting (in which the subject overcomes the loss of the object). For Freud, this constitutes a "normal" and healthy direction for experiencing loss (1964, 243). Melancholia, by contrast, prevents the subject from getting over the loss. Instead, the libido is:

> withdrawn into the ego. There, however, it was not employed in any specified way, but served to establish an identification of the ego with the abandoned object [...]. The ego wants to incorporate this object into itself,

and, in accordance with the oral or cannibalistic phase of libidinal development in which it is, it wants to do so by devouring it [249–50].

By integrating the lost other (object) within the self, this other is maintained
within the subject's psyche akin to a spectral presence that haunts. Extend-
ing Freud's theory, Abraham and Torok redefine mourning as a process of
introjection, and melancholia as incorporation. The mourner introjects
the lost love object but is able to overcome this loss by putting it into language: "Learning to fill the emptiness of the mouth with words is the initial
model for introjection" (128). I will return to this theory later. The melancholic, in contrast, is unable to metaphorize loss and instead literally "ingests"
the other. Through incorporation, Abraham and Torok argue, the subject
implements "literally something that has figurative meaning. So in order
not to have to 'swallow' [in the sense of having to accept] a loss, we fantasize
swallowing (or having swallowed) [in the literal sense of eating] that which
has been lost, as if it were some kind of thing" (126). The lost other, once
incorporated, is entombed within the self (which now functions as a crypt)
but remains still apart from the ego, which is now given the task of a
cemetery guard (159). Žižek considers this incorporation of the other into
oneself as materializing a symbolic debt on account of a sin or crime committed in the past by the love object (25). In this logic, "we can conclude [...]
that the primary aim of the fantasy life born of incorporation is to repair —
in the realm of the imaginary, of course — the injury that really occurred
and really affected the ideal object" (134).[2] The traumatic potential of
having the ideal object's offence revealed is therefore kept locked within, and
barred from, the subject's consciousness in order to maintain the object's
"innocence."

As long as the "crypt" remains intact, loss is unconsciously preserved
within the subject. But in the event that its walls are breached, for example,
"as a result of the loss of some secondary love-object who had buttressed
them" (136), the phantom housed within the self now overcomes the ego to
"possess" the subject who, in turn, now serves as their embodiment.[3] Abraham and Torok term this mechanism of exchanging one's identity for a fantasmic identification with the love object, "endocryptic identification":

> In endocryptic identification, the "I" is understood as the lost object's fanta-
> sized ego[...]. The "I" stages the words, gestures, and feelings — in short, the
> entire imaginary love — of the lover who mourns for his forever "dead" object
> [148].

This theory has interesting significance when framed within a family romance.
As a child often "endocryptically identifies" with his or her parent(s), the trans-

mission of family secrets or phantoms (usually shameful ones) can transform the former into a repository and guardian of the latter's unspoken history which sometimes is not even known to the "cemetery guard" him- or herself. This locks the child within perpetual mourning — or melancholia — because the child, simply because s/he does not know of his/her parent(s) secret, cannot lay the latter to rest. As Andrew Ng, drawing on Abraham and Torok, explains, "the secret is buried in [the child], but he is not the secret's owner, thus lodging an other within his self. He is 'traumatised' because the secret cannot be cathected from his psyche, positioning him instead in an endless loop of returning to the point of the secret" (110). More insidiously, this looping does not merely end with a single generation, but actually conditions the fate of several generations to come, giving rise to endless fractured lives. In a similar respect Derrida, in his introduction to Abraham and Torok's *The Wolf Man's Magic Word*, explains that "incorporation is never finished" because the endless repetition the phantom (or secret) gives rise to is inscribed in the contradictory structure of the process of incorporation:

> By resisting introjection, it (incorporation) prevents the loving, appropriating assimilation of the other, and thus seems to preserve the other *as* other (foreign), but it also does the opposite. It is not the other that the process of incorporation preserves, but a certain topography it keeps safe, intact, untouched by the very relationship with the other to which, paradoxically enough, introjection is more open [1986, xxi–xxii].

The insoluble contradiction between preserving the other *as other* and preserving the other *as self* prevents incorporation from ever concluding.[4] Then, there is the "structural multiplicity in the cryptic incorporation," the fact that "the crypt must incorporate *more than one* [indeed all those involved in the secret] and behave toward it more *than one way*" (xviii), so that different repressed materials are activated. Hence, the promulgation of secrets/phantoms over generations, exploding in multiple forms of often pathological problems, becomes inevitable.

Introjection, by contrast, is successful mourning. When introjection occurs the subject is able to finally articulate the secret/phantom and dispel it. This linguistic performance exorcises the ghost that has been haunting the subject and loss is finally accepted and overcome. The narratives of traditional Gothic romances seem to privilege introjection through the explication of the secret which has mobilized the events in the first place. As Anne Williams contends, the "resolution of the conventional Gothic mystery coincides with the revelation of a particular family secret, usually a hitherto unrecognized aspect of family relationship" (45).[5]

Filial Piety in Confucian Tradition

The psychoanalytical views on mourning and melancholia discussed above, however, take on a very different configuration when approached from a Confucian perspective. If Western understanding of mourning is to relieve the mourner of the object through a mechanism of "forgetting," the Eastern (or more specifically, Chinese) injunction to remember the dearly departed for as long as the subject is alive, is curiously akin to Freudian melancholia. To understand this, it is important to revisit the cultural imperative of filial piety that underlies Confucian ideology and structures the Oriental family systems. In 1949 anthropologist Francis L.K. Hsu describes the modern Chinese community as a social organization grounded on the Confucian rule of *hsiao*, filial piety, which consists of serving one's parents when they are alive, burying their bodies when they die, and remembering them afterwards (207).[6] After a good coffin and a tomb are procured, the family must commence a ritualized expression of grief through ascetic observances (mourning robes, wailing, prayer, and fast), and offerings to satisfy the needs of their predecessors: "In dealing with the dead, if we treat them as if they were entirely dead, that would show a want of affection, and should not be done; or, if we treat them as if they were entirely alive, that would show a want of wisdom, and should not be done," says Confucius in the *Book of Rites*, one of the six classics in which he restores the value of rituals and propagates the rules of propriety as a way of moral improvement (II. i., iii., 3).[7] Still these "spiritual intelligences" behave as living people (Harrell 527), and make certain demands on their living relatives such as for edibles (grain or fruits, so that they are free from hunger), for money (to satiate their materialistic desires), and for a house (to shelter them).[8] The souls of the dead, now separated from the bodies, abide in spirit tablets inscribed with their surnames, names, and ranks at the time of death (*shen-chu*). The first tablet, made of silk, is temporary. It is "fastened up under the eaves above the steps on the east," and carried by the eldest grandson in an elaborate funeral procession. After the internment, this tablet is burned and its inscription is transferred to a permanent one made of wood before which, at the family altar, offerings are presented from generation to generation (*Li Ki*, II, ii., i., 26). In time, these ancestral tablets will accrue, and whenever the principle male member of the family — usually the oldest son — goes travelling, he takes "(one of) those tablets along with him, conveying it in the carriage of Reverence, thus intimating how it was felt necessary to have with him that object of honour" (II, v., i., 24). In wealthy families, the spirit tablets are gathered under the roof of the clan shrine-temple, and it bodes ill for the family to fail in its duties towards these ancestors. Neglect is usually punished with bad fortune. Having said this however, the spirits of ancestors can be malicious for no apparent reason as well (Ahern 200).[9]

Family Secrets

It should be evident from the discussion above that for the Chinese, mourning is a prolonged activity requiring constant "incorporation" of the departed into the family structure itself. Because ancestors are deeply revered, they remain a constant fixture in any Chinese family makeup, whose duty it is to uphold the continuation of their phantom presences. I say phantom here, because the "housing" of these ancestors entail that the "children" also preserve their secrets. In Sky Lee's novel, the preservation of dark pasts has a more profound significance because the children literally *embody* their parents' shameful and unspeakable secrets. An outline of the narrative's protagonist's family tree will evince this.

Disappearing Moon Cafe begins in Vancouver at the end of the nineteenth century. We are introduced to Wong Gwei Chang, Kae Ying Woo's (the protagonist) great-grandfather. He is gathering the bones of dead Chinese workers along the Canadian Pacific Railway in order to send them back to China for burial. At that time, family and district associations were busily involved in the business of returning bodies, which were exhumed and painstakingly prepared for shipment to China.[10]

Chang falls in love with Kelora Chen, a Native Indian woman, but whom he later abandons to go back to China, where he marries another woman. Internal revolts and famine, however, force Chang and many others to return to Canada. Arriving in Canada once again, he sets up the "New Disappearing Moon Cafe" which, during the 1920s, is the largest and most popular Chinese restaurant in Vancouver. In 1911, once he has saved money enough to pay for the tickets of his new wife, Lee Mui Lan, and his son, Wong Choy Fuk, he sends for them. Transplantation does not negate Chinese tradition, and Lee Mui Lan, who is obsessed with the need to marry her son to an authentic Chinese woman, imports Chan Fong Mei from China. The marriage proves infertile, but Mui Lan finds him a concubine, Song Ang, to bear sons: "our customs are clear and practical too. If the first wife cannot bear a son, then she stands aside for another. That way, the family is assured of a yellow, 'lucky' road" (60), she explains to her daughter-in-law. However, Fong Mei feels aggravated by this loathsome living arrangement, and starts an affair with Wong Ting An, who turns out to be the son of Gwei Chang and Kelora. In 1926 two babies are born, Beatrice, daughter to Fong Mei and Ting An, and Keeman, son to Song Ang and seemingly Choy Fuk (seemingly, because we later discover that Fuk is sterile). Three years after Beatrice, Suzanne is born. Beatrice marries her supposedly half-brother Keeman, and Suzanne gets pregnant by Morgan, son to Ting An, her own father, and a French-Canadian woman. Suzanne later delivers a baby who dies at birth, and she then commits suicide. Kae, Beatrice's daughter — and the novel's narrator — marries Henry Lee, and gives birth to Robert Man Jook Lee. "[G]iven the importance of the family as the basic organizing principle in the (Gothic) narratives," (Williams 45) and in view of the fact that I am approaching Lee's text as Gothic, the detailed information about Kae's family history becomes highly pronounced: it is a family history laced with the unspeakable sin of incest, which remains locked in the various generations' psychic vault, resulting in repetitive pathological patterns. In this sense then does Kae and her family bear the terrible mark of ancestral secrets literally upon their bodies. So, in 1987, when Kae finally decides to *write* her family's history ("I have been faithfully told, and I have also respectfully remembered," she declares [19]), is it a performance to face her family phantoms and exorcise them once and for all? Or is writing a compliance with her debt of filial piety, which thus sustains familial melancholia? The rest of the essay will seek to answer these questions.

The Memories of Kae Ying Woo

That the dark secret of Kae's family has remained largely undisclosed for a long time is principally the result of apathy. The struggle to assimilate and adapt to a new cultural and national identity has taken precedence over family ties, and family history has become ignored in the pursuit of carving individualistic historical niches. In the novel, integrands of the second generation continue to either remain nostalgic of the past (Fong Mei), or wish to forget it altogether (Choy Fuk), or attempt an uneasy negotiation between past and present by integrating the two (Ting An). Their choices are made manifest through the kinds of spaces they frequent, which explicitly reflects their psychic identifications. As the narrative informs us:

> Disappearing Moon Cafe was divided into two front sections, with the kitchen and the storeroom at the back. The dining room was the largest in Chinatown, perhaps the most beautiful in all of Vancouver, with its teak carvings on the pillars and gateways[...]. It was a nostalgic replica of an old-fashioned Chinese teahouse[...]. However, Choy Fuk liked the more modern

counter-and-booth section better. [...] except for the customers, his mother, and perhaps the cacti, there was nothing Chinese about it [32].

Fong Mei prefers the dining-room, a bristling space covered with ornament and filled with the tumult of memories. Choy Fuk, however, inclines towards a diaphanous room devoid of history and designed for the purposes of utility only. Ting An, by contrast, glides between these two sections.

The endeavour to assimilate nationalistically and culturally becomes even more pronounced in the third generation. Losing their ethnic memory and aggregating into the mainstream (read dominant) society, these individuals try to become as "Canadian" (read White) as they can. Beatrice, for examples, grows "thoroughly small-town Canadian" (164). She abandons Chinatown, "and never looks back" (145). Suzanne feels incarcerated at home (212) and hates "all the years of dressing [...] up like monkeys and [being told] to behave like good little girls" (202). Morgan never steps into Chinatown for fear that "he might get mistaken for a Chinaman himself" (172). From a Confucian perspective, their disregard of the past, and the neglect of their duties to the dead provide the necessary conditions for the fantasmic return of ancestral spectres. From a psychoanalytical perspective, this refusal to acknowledge the past ironically preserves it, which resurfaces to "disturbs" the subject at the level of the unconscious.

In the narrative, it is Kae — a third generation daughter — who is most aware of her haunted status. This prompts her act of writing in order to "face" her phantoms. But what has triggered this sudden "return" of the phantom after it has lain dormant for so long? The answer, I propose, may lie in another form of melancholia that beseeches her, and all other hyphenated individuals who struggle with liminal identities. The process of acculturation, or assimilation, has often been theorized as an act of personal relinquishment whereby minority subjects are enjoined, albeit unconsciously, to renounce themselves. On renouncing an original cultural identification that is degraded by one's current culture but impossible to dissolve as it is the very foundation of the self, the racialized subject becomes, as Ann Cheng explains, "actively melancholic" (40) in that what she attempts to exclude has become buried within her psyche but not forgotten.[11] Cheng further argues that "[R]acial melancholia [...] has always existed for raced subjects as a *sign* of rejection [of loss] and a psychic *strategy* [repression of consciousness] in response to that negation" (20). The loss is rejected and, as already noted, barred from consciousness until the walls of the crypt are breached by a second destitution, which will bring the first to consciousness (Abraham and Torok 141). When awareness of loss is thus awakened in the acculturated subject, the wound reopens.

This reopening precipitates the need to recover one's roots in order to secure the half of the self the ethnic subject has rejected.

Hence, two forms of melancholia — one incorporation, the other racial — seem to set off Kae's desire to finally expose her family phantoms, and by doing so, consolidate her identity as both Chinese and Canadian. Racial melancholia propels the various generations of Kae's families to deny their cultural and familial roots, directly locking the family within the vault of their incestuous (refused-)memory and history. But a concerted attempt to rediscover one's past would entail the disclosure of dark family secrets that is not only an unfilial act, but one which can potentially disrupt one's fragile sense of identity; yet to do so is also a powerful means to overcome racial melancholia. Kae's desire to rediscover her past demonstrates her struggle to dissolve her sense of unbelonging within the dominant group by consolidating for herself a subjectivity rooted in her own ethnic and cultural identity. In *Disappearing Moon Cafe*, it seems that to surmount racial melancholia requires the acknowledgement of the incorporation of phantoms.

This may explain why Kae, who has more or less successfully assimilated into the ideational content of the Canadian identity, and who has, in the process, largely relinquished traditional Chinese modes of self-actualization, is compelled to become the carrier of "the big secret" (191). But the narrative suggests however, that a specific event in her life actually triggered this sudden shift. Kae becomes pregnant, and it is during this extremely emotional time of gestation that she regains a sense of intergenerational continuity, and turns against the grain of assimilation to which she has so far consented. After a difficult delivery, she decides to cease resisting her past, but begins to cultivate remembering instead (incidentally, birthing as the originary moment of transformation is, in Anne Williams's view, a Gothic motif [158]). The expulsion of another body from within her (parturition), which I read as symptomatic of a "second loss," is what that jolts the first loss (through acculturation), which has hitherto remained repressed, into consciousness.

This view finds substantiation in Derrida's *Mémoires: For Paul de Man*, in which he elaborates a theory of melancholia as pregnancy. According to Derrida, the incorporation of the dearly departed object within the self is akin to pregnancy. This "other" is now "part of us, included 'in us' in a memory which suddenly feels greater and older than us [...] greater *with* this other, greater than itself, inadequate to itself, pregnant with this other" (1989, 37). Pregnancy, Derrida argues, is a "faithful interiorization [that] bears the other and constitutes him in me (in us), at once living and dead. It makes the other no longer quite seem to be other, because we grieve for him and bear him in us, like a child, an unborn child, like a future" (35). Derrida negotiates the trauma of de Man's loss by imagining that he is "pregnant" with his friend. He keeps the other, who is and is not other-than-self after interiorization, within, "into the pocket of a cyst" (1986, xxxviii), but without completely assimilating him. There his friend lies, far from dormant, filling Derrida like a fetus and conditioning his words. Appropriating Derrida's fecund theory, Erin Soros, who argues that all analysis of encryptment expresses a fantasy of pregnancy, affirms that "pregnancy functions as a form of encryption — an act of keeping a secret and a refusal to mourn. The trauma is pocketed within her womb[...]. [Its memory] fills her belly like a word holding all she cannot say [...] only to be expelled, screaming its first sound through her second mouth" (7).

Based on the theories discussed above, one may argue that the child which is growing within Kae comes to symbolize, at least for her, the memories of her familial past — her womb transformed into a silk cocoon for their secrets, like a first memorial tablet, and her foetus into the phantom enclosed within it. As such, it follows through labor, she figuratively delivers the ghosts (at one point in the narrative, Kae calls her baby a "dead ghost" [49]) of her heritage to exposure, expels her familial trauma, and expiate guilt (theirs and hers) — all performed through the first "screaming" of her "second" mouth (her child).

But Kae's delivery metonymically impels another mode of "labor," that is, through writing. Like pregnancy and parturition, writing entails the "holding in" of other identities (phantoms) within the self which must be eventually expelled in the act of scripting. Kae writes in a painful attempt to repair the offences of her ancestors. "I've landed up paying dearly for their deeds," says Kae, referring to her grandparents' transgressive history of incest (31, 132), the shame which has infected the whole Wong family, unleashing a long history of substance abuse, social phobias, eating disorders, domestic violence, and, even suicide. Because the *Li Ki* prohibits marriage between individuals of a similar surname or related within the fifth degree of kindred (Appendix to Book I), this crime of incest has long been a well-kept secret. As long as the secret remains undisclosed, "then it never existed" (Lee 161). Yet, the unspeakable gets spoken in the narrative.[12] Kae discovers that in 1923, the Canadian law against Chinese immigration forced a rapidly diminishing Canadian-Chinese community to withdraw "into itself ripe for incest" (147). The prevalence of incest in this community was exposed to reflect the fear of contagion by the racial other (that is, the white) that had affected both sides of the Vancouverite contact zone at the end of the nineteenth century. For this declining group, incest was the means to bind the Chinese community together and to ensure the purity of racial blood. But rather than construing incest as an "evil," Kae recasts it as her *source of authority* to memorialize her ancestors, especially the female ones who are normally obscured by Chinese patrilineal systems. If, according to Freud in *Totem and Taboo* (1913), incest is what destabilizes the father-son knot, and that the renunciation of this "crime" guarantees the patriarchal imperative, then it makes sense that Kae would want to "unearth" this family secret as a way to articulate her matrilineal past into textual being. Kae deploys the narrative of incest to make the mother the ultimate guarantor of continuity and identity: "By parents she naturally meant her mother and her grandmother" (169). Obsessed with origins and authenticity (128), when Kae realizes that the family story cannot be found in her "fathers," she reassigns the role of memory to women through whom she will now seek historical authentication, for it is women who "always want to dig beneath the surface" (39). Kae's exposure of her family's unsavory history thus directly violates the sanctity of ancestral secrets which must be upheld and protected, as well as the patrilineal assumptions of the old Chinese kinship system, which prescribes mourning and filial worship as responsibilities of sons (*Li-Ki* II, i., i.). Also, her attempt to make sense of the world through female ancestors has curiously Gothic overtones, one which Anne Williams, in her designation of female Gothic, sees as an assertion of the female self "nurtured outside the conflict of fathers and sons" (Williams 139), and against the "assumptions of patriarchal culture" (138).

That Kae incorporates her female ancestors into herself, and who are then given articulation, are suggested by the indeterminacy of the choice of pronouns and points of view in her writing. For example, when recalling Suzanne's suicide, the recount begins in the third person but then subtly shifts to the first: "Suzie is on the verge of death again; her labour long and hard[...]. The baby is struggling, pitching about inside of me. Oh, this pain! If I had a razor" (206). This abrupt textual slippage implies Kae's fantasmic identification with her aunt, which directly demonstrates a testimony of incorporation. And Suzanne is not the only spectral "citation" that intermittently emerges from Kae's "I." Ultimately, in effect, Kae's writing is a dialogue with citations from the dead which she has inserted ("or incorporated") into herself and her text. In the novel, this notion of various ancestral phantoms residing within the "I" is most obviously noted by Hermia, Kae's friend, in a series of questions:

> Do you mean that individuals must gather their identity from all the generations that touch them — past and future, no matter how slightly? Do you mean that an individual is not an individual at all, but a series of individuals — some of whom came before her, some after her? Do you mean that this story isn't a story of several generations, but of one individual thinking collectively? [189].

Whether it is an individual thinking for a collective, or a collective thinking through the individual, for Kae, subjectivity is dependent on the presence of the collective within the self, and premised on a dialogic relationship with this collective. The self is a sedimentation of imagos (or spectres) with which she identifies and nourishes, and which in turn, nourish her into signification. Through writing then, Kae becomes simultaneously impregnated by the ghosts of her ancestors, and delivered of these same ghosts. Since this process of "endocryptic identification" with someone else's words and affects entails the disappearance of hypertrophied individualism that constitutes the subject model in mainstream Western society, for theorists such as Abraham and Torok, this identification is symptomatic of self-destruction (142). But *Disappearing Moon Café* provides a alternative model: instead of being "destroyed" because she allows ghosts to use her as home and conduit, Kae is actually sustained and provided with a healthy sense of self and belonging.[13]

Having unveiled the unspeakable history that has haunted Kae's family — the "lousy story that could have been thrown into the wastepaper basket a long time ago" (Lee 132) — it seems that the phantoms can be finally exorcised, in the way Abraham and Torok would have it (128). Huggan seems to take this view when he claims, with respect to Lee's narrative, that "in the third generation of granddaughters is the burden of the unspeakable past finally cast off" (86). I beg to differ however. The family's history of incest may be have been revealed, but the narrative seems to suggest that there remains other undisclosed secrets which, because they are deposited within the vault of maternal memory, will remain forever buried. A diary entry written by Kae in 1986 provides a crucial clue:

> "You don't know, A Kae," whispers my mother, "but there has been much trouble in our family. It's best that what I tell you does not go beyond these four walls."
> Thus the story — the well-kept secret that I had actually unearthed years ago —finally begins to end with me with the birth of my son, Robert Man Jook Lee, on April 29, 1986. It took quite the sentimental occasion for my mother to finally loosen a little of her iron grip on her emotions in order to reveal a little of her past that she thought so shameful — the same past that has shaped so much of my own life, with evil tentacles that could have even wormed into the innocent, tender parts of my baby. No, no, it will not be so unless I make it so. And I will leave it boxed in our past — mine and my mother's, the four walls that we share! [23].

Kae's diary entry gives the impression that the mother has not fully divulged everything about the family's past to her, and that she (the mother) harbors another secret, still psychically interred in her, about which nothing can be determined. In fact, greater than the sin of incest, this other "secret" proves much more harrowing, and hence even more unspeakable. As Kae relates of this secret: "the final reckoning [will always be] deeply buried within my mother ... [who] still needs that margin of silence from the guilt and the pain" (179–80). Kae demands that her mother tells her the "truth"(180), but is refused, compelling Kae into a debt to which she is incognizant. Unlike the story of incest, which upon knowing, sets Kae free and explains her family's disturbing past, the mother's story, if unveiled, can prove treacherous. Seto Chi, Kae's mother's housekeeper, seems to understand the gravity of this other, indeterminable story, and the need to preserve its silence. Once confronted by Kae who insists that she reveals the secret, Chi angrily replies: "No, you don't [...] you want to hear about smut, and the guilt. And who is to blame for the little lost babies[...]" (132). Clearly, Chi has intuited that Kae's interest in the family history arises from more prurient reasons than from a genuine desire to understand her family's past. Chi refuses to satiate Kae's voyeuristic needs, allowing the "secret" to persist as a kind of monument to the ancestors.

Kae could have relinquished her mother's furtive tale as unimportant, but instead, she faithfully records the unspoken, because *she realizes the debt she owes her mother for not divulging the story*. Kae comes to acknowledge that it is the gift of her mother's silence that has nurtured her writing, confessing that "a great work of art is supposedly prepared within the silence of the heart" (191). Henceforth, she will write in order to *continue* her family's (or more specifically, her mother's) lineage; she will consciously embody melancholia because, as a woman and mother, and therefore the keeper of the family's inheritance (be they unspeakably shameful) she can function as both the upholder of her ancestral history (and hence, perform filial piety), as well as protect her son (the next generation) from becoming infected by his ancestry's venom. As noted, because dark secrets are the repository of womenfolk, that Kae decides not to pursue her mother's secret suggests that it will end with her (Kae), and that her son will be spared this burden. Furthermore, the birth of Kae's son also connotes the breaking of the vicious loop which has thus far confined her family in a secret history of shame. Unlike his mother and grandparents, this boy is not a product of incest or adultery.

The journey that opens the novel also concludes it. Kae relinquishes her job in Vancouver and migrates to Hong Kong. When asked by Hermia if she would rather live a great novel or write one, Kae answers, "I'd rather live one" (216). In her quest to rediscover family history in order to paradoxically free and preserve it (and her), this final passage home may not be so surprising after all, but a logical culmination. Travelling, in fact, also implies a loss that reopens the space for new ingestions and the re-animation of other memories, a point which Derrida also postulates when he writes that "incorporation is never finished" (1986, xxi.). As Confucius mandates, Kae feeds and houses her dead ancestors. Her feeling of guilt persists because it signifies acknowledgement of, and possession by the past. In Confucian belief, the ancestral debt can never be fully be paid because it would mean a cessation of self and history (or an oblivion), so intricately is the self tied to his or her past.

Notes

1. In *The Coherence of Gothic Conventions* (2001), Sedgwick makes the link between the Gothic and psychoanalysis on the grounds of their imaginary topographies. See also Joey Castricano (2001) on the Gothic topoi that have appeared in psychoanalytic work and in Derridean discourse.

2. Abraham and Torok see fantasy as "all those representations, beliefs, and bodily states that gravitate toward [...] the preservation of the status quo" (125). Since this preservation is sought for and maintained at the cost of transforming the world, incorporation inheres a very profound mode of fantasizing.

3. A phantom is the carrier of secrets. I will use the terms "phantom" and "ghost" when talking about the incorporated object.

4. The contradiction is typical in every love relationship formed by the ego. See Freud (1964, 256).

5. In fact, the practice of writing the Gothic seems to have certain therapeutic qualities attached to it which aids the writer to overcome his or her own sense of melancholia. Likewise, Sedgwick underscores the autobiographical underpinnings of the Gothic novel, and suggests that its writers subconsciously abort their interior ghosts by triggering their revival through composition (Sedgwick 13). For example, H.P. Lovecraft claims that his art helped him discharge from his mind "certain phantasmal shapes which would otherwise haunt" him (Lovecraft 23).

6. Hsu's study may be related to the modern Chinese community, but the various Confucian principles outlined in his work have been in practice throughout China since ancient times.

7. The other five are: the *Book of Music, the Book of History,* the *Book of Poetry,* the *Book of Changes,* and the *Spring and Autumn Annals.* All six books help establish a good government (Xinzhong 51). James Legge translates the *Book of Rites,* or *Li Ki,* in two volumes. I will follow in Legge's example of keeping the Chinese title; citations are made according to the book number (the volume is subdivided into 10 books), section number, part number, and finally, paragraph number. Hence, a citation that reads (II, i., iii., 3.) suggests that the excerpt is from Book II, section 1, part 3, and paragraph 3).

8. In Chinese beliefs, the dead continues to desire the kinds of material comfort that they enjoyed, or did not have, while they were alive. These desires can be satiated through paper replicas of houses, money, household items and other luxury items (such as jewelry, fancy cars, and even servants) which will then be collectively burned as offerings to appease the dead. Provision for shelter is most crucial for homeless spirits (that is, those who have died away from home, or who have been improperly buried).

9. Since industrialization became the Communist political system's priority after 1949, when the People's Republic of China was established, traditional values and behavior were attacked as being "backward." The totalitarian government repressed religious freedom and disrupted the Confucian-sanctified familial systems based on self-governing clans. When the old funeral rites were condemned as a waste of money and cultivable land, burials at sea were initiated. In 1956 Mao Zedong signed a proposal advocating cremation in China. Yet, despite adversities, Confucianism survived the impact of the Cultural revolution. According to Adam Yuet, writing in 2005,

> The reform era (from the early 1980 onward) of the People's Republic of China has witnessed a massive re-emergence of ostensibly traditional Chinese folk beliefs and practices. [...] all of a sudden people are busy rebuilding or renovating temples, ancestral halls, and graves that were torn down during the Cultural Revolution, reconstructing family genealogies that were burnt by the Red Guards, re-enacting long suppressed rituals around births, weddings, and deaths, going to temple festivals, reading ritual handbooks and consulting fortune-tellers and geomancers, praying

for male babies, or simply thinking feudalistic thoughts. (See also studies by Harell [1979] and Xinzhong [2000])

For Yuet the return to old religious customs and practices is partly the result of diverse political interests in the temple as a valuable economic resource (3). But from a psychoanalytical perspective, this "return" also suggests the work of melancholia embedded within political ideology, of which a critical study remains entirely unexplored.

10. Yet, despite the importance of burial at home for the early Chinese emigrants, in 1936 the reburial custom stopped following a series of international events. The invasion of China by the Japanese, World War II, and the internal Communist-Nationalist conflict closed the borders of the nation to the mortal remains of Chinese immigrants. See Nelson (1993) for further elaboration.

11. Although Cheng constructs the racialized identity as melancholic she does not agree with the view that assimilation entails the evacuation of one's racialized self, but instead examines assimilation as a form of occupation and embodiment of the raced other, "almost a bodily incorporation of the other" (79).

12. On the unspeakable as a motif in Gothic fiction, see Sedgwick (97–139).

13. Almost as if to carry through the metaphor of ingesting as symptomatic of melancholia, Kae expressly describes her stories as digestible units swallowed through her own process of writing: "I thought that [...] the intricate complexities of a family with Chinese roots could be massaged into a suant, digestible unit. Like a herbal pill — I thought I could swallow it and my mind would become enlightened [...]. So, having swallowed the pill, here I am, still waiting. For enlightenment" (19–20).

Works Cited

Abraham, Nicolas, and Maria Torok. 1994. *The Shell and the Kernel.* Trans. Nicholas Rand. Chicago: University of Chicago Press.

Ahern, Emily M. 1973. *The Cult of the Dead in a Chinese Village.* Stanford: Stanford University Press.

Botting, Fred. 2001. "Introduction." *The Gothic.* Ed. Fred Botting. Cambridge: D.S. Brewer, 1–7.

Calder, Alison. 2000. " Paper Families and Blonde Demonesses: The Haunting of History in Sky Lee's *Disappearing Moon Cafe.*" *Ariel* 31, 4: 7–21.

Castricano, Joey. 2001. *Cryptomimesis. The Gothic and Jacques Derrida's Ghost Writing.* Montreal & Kingston: McGill-Queen's University Press.

Chau, Adam Yuet. 2005. *Miraculous Response: Doing Popular Religion in Contemporary China.* Stanford: Stanford University Press.

Cheng, Anne Anlin. 2001. *The Melancholy of Race.* Oxford: Oxford University Press.

Chu, Julie Y. "Card Me When I'm Dead: Identification Papers and the Pursuit of Burial Rights in Fuzhou, China."<http://www.irmgard-coninxstiftung.de/fileadmin/user_upload/pdf/roundtable 07/Chu.pdf> (Accessed 30 Jan. 2007).

Derrida, Jacques. 1986. "Foreword: Fors: The Anglish Words of Nicholas Abraham and Maria Torok," in *The Wolf Man's Magic Words.* Nicholas Abraham and Maria Torok, trans. Nicholas Rand. Minneapolis: University of Minnesota Press, xi–xlviii.

_____. 1989. *Mémoires: For Paul de Man.* New York: Columbia University Press.

Ellmann, Maud. 1993. *The Hunger Artists.* London: Virago.

Freud, Sigmund. (1964) "Mourning and Melancholia (1917)," in *The Standard Edition of the Complete Works of Sigmund Freud,* vol. 14. Trans. James Strachey. London: Hogarth Press, 243–58.

_____. *Totem and Taboo* (1913). Trans. James Strachey. New York/London: Routledge, 2000.

Groddeck, Georg. 2001. *Las tripas.* Trans. Ángel Cagigas. Jaén: Gráficas La Paz.

Harrell, Stevan. 1979. "The Concept of the Soul in Chinese Folk Religion." *Journal of Asian Studies,* 38. 3: 519–28.

Hsu, Francis L.K. 1949. *Under the Ancestor's Shadow.* Leyden: E.J. Brill.

Huggan, Graham. 1994. "The Latitudes of Romance: Representations of Chinese Canada in Bowering's *To All Appearances a Lady* and Lee's *Disappearing Moon Café.*" *Canadian Literature,* 140: 34–48.

Lee, Sky. 1991. *Disappearing Moon Cafe.* Washington: Seal Press.

Legge, James, trans 1885. *The Li Ki or the Collection of Treatises on the Rules of Propriety or Ceremonial Usages. The Sacred Books of the East.* Oxford: Clarendon Press: <http://www.sacred-texts.com/cfu/liki/index.htm> (Accessed 10 Sept. 2006)

Lovecraft, Howard Philips. 2000. *The Annotated Supernatural Horror in Literature.* Edited by S.T. Joshi. New York: Hipocampus Press.

Nelson, Judy. 1993. "The Final Journey Home: Chinese Burial Practices in Spokane." <http://www.narhist.ewu.edu/pnf/articles/nelson/html> (Accessed 10 Sept 2006)

Ng, Andrew Hock Soon. 2004. *Dimensions of Monstrosity in Contemporary Narratives: Theory, Psychoanalysis and Postmodernism.* Basingstoke: Palgrave.

Sedgwick, Eve Kosofsky. 1986. *The Coherence of Gothic Conventions.* New York: Methuen.

Snitow, Ann Barr. 1983. "Mass Market Romance: Pornography for Women Is Different." *Powers of Desire: The Politics of Sexuality.* Ed. Ann Barr Snitow, Christine Stansell, Sharon Thompson. New York: Monthly Review Press, 245–63.

Soros, Erin. 1998. "Giving Death." *differences* 10, 1: 1–29.

White, Hayden. 1992. "Historical Emplotment and the Story of Truth." *Probing the Limits of Representation: Nazism and the "Final Solution."* Ed. S. Fiedlander. Cambridge: Harvard University Press, 37–53.

Williams, Anne. 1995. *Art of Darkness. A Poetics of Gothic.* Chicago and London: University of Chicago Press.

Xinzhong, Yao. 2000. *Introduction to Confucianism.* Cambridge: Cambridge University Press.

Žižek, Slavoj. 1993. *Looking Awry: An Introduction to Jacques Lacan through Popular Culture.* Cambridge, Mass: MIT Press.

7

The Ghostly Rhetoric of Autobiography: Maxine Hong Kingston's *The Woman Warrior* as American Gothic Narrative

Carol Mejia-LaPerle

In her autobiography, *Woman Warrior,* Maxine Hong Kingston gathers her childhood memories of being a Chinese-American girl in Stockton, California — memories that merge the fantastic productions of an active imagination with the banalities of everyday existence. The process of this gathering is such that "we cannot find the seams where a myth leaves off and a life and imagination begins" ("Personal Statement" 24). Indeed, the formation of a "woman warrior" is traced throughout the text as a negotiation of legends and tales that are no less real than the daily maxims of young Kingston's mother or the oppressive heat of the family-owned laundromat. Appropriately, Kingston's subtitle—*The Memoirs of a Girlhood Among Ghosts*— captures the relationship between the promise of a chronicled life implicit in the genre of autobiography, and the problematic retrospection that exploits, even while it resists, the parameters of the genre. I am interested in examining the relationship between memoir and ghosts, the possible reciprocity between the telling of memory and the evanescent shapes that haunt the telling. Indeed, the subtitle reminds us that this connection is itself ephemeral; after all, this is a narrative full of ghosts though not a conventional ghost story, a whispering of mysterious family secrets that unsettle but do not necessarily frighten. Rather, the ghosts in Kingston's memoir function to express and complicate the Asian-American experience of minoritization. Informed by recent insights in American gothic criticism, this study attempts a nuanced interrogation of Kingston's self-representation as an Asian-American girl who ultimately writes her self despite, and through, her ghosts.

In an interview with Susan Brownmiller, Kingston reveals that "It was her conscious writer's craft that led her to use an English word —'ghosts'— to represent both the spirit demons that haunt her Chinese ancestors and the pale face Americans that her uprooted family must cope with in California" (in Brownmiller 178). The double function of ghosts as a personification of a cultural and familial past, as well as an embodiment of the family's wariness of a dominant white culture, is also noted by Gayle Sato: "Ghosts define two antithetical worlds that threaten the narrator's sense of a unified self. How is she to articulate her own location, which is "Chinese-American," when history, tradition, and family have formulated "China" and "America" as reciprocally alien territories?" (139).

Significantly, Eric Savoy defines American gothic as concerned with the self-conscious fragmentation that Sato notices in Kingston's text. Savoy claims that "Gothic texts return obsessively to the personal, the familial, and the national pasts to complicate rather than to clarify them, but mainly to implicate the individual in a deep morass of American desires and deeds that allow no final escape from or transcendence of them" (169).

Kingston's memoir is in unique dialogue with Savoy's theorization of American gothic narratives since in the process of narrating her "self," through the contexts of an elusive Chinese ancestry on the one hand and an inescapable American acculturation on the other, Kingston enacts the fragmentation of a culturally hyphenated subject. This essay premises that Kingston employs Gothic features not as accessories to her story, but as part of the complex vocabulary of self representation, revealing that ghosts have significant implications for an Asian-American autobiographer.[1] Consequently, my reading also asks how gothic elements inform and express the anxieties of a minority discourse. I am interested in the coexistence of divergent cultures within Kingston's memoir — her Chinese ethnicity and her American citizenship — and the ghosts' ambivalent roles in representing that coexistence. Ghosts reveal the anxiety, and the potentiality, of her fragmentation.

Thus, the term gothic is here employed not in the popular understanding of tropes of terror but rather as the critical theorization of a malleable, hybrid discourse that disturbs and disrupts the written text (in this case an autobiographical narrative of an Asian-American) even as it enables that text to convey symbolic relevance in what is strange, othered, unknown. Within the literary form of Kingston's autobiography, ghosts function not as conventions of a genre but rather as expressions of the complexities of one's past, and the troubling ghostliness of one's experience of recalling the past.[2] In other words, gothic is not simply a form of escapist entertainment — as in the popular and often overused understanding of the term as generic or thematic — but is rather a theoretically conscious discourse representing repressed communal and personal anxieties. As Teresa Goddu claims, "Instead of fleeing reality, the gothic registers its culture's contradictions, presenting a distorted, not a disengaged, version of reality" (Goddu 3). The idea of gothic elements as "version(s) of reality" may seem contradictory; after all, part of recognizing gothic elements is through their fantastic effects. However, it is precisely through the suspension of realistic representation that gothic profoundly comments on reality. As Jerrold Hogle observes, gothic is the gesture "whereby the most multifarious, inconsistent and conflicted aspects of our beings ... are 'thrown off' onto seemingly repulsive monsters or ghosts that both conceal and reveal this 'otherness' from our preferred selves as existing very much *within* ourselves" (Hogle 295). Hogle's discussion of the function of gothic narratives illuminate Brave Orchid's experience in China, wherein ghosts embody, and thus release, the internal anxieties that haunt the women of Kingston's narrative.

Brave Orchid's story is the story of Kingston's mother prior to the family's migration to America. As she recalls her time in the medical academy for women, training to be a well-respected doctor and midwife, Brave Orchid recounts the incredible story of the female students defeating a "Sitting Ghost" — a supernatural embodiment that I argue is both representative of an external terror and reflective of a woman's complex inner life in the way that William Veeder observes as implicating "repressed emotions and [...] foreclosed social issues" (Veeder 23). Kingston narrates her mother's terrible confrontation with the Sitting Ghost:

> She did not know whether she had fallen asleep or not when she heard a rushing coming out from under the bed. Cringes of fear seized her soles as something alive, rumbling, climbed the foot of the bed. It rolled over her and landed bodily on her chest. There it sat. It breathed airlessly, pressing her, sapping her. "Oh, no. A Sitting Ghost," she thought. She pushed against the creature to lever herself out from underneath, but it absorbed this energy and got heavier. Her fingers and palms became damp, shrinking at the ghost's thick short hair like an animal's coat, which slides against warm solidity as human flesh slides against muscles and bones. She grabbed clutches of fur and pulled. She pinched the skin the hair grew out of and gouged into it with her fingernails. She forced her hands to hunt out eyes,

furtive somewhere in the hair, but could not find any. She lifted her head to bite but fell back exhausted. The mass thickened [Kingston 69].

What is interesting about this confrontation is the pressure that the ghost exerts; it is power that is not combative but destroys by "pressing" and "sapping," thus turning her own energy against her. Brave Orchid's efforts — pinching, gouging, grabbing, biting — are futile because the more energy she exerts, the more the ghost presses and thickens. The ghost is described in fleeting fragments — heavy, eyeless, furry. Indeed, the fact that the ghost can only be perceived using limited, broken perceptions adds to the surreality of the specter. But the confused, fragmentary apprehension of the ghost does not take away from its terrible and immediate threat. This is a woman alone in the dark, threatened while in bed and thus in her most vulnerable position. The story is on the brink of a rape narrative — a woman's sense of safety and autonomy stripped by physical force. Eugenia Delamotte describes this kind of traumatic experience as one's confrontation with an "oneiric setting," for a spectre inhabits an

> oneiric world, set apart from diurnal reality, [but] *is* that reality: not simply in the sense that it expresses the heroine's psychological state but also in that it represents her social situation, with its dominant power relations stripped of their civilized disguise. The conflicts and terrors that reign in that world reveal her place in society, her relationships, her special vulnerability [Delamotte 165].

The ghost reveals an indefinable apprehension that the women must face: the "vulnerability" of their "social situation" — as women practicing the predominantly male profession of medicine — is expressed through the ghost's hauntings. Earlier in the text, the female students disclose that the room's haunted repute is due to a "series of hauntings that had made [the room's] inhabitants come down with ghost fear that shattered their brains for studying" (Kingston 65). It is ultimately the "shattering of their brains" that makes the room an "oneiric" world, the ghost's ability to destroy intelligence that arouses the greatest fear. The ghost represents, for these young women, not just an external threat, but also an internal anxiety about their position as aspiring doctors in a society that would render their professionalism — and the privileged independence it implies — threatening to a system of gender inequality. It is therefore significant that Brave Orchid keeps the ghost at bay by chanting her lessons: "She then ignored the ghost on her chest and chanted her lessons for the next day's classes. The moon moved from one window to the other, and as dawn came, the thing scurried off, climbing quickly down the foot of the bed" (Kingston 71). The act of chanting her lessons protects Brave Orchid from further harm, while reinforcing her commitment to the medical knowledge that empowers her. The ability to learn, that she exercises as she studies, becomes the very tool to overcome the pressures against her endeavors.[3]

Surviving the ghost's visit, she enlists a community of women to exorcise the Sitting Ghost:

> The smoke curled in black boas around the women in their scholars' black gowns. They walked the ghost room, this circle of little black women, lifting smoke and fire up to the ceiling corners, down to the floor corners, moving clouds across the walls and floors, under the bed, around one another [...]. When the smoke cleared, I think my mother said that under the foot of the bed the students found a piece of wood dripping with blood. They burned it in one of the pots, and the stench was like a corpse exhumed for its bones too soon. They laughed at the smell [Kingston 75].

In the collective act of "cleaning" the room of the Sitting Ghost, the women's anxiety about the "shattering of brains" is also exorcised. The "scholars' black gowns" is not just a uniform for the school but a sign of their solidarity as a community protecting themselves and guarding the place of their learning. The smoke they create is effective by its sheer volume — an amount that would not be possible with just one person. Most significant is the laughter they share. After this gathering, they are no longer a group of cowering women, fearing and thus restricting themselves from certain parts of the dormitory. The smell of the corpse is now a cause to celebrate since it not a sign of their vulnerability, but proof of the ability to transcend their own fears and apprehensions.

But what happens when Brave Orchid migrates into a new environment? Looking into the American landscape, Brave Orchid finds that ghosts are not just stirrings in the night but are, in fact, the main inhabitants of this "ghost country." Theorizations in American gothic invite a productive interrogation of Kingston's use of ghosts to portray her mother's reaction to America. Teresa Goddu explores American gothic discourse as a product of the American nation-building experience:

> Moreover, in its narrative incoherence, the gothic discloses the instability of America's self-representations; its highly wrought form exposes the artificial foundations of national identity. However, while the gothic reveals what haunts the nation's narratives, it can also work to coalesce those narratives. Like the abject, the gothic serves as the ghost that both helps to run the machine of national identity and disrupts it [Goddu 10].

Goddu's postulation of a "haunted" national identity shows the inherent complications in nation building, thus revealing the fissures of a constructed national unity. The "narrative incoherence" of ghosts — the disorientation and uncertainty they symbolize — expose the anxieties of the immigrant experience. These anxieties are pertinent for Chinese immigrants who encounter cultural exclusions that frustrate their participation in American self-representation and disrupt their attempts at cultural authenticity within, rather than despite, an American assimilation. In other words, the hegemony of a dominant white culture facilitates its unified view of America at the expense of excluding certain ethnic communities. Sau-ling Cynthia Wong notes that Chinese Americans are often the objects of this exclusion since they:

> are placed in the situation of permanent guests who must earn their keep by adding the spice of variety to American life — by selectively maintaining aspects of traditional Chinese culture and language fascinating to whites. In the terminology of Werner Sollors, if the essence of the American experience is the formation of a society based on "consent" rather than "descent," Chinese Americans have clearly been (and still are) excluded from participation in "consent" by the dominant group's insistence on the primacy of their "descent." [...]. Demanding "representativeness," the Chinese-American critics of Kingston differ from the white literary tourists only in the version of cultural authenticity subscribed to [Wong 42].

Wong alludes to Chinese American critics who claim that Kingston's inclusion of ghosts in her autobiographical narrative indicates a commodification of her Chinese descent.[4] This essay responds to this charge by arguing that ghosts are not exoticized additions for the fascination of a white culture but function to personify the fissures of an American identity, forcing us to acknowledge the fictions inherent in any view of cultural authenticity. By expressing the multiple ways that ghosts exist in her childhood, Kingston explores the implications of Sollors' concept of "descent" and in doing so, meditates on what it means to be Chinese *and* American. Kingston's girlhood among ghosts recounts her negotiation of a Chinese ancestry and an American acculturation, while productively questioning the idealized and unified category of "American."

The use of current theorizations of American gothic discourse is likewise a dialogue with critics who deem Kingston's narrative of fragmentation as the result of the oppressions of being Chinese within the American culture.[5] Indeed, many critics tend to attribute the dilemma of Kingston's cultural hyphenation to her Asian identity, as if Asian in the Asian-American nominer is the categorical cause of her marginalization. However, much of the pressures in the text are caused by her feelings of alienation from the *two* cultural frameworks competing for her attention and requiring her careful arbitration. While this essay is invested in the implications of Kingston's Chinese ethnicity, it also explores how that ethnicity uniquely informs the fragmentation of an Asian-American whose American-ness is no less problematic, no less "ghostly," than the Asian adjective that persistently qualifies her American identity.

This fragmentation pervades Kingston's life from childhood: she appears to the culture at large as a foreign minority, while her mother insists that she is already too much like the inhabitants of the ghost country. Kingston recalls that, "we had been born among ghosts, were taught by ghosts, and were ourselves ghost-like. [Our parents] called us a kind of ghosts" (183). By their exposure to American culture, the children are themselves turning into the "other" that Brave Orchid ambivalently critiques, and yet dismisses as inevitable. Steven V. Hunsaker observes that "Insubstantiality [...] seems to be at the heart of what Brave Orchid means when she calls her children 'ghosts.' The implication is that their foreign experience, the simple fact of living in a new and inferior land, has somehow deprived them of things needed to make one whole" (Hunsaker 98).

Indeed, the accusation of insubstantiality is one that Kingston negotiates as a feeling of deficiency. It is the sense of lack or ignorance that R. Radikrishnan has called "ghostly:" "the diasporic/ethnic location is a ghostly location where the political unreality of one's present home is to be surpassed only by the ontological unreality of one's place of origin" (765). Facing the charge of being ghostly (or too "American") by her mother, yet experiencing America as an ethnic minority, Kingston confronts a bankruptcy of cultural ethos that ghosts express and reveal not just for Kingston, but for the American experience. The ghosts in *Woman Warrior* embody the anxieties of the hyphenated subject, rendering the author and the subject of this narrative as, literally, writing contradictions.[6] Both cultural identities embodied by young Kingston are inherently compromised by the simultaneity of her parent's anxious preservation of Chinese culture, and the stereotypes manifested in an American representation of this culture.

It is thus as a means to conquer the trauma of dislocation, as a way to manage her cultural and personal vulnerability, that Brave Orchid resists a threatening American landscape. E.D. Huntley notes that "Kingston's texts occupy an increasingly significant cultural space, inhabiting the invisible borderlands between China and America, the geography of the immigrant nation, the country of diasporic people who have lost a homeland and yet have not full gained a new country of the heart" (Huntley 40).

Ghosts express the nature of the diasporic displacement by giving name to the invisible cultural boundaries that mark the family's interaction within an American cultural experience.[7] Kingston's mother tells her,

> Lie to Americans. Tell them you were born during the San Francisco earthquake. Tell them your birth certificate and your parents were burned up in

the fire. Don't report crimes; tell them we have no crimes and no poverty. Give a new name every time you get arrested; the ghosts won't recognize you[...]. Ghosts have no memory anyway and poor eyesight [Kingston 184].

Since ghosts are easy to trick, misinformation keeps them at bay. Ultimately, this tactic keeps Brave Orchid's own subjectivity from being absorbed into a cultural vacuum that would render her known, and therefore assailable. Eric Savoy discusses the way American Gothic disrupts "the seamless authenticity of national narrative [...] by the irruption of 'another history'" (Savoy 7). In her mother's advice to refuse to give a birth certificate and to withhold real names, Kingston depicts a tactical representation of history. The tactic of refusing to give the details of one's past is itself the history of the Chinese immigrant experience. Indeed, this seems to be the ultimate irony: within the context of American assimilation, it is the Chinese who have remained ghosts, whose status can be rendered tenuous, ephemeral. In speaking of Americans as ghostly, Kingston's mother resists a hegemonic culture that treats *her* like a ghost. Ghosts therefore reveal what Radikrishnan has identified as a confirmation of minoritization: "Thus in the American context (the so-called 'nation of nations') of ethnic hyphenation, the passage into citizenship is also a passage into minoritization" (764). It is the Chinese who are hardly "official" people in this society because they are rendered incessantly anonymous by an indifferent American (that is, white) community that, throughout the text, hardly bothers to distinguish Chinese individuals from the group stereotype.[8] The metaphoric invisibility of racial minoritization finds its fullest yet most ambivalent expression in the vocabulary of ghostliness that pervades the text. It is not, after all, the scariness of ghosts that is their most relevant quality, but rather the feeling of otherness inherent in every interaction, the persistent reminder of the family's marginalized existence in American culture.

When Kingston describes her childhood full of ghosts, she recalls an American landscape full of the frightening unknown:

But America has been full of machines and ghosts — Taxi Ghosts, Bus Ghosts, Police Ghosts, Fire Ghosts, Meter Reader Ghosts, Tree Trimming Ghosts, Five-and-Dime Ghosts. Once upon a time the world was so thick with ghosts, I could hardly breathe; I cold hardly walk, limping my way around the White Ghosts and their cars [Kingston 97].

This passage uniquely expresses the experience of an uncanny, potentially hostile, environment. The word ghost is the common denominator to ground the vast and confusing complexities of American life and modern technology. Eric Savoy theorizes on the prevalence of ghosts in the literary landscape when he claims that "Especially important in this tradition of verbal devices is prosopeopieia, or personification, by which abstract ideas (such as the burden of historical causes) are given 'body' in the spectral figure of the ghost" (Savoy 168). Kingston's childhood uneasiness is certainly expressed through her delineation of ghostly figures, cumulatively articulating the opaque yet intriguing face of American life. But instead of representing the "burden of historical causes," the ghosts of Kingston's girlhood are the figures stirring within a modern world. Yet these figures are as ephemeral and mysterious as the ghosts of a troubled history; that is, Kingston experiences these modern figures *as* ghostly specters of an abstracted environment. She recalls her difficulty to breathe — a physical reaction to a personal crisis of cultural exclusion. Furthermore, this crisis results in a literal handicap; "limping [her] way" signals a feeling of disability that pervades her recollection of the past. The dominant white culture is the unknown and unknowable "other" of the Chinese vocabulary of ghosts, even while it ultimately constitutes the center of immigrant existence and thus establishes the norm of American identity — a normalized identity that Kingston remembers as causing physical pain and emotional exclusion.

By employing ghosts to comment on the American experience, Kingston furthermore problematizes the claimed hybridity of America gothic criticism. While American Gothic theorists explore ghost narratives as expressions of the anxieties of an immigrant nation, there remains what Radikrishnan calls "an ideologically tacit nominal qualifier" (753) — a European subtext that pervades critical approaches to American ghost narratives. For instance, David Mogen, Scott Sanders, and Joanne Karpinski, in their introduction to an American Gothic anthology, specifically attribute "frontier gothic [as] part of the American tradition that extends from the present back to the earliest reactions of the European immigrants to the New World. The gothic wilderness is a profoundly American symbol of an ambiguous relationship to the land" (20). In this theorization, one can apply Radikrishnan's observation that "even if one were to hyphenate all of these identities, one still has to face the question of unequal mediation" (754), a mediation of "western" in American Gothic that ideologically marginalizes non–European appropriation of literary discourse and cultural participation. Therefore, the ghosts in *Woman Warrior* function to complicate what American gothic might consider its precedence — a cultural and literary past traced to a western, Eurocentric tradition. Rather than outline a separate generic category of Asian gothic within an American context, *Woman Warrior* underscores that excluded in American gothic criticism is an account of the migrant traumas and the fragmented self-construction of the Asian-American. Indeed, Kingston's portrayal of ghosts undercuts the European experience as root of American ghost narratives by engaging with "the revolutionary potential of American gothic, its long history of accommodating new interventions" (Savoy 16). By using ghosts to express the problems of cultural assimilation, Kingston's autobiographical text is one of these new interventions.

Her text is likewise an intervention within the genre of memoir, for ghosts critically explore and disrupt the expectations of autobiographical narrative. Significantly, she begins her memoir with the story of No Name aunt, a cautionary tale that subversively serves as the basis for Kingston's construction of a personal ancestry.[9] In China, Kingston's No Name aunt causes — and suffers — the ultimate shame: impregnated outside of marriage, exorcised by the family and community, and ultimately driven to commit suicide. She is the object of sexual trafficking while alive and the subject of erasure in her death; yet in Kingston's memoir, No Name aunt inhabits the ghostly past Kingston seeks to retell. As a story of negation, of actual and discursive oppression, this foundation seems tenuous. However, Marianne Noble suggests that "identification with another's pain is transgressive because it makes her body and her passions physically present, undoing the erasure of female corporeality [...] to the extent that scenes of horror afford her a trope to imagine the transgression of repressive identity constructs, they subvert patriarchal repression" (Noble 166). By recalling the horrible conditions of her aunt's suicide, Kingston reinstates the forgotten woman in the world of personal memory, and in the world of the text.[10] No Name aunt is erased in the family ancestry because her sexualized body represents a curse. She is condemned to death even as she is considered the harbinger of death — her very presence a dangerous affliction for the whole family. They collectively admonish her: "Aiaa, we're going to die. Death is coming. Death is coming. Look what you've done. You've killed us. Ghost! Dead ghost! Ghost! You've never been born" (13–14). Kingston recovers her aunt's story — changes her mother's cautionary tale — by imagining a corporeal and conscious agent.[11] It is precisely by articulating her aunt's motivations that the curse is reversed, thus allowing Kingston to acknowledge the forgotten in her own familial lineage.

Consequently, by unearthing the secrets and desires of a repressed familial past, Kingston identifies her connection with her aunt. She claims, "My aunt haunts me — her ghost drawn to me because now, after fifty years of neglect, I alone devote pages of paper to her, though not origamied into houses and clothes" (Kingston 16). The pages of her memoir become the means to entitle her aunt (since "No Name" is itself a proper name) to her rightful place in the family heritage. Significantly, the reiteration of her aunt's story emerges as something Wendy Ho calls a "resurrection":

> Such a resurrection of No Name Woman is a subversive form of ancestor
> worship that would not have the authorization of the Father. It takes its form
> not with paper boats, clothes, or money to honor the dead but with the
> power of the written word, the discursive power to name and order the world
> that had predominantly belonged to males in Chinese and American society.
> Writing talk-stories, which value women's oral cultures and practices, is a
> multiple transgression of patriarchy: in naming No Name Woman and in
> breaking the family's silence about her very existence from a woman's stand-
> point [Ho 137].

The discursive power of the written word, that is itself a repetition of an orally
inherited past, substantiates a woman's standpoint in the face of oppression.
In a Chinese cultural ethos, wherein ancestor worship is the acknowledgment
of ghosts watching over one's destiny, Kingston's choice of venerating the for-
saken ghost subversively reinvents her aunt, and by extension her self, to
become powerful female forces that resist and contest the oppressions of a
patriarchal system. Ghosts emerge as the epistemological ground for Kingston's
narrated self, the very foundation for her constructed identity. However, her
appropriation entails certain risks; Kingston herself notes, "I do not think she
always means me well. I am telling on her, and she was a spite suicide, drowning herself in the drinking water. The Chinese are always very frightened of
the drowned one, whose weeping ghost, wet hair hanging and skin bloated,
waits silently by the water to pull down a substitute" [16].

Kingston reminds us that to create a subversive female lineage, and to
base one's identity on this ghostly manifestation, is to allow the hauntings of
the past to affect the present. The act of telling the self, the "product" of the
memoir that is Kingston's text, is not merely a recollection of memory, it is
a concession to the ghosts that haunt one's self-representation.[12] Although
Kingston expresses the threat of the writer being a "substitute," she is in fact
using her aunt as the substitute in the text — her aunt's ghostly presence stand-
ing-in for the author's ephemeral self-construction. This is especially
significant for a text proclaiming itself to be autobiographical, wherein the
construction of the self is manufactured from the admitted reconfigurations
of one's memory.[13] The ghosts of the text are the very materials from which
Kingston confirms and celebrates a personal ancestry, at the risk of acknowledging the fragility of her epistemological ground.[14]

Kingston's text confirms that memory is as much the product of articulation as it is the result of remembering; memory is created as well as recalled.
Sidonie Smith states that:

> The "I," something apparently familiar, becomes something other, foreign;
> and the drift of the misappropriation, the shape, that is, that the autobiogra-
> pher's narrative and dramatic strategies take, reveals more about the autobi-

ographer's present experience of "self" than about her past, although of course, it tells us something about that as well. Fundamentally, it reveals the way the autobiographer situates herself and her story in relation to cultural ideologies and figures of selfhood [Smith 47].

Kingston's memory of the "cultural ideologies and figures of selfhood" is expressed through ghosts, her past conveyed via the recollection of ghostly hauntings — in particular the female lineage based on the repressed woman of her family history. The act of writing allows the world of her present self to coexist with an ephemeral past — both inevitably haunted by ghosts. The disgraced female ghost is the ground for Kingston's "present experience of 'self'" for to narrate her memories is simultaneously to engage in the act of self-representation. Telling the past is itself a means to tell the self, creating a personal and communal history that "branches into hers."

Ghosts represent not just the unknown and unrepresentable in the world, but also the unrepresentable in the self, expressed through the reappropriation of a repressed personal history. What is troubled or unacknowledged in the material world becomes symbolic and essential in the world of memory. Because one's identity is confirmed only by a return to the past, the reality of the text is created by a selective, at times tormented, retrospection. Indeed, ghosts show us that both the past and the self are knowable only through the tenuous creation, rather than recollection, of memory. Ghosts emphasize what is constructed — therefore fleeting, undependable, ephemeral — yet this constructedness is proof of, and perhaps the only tenable foundation for, one's identity.

Through personal introspection and the creation of a cultural and familial memory, Kingston authors the autobiographical self. Ghosts embody and emphasize the complexities of her task and thus highlight the fragility of, and potential for, establishing one's identity and reclaiming one's past. Yet ghosts also stress the fact that both one's identity and past are ultimately compromised: "for to think about the contemporary Gothic is to look into a triptych of mirrors in which images of the origin continually recede in a disappearing arc. We search for genesis but find only ghostly manifestations" (Bruhm 259). Kingston risks reverting to this ghostly origin, in order to claim the present. In doing so, she reminds us of the irony that ghosts are evoked to express an underlying need for a substantial embodiment of internal conflict, to address an overwhelming desire to find wholeness from mere fragments. Yet she chooses to expose, rather than repress, these ghostly manifestations; utilizing them to confer significance to the most troubled parts of her self-construction. Ultimately, American gothic discourse's obsession with a disturbed and unknowable past is linked to the retrospection inherent in an autobiographer's narrative of the self. Both seek to find a cohesive, articulated identity but reveal, instead, ghosts that compromise, and comprise, the search.

Notes

1. Critics have noted that Gothic elements often reflect the social institutions that enable their production. As Eugenia Delamotte notices of the Gothic in nineteenth century novels, "the Gothic vision has from the beginning been focused steadily on social relations and social institutions and thus its simultaneous focus on the most private demons of the psyche can never be separated from this persistent preoccupation with the social realities from which those demons always, in some measure, take their shape" (Delamotte vii). In recognizing the Gothic as linked to a cultural and historical context that produces it, it is no wonder that culturally embedded insights on the Gothic tend to confirm the difficulty of establishing generic parameters. Fred Botting comments on the Gothic as a "hybrid" mode of writing: "The diffusion of Gothic forms and figures over more than two centuries makes the definition of a homogenous generic category exceptionally difficult. Changing features, emphases and meanings disclose Gothic writing as a mode that exceeds genre and categories, restricted neither to a literary school nor to a historical period. The diffusion of Gothic features across texts and historical periods distinguishes the Gothic as a hybrid form, incorporating and transforming other literary forms as well as developing and changing its own conventions in relation to newer modes of writing" (Botting 14).

2. Gothic is not necessarily a genre but a "language that signals a revolution within the established system. It reveals a kind of fault line within the imagination that may open up in prose or in verse, in lyric or drama or narrative, in popular or 'serious' art" (Williams 66).

3. Sidonie Smith notices that it is precisely in this story that Kingston's mother is most like a model of a woman warrior: "In her daughter's text, Brave Orchid becomes a kind of 'woman warrior,' whose story resonates with the Fa Mu Lan legend: both women leave the circle of the family to be educated for their mission and both return to serve their community, freeing it through many adventures from those forces what would destroy it. Both are fearless, successful, admired" (Smith 161).

4. The most famous voice of this argument is from playwright and social critic, Frank Chin, who accuses Kingston's memoir of catering to white stereotypes of Chinese exoticism. He states: "Maxine Hong Kingston has defended her revision of Chinese history, culture, and childhood literature and myth by restating a white racist stereotype" (Chin 29).

5. Donald Goellnicht articulates in Kingston's narrative a "double subject split": "First, when she takes on the gendered position constructed for her by the symbolic language of patriarchal and second, when she falls under the influence of discursively and socially constructed position of racial difference [resulting in a] potential double powerlessness" (Goellnicht 123). The underlying assumption of Goellnicht's analysis is that Kingston's racial difference, her Chinese ancestry, is an ideological qualifier that underlies, indeed causes, her powerless position in society. However, I suggest that the cultural matrix mapped out by Kingston's autobiography is itself more complicated than expressed in Goellnicht's "double subject split," since Kingston's troubled childhood is not caused solely by her ethnicity and gender but is rather a symptom of her fragmented negotiation between two distinct and equally problematic cultural identities.

6. The problem of language is emblematic of the experience of contradiction. The symbolic otherworldliness of ghosts reveals the difficulties of linguistic, and by extension cultural, transcommunication. Something is threatened when the "other" becomes familiar, when an unexpected connection is made, as when the Garbage Ghost mimes the language that mocks him:

> It seemed as if ghosts could not hear or see very well. Momentarily lulled by the useful chores they did for whatever ghostly purpose, we did not bother to lower the windows one morning when the Garbage Ghost came. We talked loudly about him through the fly screen, pointed at his hair arms, and laughed at how he pulled up his dirty pants before swinging his hoard onto his shoulders[...]. Steadying the load on his back with one hand, the Garbage Ghost walked up to the window. He had cavernous nostrils with yellow and brown hair. Slowly he opened his red mouth, "The [...] Garbage [...] Ghost," he said, copying human language [...]. They have learned it. You mustn't talk in front of them again [Kingston 98].

Crucial to managing the anxieties of the American landscape is recognizing that culture is permeable through language. Ghosts' cultural and linguistic distance, that the children as "a kind of ghost" could potentially bridge, is actually a cultural impermeability that Brave Orchid seeks to maintain. Cultural dislocation emerges as the inevitable result of keeping one's self "substantial," of resisting complete assimilation into the dominant white culture. The colloquial expression of "ghosts" thus consistently resists, by stressing the opacity of each other's language, an American acculturation that would render Brave Orchid's Chinese identity as marginal.

7. Gregory Pepetone discusses the troubled political function of ghost narratives within an American setting. He claims, "America's Gothic imagination is best understood as an attempt to expose and confront our own repressed contradictions" (Pepetone 20).

8. As Amy Ling notes, Chinese American's "facial features proclaim one fact — an Asian ethnicity — but by education, choice, or birth they are American. The racial features that render them immediately visible, by differentiating them from the Caucasian norm, at the same time, paradoxically render them invisible, in the metaphoric sense that Ralph Ellison used in his novel, *Invisible Man*. At certain times in history, the racial minority person in the United States has been a nonperson — politically, legally, and socially — and these traditions die hard" (Ling 20).

9. Lauren Rusk articulates the pervasiveness of ghosts in Kingston's memoir as a "colloquial expression ... that denote(s) both real people perceived as shadowy presences and, conversely, the visions of imagination and memory perceived as vital forces" (Rusk 70). Ghosts embody the "vital forces" that will substantiate and inspire Kingston's autobiography.

10. Wendy Ho observes, "It is through telling and transforming her mother's stories that she breaks her own suffocating silence, vindicates the ancestral women in her family and culture, and reclaims their names and stories for herself and for other women in socially and politically creative ways. Maxine learns to assert her identity against the institutions that seek her erasure, marginalization, and confinement as a Chinese American woman" (Ho 123).

11. This re-telling highlights what Ludwig calls the "intentionality and willfulness of the aunt's actions" (Ludwig 64); Kingston articulates, indeed invents, her aunt's agency through the written word.

12. Pattie Cowell notes that "gothic fiction is a destabilizing genre by definition, a genre whose very form prohibits a secure framework for defining the self. When traditional sources of knowing — reason and nature — are undermined, the coherence of the self is also subverted" (Cowell 128).

13. In a meta-autobiographical commentary, Philippe Lejeune offers a reflection on the epistemological risks of autobiography: "Telling the truth about the self, constituting the self as complete subject — it is a fantasy. In spite of the fact that autobiography is impossible, this in no way prevents it from existing" (Lejeune 132).

14. *Woman Warrior* critics often note the problem of identity formation within Kingston's narrative. Amy Ling articulates this most effectively in deciphering two worlds as either "occupying the space of gulf between two banks [...] and therefore truly belonging nowhere" or "having footholds on both banks and therefore belonging to two worlds at once" (177). By reminding us of the prevalence of ghosts, Kingston problematizes her arbitration between the "identity banks" of the past and the present, yet she asserts that "Unless I see her [No Name aunt's] life branching into mine, she gives me no ancestral help" (Kingston 8). Retelling the oral tales of her mother, Kingston creates a ghostly female lineage that is ultimately, and perhaps most ironically, her most stable "identity bank."

Works Cited

Botting, Fred. 1996. *Gothic*. London: Routledge.

Brownmiller, Susan. 1999. "Susan Brownmiller Talks with Maxine Hong Kingston, Author of *The Woman Warrior*." *Maxine Hong Kingston's A Woman Warrior: A Casebook*. Ed. Sau-ling Cynthia Wong. Oxford: Oxford University Press, 173–80.

Bruhm, Steven. 2002. "The Contemporary Gothic: Why We Need it." *The Cambridge Companion to Gothic Fiction*. Ed. Jerrold E. Hogle. Cambridge: Cambridge University Press, 259–76.

Chin, Frank. 1991. "Come All Ye Asian American Writers of the Real and the Fake." *The Big Aiiieeeee!: An Anthology of Chinese American and Japanese American Literature*. Eds. Jeffery Paul Chan, Frank Chin, et al. New York: Meridian, 1–92.

Cowell, Pattie. 1993. "Class, Gender, and Genre: Deconstructing Social Formulas on the Gothic Frontier." *Frontier Gothic: Terror and Wonder at the Frontier in American Literature*. Eds. David Mogen, Scott Sanders, Joanne Karpinski. Rutherford, NJ: Fairleigh Dickinson University Press, 1993; London: associated University Press, 126–39.

Delamotte, Eugenia C. 1990. *Perils of the Night: A Feminist Study of Nineteenth-Century Gothic.* New York: Oxford University Press.

Goddu, Teresa. 1997. *Gothic America: Narrative, History, and Nation.* New York: Columbia University Press.

Goellnicht, Donald C. 1991. "Father Land and/or Mother Tongue: The Divided Female Subject in Kogawa's *Obasan* and Hong Kingston's *The Woman Warrior.*" *Gender and Genre in Literature: Redefining Autobiography in Twentieth Century Women's Fiction.* Eds. Janice Morgan and Colette T. Hall. New York: Garland Publishing, 119–34.

Ho, Wendy. 1999. *In Her Mother's House: The Politics of Asian American Mother-Daughter Writing.* Walnut Creek: Altamira Press.

Hogle, Jerrold E. 2000. "The Gothic Ghost of the Counterfeit and the Progress of Abjection." in *A Companion to the Gothic.* Ed. David Punter. Oxford: Blackwell Publishers Ltd., 293–304.

Hunsaker, Steven V. 1999. *Autobiography and National Identity in the Americas.* Charlottesville: University Press of Virginia.

Huntley, E.D. 2001. *Maxine Hong Kingston: A Critical Companion.* Westport, Connecticut: Greenwood Press.

Kingston, Maxine Hong. 1989. *The Woman Warrior: Memoirs of a Girlhood Among Ghosts.* New York: Vintage International Books.

Lejeune, Philippe. 1989. *On Autobiography.* Trans. Katherine M. Leary. Minneapolis: University of Minnesota Press.

Lidoff, Joan. 1991. "Autobiography in a Different Voice: *The Woman Warrior* and the Question of Genre," *Approaches to Teaching Kingston's The Woman Warrior.* Ed. Shirley Geok-lin Lim. New York: MLA, 116–20.

Ling, Amy. 1990. *Between Worlds: Women Writers of Chinese Ancestry.* New York: Pergamon Press.

Ludwig, Sami. 1996. *Concrete Language: Intercultural Communication in Maxine Hong Kingston's The Woman Warrior and Ishmael Reed's Mumbo Jumbo.* Frankfurt: Peter Lang.

Mogen, David, Scott Sanders, and Joanne Karpinski, eds. 1993. *Frontier Gothic: Terror and Wonder at the Frontier in American Literature.* London: Associated University Press.

Noble, Marianne. 1998. "An Ecstasy of Apprehension: The Gothic Pleasures of Sentimental Fiction." *American Gothic: New Interventions in a National Narrative,* Ed. Robert Martin and Eric Savoy. Iowa City: University of Iowa Press, 163–82.

Pepetone, Gregory G. 2003. *Gothic Perspectives on the American Experience.* New York: Peter Lang.

Radhakrishnan, R. 1993. "Postcoloniality and The Boundaries of Identity." *Callaloo* 16, 4: 750–71.

Rubenstein, Roberta. 1987. *Boundaries of the Self: Gender, Culture, Fiction.* Urbana and Chicago: University of Illinois Press.

Rusk, Lauren. 2002. *The Life Writing of Otherness: Woolf, Baldwin, Kingston and Winterson.* New York: Routledge.

Sanders, Scott P. 1993. "Southwestern Gothic: On the Frontier between Landscape and Locale" in *Frontier Gothic: Terror and Wonder at the Frontier in American Literature,* eds. David Mogen, Scott Sanders, and Joanne Karpinski. London: associated University Press, 55–70.

Savoy, Eric. 2002. "The Rise of American Gothic." *The Cambridge Companion to Gothic Fiction.* Ed. Jerrold E. Hogle. Cambridge: Cambridge University Press, 167–88.

Savoy, Eric. 1998. "The Face of the Tenant: A Theory of American Gothic." *American Gothic: New Interventions in a National Narrative.* Eds. Robert Martin and Eric Savoy. Iowa City: University of Iowa Press, 3–19.

Sato, Gayle K. Fugita. 1991. "*The Woman Warrior* as a Search for Ghosts." *Approaches to Teaching Kingston's The Woman Warrior.* Ed. Shirley Geok-lin Lim. New York: MLA, 138–45.

Smith, Sidonie. 1987. *A Poetics of Women's Autobiography: Marginality and the Fictions of Self-Representation.* Bloomington: Indiana University Press.

Veeder, William. 1998. "The Nurture of the Gothic, or How Can a Text Be Both Popular and Subversive?" *American Gothic: New Interventions in a National Narrative.* Ed. Robert Martin and Eric Savoy. Iowa City: University of Iowa Press, 20–39.

Williams, Anne. 1995. *Art of Darkness: A Poetics of Gothic.* London/Chicago: The University of Chicago Press.

Wong, Sau-ling Cynthia. 1999. "Autobiography as Guided Chinatown Tour? Maxine Hong Kingston's *The Woman Warrior* and the Chinese American Autobiography Controversy." *Maxine Hong Kingston's A Woman Warrior: A Casebook.* Ed. Sau-ling Cynthia Wong. Oxford: Oxford University Press, 29–58.

8

The Asian-American Hyphen Goes Gothic: Ghosts and Doubles in Maxine Hong Kingston and lê thi diem thúy

Belinda Kong

Freud's uncanny ([1919] 1990), the notion of a frightening *unheimlich* within even the most homely and intimate of things, is perhaps his clearest trope of the foreign within our own psyches, of what makes us, in Julia Kristeva's words, "strangers to ourselves." As Kristeva (1991) argues in her book of the same title, the private psychic unhomeliness of Freud's analysis can be transferred over to the public sphere, to an examination of foreigners within social communities. Her method is to unravel renderings of the outsider figure within familiar, that is to say, "Western" and canonical texts such as Greek tragedies and the Bible, Dante and Kant. It becomes a very different discussion of the uncanny, however, when we turn to the writings of those who are themselves defined as internal foreigners, those who occupy the place of the stranger and write from the other side of estrangement.

Asian-American literature marks one such other-place of the social uncanny. Given their historical status as an immigrant population, Asian-American writers bear a not-so-elective affinity to the uncanny, and on a larger genealogical canvas, to the Gothic. For the idea of the uncanny itself emerges for Freud out of a reading of a paradigmatic Gothic tale, E.T.A.

Hoffman's "The Sand-Man." Similarly, Asian-American writers, even early on in a tradition predominated by social-realist codes, have variously turned to the Gothic for tropes of alienation and alterity. This Asian-American Gothic has its chiaroscuro, its shades of difference in sketching out the distance between Asia and America, the two sides of the Asian-American hyphen. By juxtaposing two interrelated texts — Maxine Hong Kingston's *The Woman Warrior* and lê thi diem thúy's *The Gangster We Are All Looking For*— one may argue that contemporary Asian-American literature demonstrates an intensified appropriation of the Gothic as it continually expands the representational boundaries of Asian-American identity. If Fred Botting has provocatively suggested that the Gothic is "the only true literary tradition," that by amassing disparate marginalized genres and techniques it paradoxically becomes the sole continuous thread — or the most persistent excluded insider — in Anglo-American literary history (1996, 15–16), then Kingston and lê at once coincide with this metaphor and turn it inside out by exemplifying not only internal foreigners in America but also distant diasporic heirs of China and Vietnam. Inhabiting the linguistic fabric of the United States and inheriting cultural imprints of Asia, but fully enclosed by neither tradition, their Asian-American female *bildungsromans* enfold a doubled — we might say hyphenated — Gothic.

Ghostly Ambivalence

In recalling a "Girlhood Among Ghosts," *The Woman Warrior* (Kingston 1976), by its very subtitle, announces a generic relation to the Gothic. This relation accrues bicultural emphasis when we note that the Chinese word for "ghost" (*guei/kuei*) is also commonly used in reference to ethnic non–Chinese. In translating *guei/kuei* as "ghost" rather than the more insulting "devil" or "demon," Kingston certainly defuses some of the Chinese cultural offense directed at racial others.[1] More thematically significant, though, is how her translation accentuates the connection between the foreign and the spectral as cultural synonyms. While critics have not failed to remark on this link in Kingston's writing (Kim 1981; Li 1988; Wong 1993), none has probed her text's apportioning of cultural identity across its many invocations of the ghostly. In this section, I will suggest that, on Kingston's Gothic economy, ghosts function as figures of cultural singularity: they are characterized as either Chinese or American, never both. Exploring Kingston's banishing of specters from the hyphen's domain will in turn reveal the larger accents of cultural self-definition in her seminal Asian-American *bildungsroman*.

The Woman Warrior pursues its ghosts ambivalently. In one direction are the literal ghosts, figures of the otherworldly who are consistently marked as Chinese. These may be familial forebears, such as the self-drowned no-name aunt and her newborn child. Or they may be narrative fragments passed down through the mother's talk-stories of her life in pre-communist China, such as the Sitting Ghost (which Brave Orchid as a young woman warrior herself vanquishes), the "holeless" infant on the toilet seat (a perverse return of that earlier "sitting" ghost), or other grotesque "nightmare babies," whose faces Brave Orchid may or may not have turned "into the ashes" as a doctor-mid-wife, and which return in America to haunt the narrator's dreams. From these familial and cultural remnants of the past, not only does the narrator inherit an understanding of Chineseness that is thickly knotted with the Gothic, but she comes to fear inheriting, unbeknownst to herself, the cultural tendency toward infanticide. Thus, in her nightmares, "in a blink of inattention," she mislays one baby and has to "stop moving, afraid of stepping on it," or she imagines herself unintentionally scalding another with hot water until "its skin tautens and its face becomes nothing but a red hole of a scream" (Kingston 1976, 86–87). Against Chinese cultural identity as much as its phantoms, the narrator finds herself adopting a stance of constant vigilance, for a lapse might lead her to become a phantom herself (perhaps pulled down as a "substitute" by the no-name aunt) or, worse, repeat the very practices that threaten to spectralize Chinese women and girl-infants.

Ghosts as signifiers of Gothic horror, then — as a return of the past, a manifestation of the supernatural, an inheritance of guilt — belong to a Chinese order of things. The narrator separates this class of specters from her American reality by cordoning it off to the realms of metaphysical otherness or else the unconscious: "To make my waking life American-normal, I turn on the lights before anything untoward makes an appearance. I push the deformed into my dreams, which are in Chinese, the language of impossible stories" (87). This attempt to designate the "deformed" as strictly Chinese reflects the text's larger effort to disentangle Chinese-American identity from pure Chineseness, to hold at bay the latter by spectralizing its alterity. In this vein, Chinese spirits are summoned with tragic, transgressive, and grotesque overtones. Even the Sitting Ghost, arguably the most innocuous and droll variant of this class of unnatural beings, is hyperbolically described in Brave Orchid's embellished account as "want[ing] lives" and "surfeited with babies," its exorcised remains "a piece of wood dripping with blood" (74).

In the other direction of ghostly ambivalence, however, the fearsome excesses of Chinese specters are tempered by the comic relief of metaphorical American ones, which function to deflate the haunting remnants of China.

Rather than transgressive apparitions from the other side of life, American ghosts disturb with an all too "nosy" corporeality:

> But America has been full of machines and ghosts — Taxi Ghosts, Bus Ghosts, Police Ghosts, Fire Ghosts, Meter Reader Ghosts, Tree Trimming Ghosts, Five-and-Dime Ghosts[...]. We were regularly visited by the Mail Ghost, Meter Reader Ghost, Garbage Ghost. Staying off the streets did no good. They came nosing at windows [97–98].

Associated with machinery and modernity, American ghosts belong to an order of the now, a suburban social order that, for all its strangeness, the text frequently casts in high comic terms. Their visitations, unlike those of their Chinese counterparts, do not substantially threaten to break down the narrator's demarcation between the homely and the unhomely: they may knock, they may peep, they may even trespass onto the premises, but their existential gravity is always exterior, their actions a banal carrying out of professional roles rather than a genuine lapsing of natural limits and boundaries. We may say that this class of American spooks, far from signaling the uncanny, is merely mock–Gothic: they are farcical elements in the daily drama of cultural disorientation in an immigrant family's narrative. As distinctly as Chinese ghosts belong to an order of metaphysical otherness and cultural ancestry, so American ones inhabit a landscape of the temporal present and the cultural everyday. If the Gothic has been formulated as evocative of both "terror and laughter" (Botting 1), Kingston's American ghosts, producing none of the former but the latter in abundance, may aptly be called the Gothic-comic.

These polarized representations of the spectral — Chinese Gothic-tragic on the one hand, American Gothic-comic on the other, with grotesquery and horror aligned principally with the former side of the hyphen — underscore how Kingston's text defines Asian-Americanness in fearful opposition to Asianness. While America may also have its cultural mysteries, its alterity is much more domesticated and normalized, certainly made much safer and more easily assimilated by comic laughter. Indeed, Kingston's text suggests that Asian-American identity would be held in suspense so long as the narrator lives in the Gothic manor of a childhood house that is presided over by the animating spirit of Brave Orchid, that vital transmitter of things Chinese and monstrous, that paragon of the "emigrant generation" against which the narrator must forge her difference. This manor has its madwoman (Moon Orchid), its infectious and suffocating bad humors ("When I'm away from [this house ...] I don't get sick. [...] I don't get pneumonia, no dark spots on my x-rays" [Kingston 1976, 108]), and of course, its eruptions of the phantasmal (nightmare babies and other visions). Little wonder, then, that Kingston's *bildungsroman*, though divided into five chapters like Joyce's *Portrait of the Artist as a Young Man*, is anything but a straightforward portrait of the artist as a young woman, and she remains unnamed throughout the Gothic confines of a house and text overcrowded with Chinese remnants. Still, though evacuated of the ghostly, Kingston's hyphen is not wholly untouched by uncanny operations. As we shall see, her hyphen is now left open to host another apparition of the Gothic: the double.

Hyphen's Falling

Arguably one of the most chilling moments in *The Woman Warrior* is the narrator's encounter with, and torture of, the silent girl in the book's concluding chapter, the section most divested of ancestral karma and most centrally concerned with the narrator's development from child to young adult to poet, hence also the section that presents most fully the text's vision of a distinct Asian-American identity. This scene is riddled with signs of the otherworldly and the underworldly: the setting is an empty basement restroom, the time, that transitional crepuscular hour when darkness begins to descend but has not yet fully consumed the dying daylight. The torture episode itself is significantly preceded by the narrator's first climbing the fire escape "upside down," turning the world topsy-turvy, then crossing over to the "forbidden places" of the boys' playground before returning, more masculine and aggressive, to confront in the girls' yard "the quiet one." In keeping with the text's cultural polarizing of ghosts, this uncanny encounter takes place in a Chinese rather than an American school (172–178).

Numerous details point to the doubling motif. Both the narrator and the silent girl remain unnamed; both struggle with voice, with speech; both are perceived by their classmates as unathletic and weak, both the last ones chosen for sports teams; and both linger on too long, alone and apart from their respective sisters, in the space of the otherwise abandoned. Like a shadow, the quiet girl trails after the narrator into the underground lavatory, a place of mirrors and the facing of mirror images. Rhetorical echoes further bind the two girls: the quiet girl's "wheezes" on a plastic flute remind us of the narrator as musician-poetess of the chapter's title ("Song for a Barbarian Reed Pipe"), and the description of the girl as "the familiar, the weak, and the small" recalls, just a few pages earlier, the scene at the drugstore in which the narrator tells herself to be "cute and small" because — the next sentence doubles these words by repetition — "[n]o one hurts the cute and small" (170). As well, when the narrator looks into the quiet girl's face so as to "hate it close up" (175), we hear another long-distance near-echo of her own phrase regarding the omnipresent misogyny of her Chinese relatives: "I had to get out of hating range" (52). But in this moment of inversions, the narrator becomes not victim but aggressor, the femme fatale to the silent girl's fair maiden.

Given such prominent signs of femaleness under siege, the subsequent scene of torture may be readily read in terms of the narrator's gendered self-loathing, her terror at coinciding with or growing into this projected female double of the voiceless girl, and her desire to destroy the negative self-image by wrenching a name out of her own obstinate silence. As she kneads, squeezes, and pokes at the girl's face, noting with furious disgust the girl's "flower-stem neck," "papery fingers," and plastic "squid"-like flesh, she begins to take on abject qualities herself until she, too, finally breaks into violent sobs. With their two voices "bouncing wildly off the tile, sometimes together, sometimes alternating," the very attribute that the narrator accentuates as her chief difference from the girl — her own vocality versus the other's muteness — is rendered moot.

That some psychic conflict about gender is at work here seems only too obvious, especially since the narrator wears her female ambivalence very much on her sleeves. At the same time, of course, Kingston is dramatizing a struggle with cultural identity, one that involves defining a unique "Chinese-American feminine" apart from the more culturally singular Chinese or American variety. Contrary to expectations, the Chinese woman is *not* characterized by silence on the gender codes of this text, which cuts across stereotypes of both Oriental demureness and Western self-assurance by overtly aligning "Chinese-feminine" with "loudness" and "American-feminine" with "softness" and "whispers"— with classist overtones, to be sure, but also the uncommon implication that only hyphenated Chinese-American femininity is associated with a quietness quieter than both (171–172). Given this apportioning of culture, gender, and volume, we can say that the narrator's encounter with her double stages a confrontation between two cultural forms of femininity: one, Chinese-American feminine and inaudible; the other, Chinese-feminine and "strong and bossy." In effect, by externalizing and expunging the former from herself, the narrator falls *backward*, that is, onto the Chinese half of the hyphen.

That a number of Asian-American critics have been inclined to read this episode in the opposite direction — as the narrator's attempt to assimilate into "mainstream America" and hence as a falling forward of the hyphen — underscores the tendency in Asian-American criticism to concentrate on American racial politics, on Asian-America's struggle against racism and its writers' efforts at "claiming America" by writing within but against the canon. This dual critical emphasis on ethnic resistance on the one hand and American priority on the other sets up some comfortable grooves for such arguments as

Sau-ling Cynthia Wong's and David Leiwei Li's, who both interpret Kingston's doubling scene primarily in relation to American racism. For Wong (86–95), the "racial shadow" is a direct consequence of "white society's" perpetual othering of Asian-Americans, and for Li (509), it embodies the narrator's failed attempts at assimilating "hegemonic cultural categories" of white femininity such as the cheerleader and the pom-pom girl. More broadly, Wong makes this argument not just for Kingston but for Asian-American literature in general (and all ethnic American writing, for that matter) whenever the racial shadow surfaces, for she regards the trope's prevalence as symptomatic of "white society's refusal to distinguish between Asian American and Asian," a racist conflation that comes to be "internalized uncritically" by Asian-American protagonists who are henceforth "plagued by a misgiving that they are tainted by an indelible 'Asianness'" which they must then purge through projection. If Freud compares the fractured ego to a piece of crystal that splinters, "not into haphazard pieces," but along "lines of cleavage into fragments whose boundaries [...] were predetermined by the crystal's structure" (Freud 1966, cited in Rogers 16), then for Wong and Li, the prime predeterminant for Asian-American psychic disintegration is inexorably white racism, with the cleavage dividing neatly along racial lines. For both critics, white racism is never in doubt, nor whiteness's culpability.

Ironically, this way of carving out the fracture lines of psychic doubling ends up seeing Asianness through whiteness's eyes once more.[2] To avoid recentering America yet again as the primary analytical lens, a kind of self-imposed catch-twenty-two that locks the critic into an incessant agon between white oppression and ethnic marginality, we can attend instead to a less politically ready-at-hand suggestion raised by Kingston's scene: that "the other" whose eyes sunder and double may be neither white nor American but Chinese and female, that the tape which measures her narrator's Chinese-American soul with contempt and pity may belong not to the racial other but to her own racial and gender ideal. From this new and somewhat peculiar perspective, which is opened up by our very inquiry into the Gothic and which defamiliarizes customary ways of reading the Asian-American hyphen, the most violent alterity is also the one most idealized and potentially self-coinciding, which is none other than the fortuitous titular figure of Kingston's text — the woman warrior.

Pretexts and Aftertexts

On this reading, we can highlight Kingston's innovations on the Gothic via two American intertexts. First, we observe that the quiet girl's obstinate inertia not only resembles but magnifies the passive non-compliance of Melville's Bartleby ([1853] 1949), for her refusals fail to be channeled into even a signal phrase, his "I prefer not to" reduced in her to a bare muteness. Likewise, Bartleby's unyielding resistance to the word of law and symbolic paternality accrues both bicultural and feminist overtones in Kingston, whose narrator comes to assume the role not just of a tyrannical cultural teacher (the Chinese school being the setting of cultural pedagogy) but also of an overexacting and wounding parent, roles inhabited most fully in the text by Brave Orchid. Thus, Melville's use of the double as outsider and pacifist dissident to patriarchal law becomes revised, on Kingston's treatment, as the hyphenated descendant's persecution by cultural matriarchy's fierce imperatives.

Aside from Bartleby, a second and more unlikely precursor to the silent girl is Poe's William Wilson. Unlike Kingston's, Poe's double is a near-exact one, sharing everything from his narrator's name and age to his facial features and physique; however, as in Kingston's text, the one distinguishing trait between them is voice: William Wilson's double has a "singular whisper [...] the very echo of [his] own" (Poe [1839] 1977, 67). Poe's tale therefore serves as a pretext to Kingston's motif of vocal doubling, since he too transfers the visual suggestions of the shadow over to its oral counterpart of the whisper or echo. But I evoke Poe in relation to Kingston here for a more oblique convergence: the coinciding first initials in both their works' titles. "W," of course, is itself a doubled letter, born from the fission of a single parent ("u"). It is intriguing that Poe further doubles the doubled-"u" with a doubled "w" for his doubles' name. Conspicuously, too, "William Wilson" plays on connotations of free will and self-mastery as well as descent and ancestry; indeed, the name is self-spawning and contains its own patronymic.

Poe's name play directs our attention to the doubled "w" in Kingston's title and allows us to speculate on its range of referents. Here as with Bartleby (another name with a doubled letter and sound), we note that Kingston's engagements again follow more female lines. The woman warrior, as a powerful and empowering feminist figure, is incarnated in not just Fa Mulan but also Brave Orchid as exorcist and Ts'ai Yen as nomadic fighter. Nor is the narrator exempt from the title, for already in the second chapter we see her projecting herself into the Mulan legend to act out the role vicariously through borrowed imagination. Less obviously, though, this figure of double-"w" can also be projected onto the very scene that stages a doubling in the text — the very scene where the narrator comes to enact most fully, in real rather than fantasy life, the woman warrior ideal. Nowhere else do we see her act with such physical aggression. If we carry over our earlier suggestion that the narrator adopts here the role of Chinese maternality, the implication is that this latter ideal, rather than whiteness or America, constitutes the prime determining force of psychic doubling. The crystal breaks most sharply, not between "Chinese" and "American," but between "Chinese" and "Chinese-American."

In this light, let us return to the book's title and the earlier comment about its fortuitousness. As Kingston once pointed out in an interview, the choice of her memoir's title was the publisher's rather than her own, for she never meant the woman warrior to stand as dominant trope or ultimate end for either her narrator or Chinese-Americans at large.[3] That she gives pride of place to the Mulan legend only in the second chapter, and as a childhood fantasy that fails the narrator in everyday life, should sufficiently indicate that it is a model to be surpassed in adulthood. Kingston's claim is further borne out by her closing the memoir on a note of peaceful reconciliation, with a story of the exile harmonizing the music of the other with words of her own origins and thereby "translating" a narrative of violent captivity and wartime displacement into one of cultural inclusion and mutual attentiveness. Indeed, the final images Kingston leaves us with — Ts'ai Yen as singer, mother, and poet, first "ringed by barbarians," then re-enfolded by the Hans (Kingston 1976, 209) — anticipate themes that will become central to her later work, themes of peacemaking through language, of reaching beyond cultural differences to arrive at a shared humanity through displacements and detours.[4] In the retrospective light cast by Kingston's aftertexts, we may regard the torture episode as an ironic inaugural point of her turn away from the warrior ideal. As the narrator's mysterious post-torture illness intimates, the woman warrior is now a diabolical double, a self-wounding rather than a self-empowering model: it perpetuates victimization and does little to assuage the hyphen's fragmentation. "Nothing changed," the narrator remarks matter-of-factly, except perhaps for another doubling: the "head line" on her palm has broken in two (182).

Joining the two foregoing discussions of Kingston's text, we may say that, whereas Chinese ghosts are perceived by the narrator as a form of Gothic alterity, the doubling episode reverses the representational lens and brings into focus the Chinese-American child as seen through the implied eyes of a Chinese mother *qua* woman warrior. Examining these two seemingly opposite tropes of the Gothic alongside each other, we become aware of Kingston's consistent casting of Chineseness as the most terrifying, threatening, and wounding alterity to the Chinese-American subject. Indeed, the text thrusts away from each other the two sides of the hyphen with such force that it is almost unavoidable the hyphen would, even if only momentarily, fall apart and not hold. If *The Woman Warrior*'s vexed relation to Asianness gives some leverage to the America-centric reading, a more recent Asian-American female *bildungsroman* I will now turn to, lê thi diem thúy's *The Gangster We Are All Looking For* (2003, henceforth *Gangster*), will render this inclination altogether untenable. On lê's self-spectering model of the Asian-American Gothic, America-centrism will become the object of exorcism.

Hyphen's Shadow

That *Gangster* palimpsests itself on Kingston's memoir can be observed in lê's adoption of an unnamed narrator and a five-part bildungsroman structure as well as her pervasive invocations of ghosts. lê's spectral, however, is much more personal and proximate: against the cultural singularity and polarizing of Kingston's ghosts, lê brings the ghostly into the Asian-American hyphen itself, the very realm that her predecessor had tried to exorcise.

If the childhood home of Kingston's narrator conjures up images of a Gothic mansion continually under siege, both from without by racially foreign presences and from within by ancestrally haunting ones, this home, at least, stays put; for the purposes of her own self-definition, this house anchors the point of maternal origin from which Kingston's narrator ultimately flees but to which she nonetheless intermittently returns. Such a geographically anchored site of the home, however, is repeatedly denied lê's narrator. For the latter, temporary formations of home are either ironized, retracted, or demolished, from her expulsion from the Russells' house, her first foster home in America, which is shown to be as insubstantial and fragile as her hosts' glass menagerie or their very surname that echoes the "rustling" sound of the butterfly in the paperweight (lê 2003, 25 and 27), to her family's eviction from the converted Navy bungalows, which are torn down to make way for more upscale "condominiums, town houses, family homes" (96–99). While Kingston's Asian-American *bildungsroman* is premised on an American nativity and childhood, lê's takes one generational-historical step back, as it were, by narrating an Asian-American girlhood that begins with the narrator's arrival in America, literally "washed to shore" (3), from an other-place.

Indeed, lê's narrator seems to be born of the sea, a child of water. As lê informs us in the epigraph, "In Vietnamese, the word for *water* and the word for *a nation, a country*, and *a homeland* are one and the same: *nu'ó'c*." Yet in her text, this synonymous relation, instead of domesticating or stabilizing water, by contrast floods out the endurance and intimacy implied in the concept of home. The novel thus opens with a reference not only to constant motion and relocation but to water as the source of origin, of the girl and her father being connected to the four boat-uncles "not by blood but by water" (3). With origin narratively displaced from land to sea, lê effectively undermines any impulse to idealize Asia as the girl's grounding point of identity. This implication is reinforced by the scene in the American classroom, where the teacher introduces the girl to other students by pointing to a globe but she can only register Vietnam as "an S-shaped curve near a body of water," a bare stroke that gains shape only *via* its proximity to the sea (19). Through these interlinked episodes of geographic flux and dislocation, lê poignantly suggests that, for the Asian-American subject dispossessed of both a native claim to America and a socio-political claim to Asia, homeliness is not pregiven — which is to say, that all spaces can take on the quality of the unhomely. If Freud's uncanny is defined as a return of the repressed, as the frightening experience of encountering the resurgence of one's own disavowed past in an exteriorized form, *Gangster* puts the Asian-American immigrant in the place, not of the subject who confronts her own uncanny, but of the uncanny to the native subject. Turning inside out Kingston's model of the Asian-American child's doubly Gothic home, lê portrays her narrator as the alien specter who knocks on the door as much as the domestic one who disturbs, like an unwelcome guest, the interior of America's house. That is to say, lê puts the ghost within the space of the hyphen and gives us a narrative of Asian-America's internal alterity.

What may appear to be the one salient exception ultimately reaffirms this insight — the figure of the narrator's drowned brother. His uncanny return seems at first to occur in anything but a Gothic setting. Walking home from the corner store one summer Sunday, the girl, however, has three preliminary encounters. First, the man at the liquor store mimics the girl's greeting and tone of voice, and she, laughing at his echoes, mentally names him thrice: "You bird. You parrot. You Polly" (72). The echo, as we noted with Kingston, can function as an oral counterpart to the visual metaphor of the double as shadow. Second, a bum at the street corner refuses to cross even after the light changes, staying behind to push the button again and to "[keep] waiting" despite the girl's hailing from "the other side of the street" (73). The bum's posture of stunned immobility suggests a lost immigrant or kin, someone who fails to make the crossing from the old homeland to the new and yet remains in place at the borderline, waiting for a signal that will unbind him. Finally, the name scratched into the sidewalk — "RAMONE," with a pair of palm prints "pressed deep into the cement" — not only evokes a tombstone and foreshadows the brother's grave in Vietnam at the novel's end but also summons to the girl's mind the image of "a boy kicking his shoes off and doing a handstand, the sun reflecting off the soles of his bare feet" (74), which in turn recalls the diving boys who disappear into the swimming pool with only the "pale soles of their feet" visible (55). This recurring image of boys flying headlong into water gives visual form to the language, posthumous and speculative, that describes the missing, unseen scene of the brother's death: "The boy jumped from boat to boat. [...] He plunged straight down [...] into a hole in the water" (145–146). One last detail in this episode merges the contrasting figures of the stationary bum and the aerial boy divers: some glass scattered across the girl's path catches the sunlight and makes the road "sparkle like a long black river" (74). In the reflection of this illusory Styx, the sepulchral appearance of "RAMONE" suddenly takes on watery associations. We may hence decipher the enigmatic name as an inverted version of "oceanic one" (*ram* as the Spanish word for "sea," *mar*, spelled backward), that is, the brother left behind at sea.[5]

Even this most ordinary and innocent of days in southern California, then, can throw up dangerously haunting fragments that recollect the past and the oceanic passage for the girl. Closely attendant on these uncanny foreshadows is the episode of the brother's return:

> What happened next was just a feeling. Like heat or hunger or dizziness or loneliness or longing. My brother, making no sounds and casting no shadow, was walking behind me. There, again, was the familiar feeling of warmth, of his body beside my body. [...] I had been waiting for him but something kept me from going to him [74].

Like the bum at the corner, symbolically the place of her brother, the girl is now in the position of the waiting, the unmoving. Intriguingly, the brother's ghost "cast[s] no shadow" but trails after her like her shadow, a relationship that is recalled again later when the girl, told by her mother to "[s]top dancing with [her] shadow," explains that she is dancing with her brother (148). The brother as a twin-like companion to the girl — her mirror image and shadowy double — is further emphasized with such parallel phrases as "his body beside my body" and "whose body my body will recall" (154), rhetorical constructions that intimate a symmetry between the two siblings. Anadiplosis is further threaded through the girl's reimagining of the oceanic hole that swallows her brother, accreting to his death an afterlife: "the hole became a room and the room was in a house, a house exactly like the one I was lying in [...] except that it was underwater" (146). Duplicating "room" and "house" across the commas, this sentence and others repeatedly position the girl and her brother in mirror-image spaces, just as she pictures them carrying out mirror-image lives with the surface of the water as the mirror's thin edge and their divider.

By the logic of doubles, if the brother's afterlife is one form of living beyond Vietnam, then the girl, as his other self, by extension lives out an alternate afterlife to Vietnam in America. On lê's handling, the diasporic life of the Asian-American child embodies, not the antithesis to Asia, but rather its strange posthumous continuation, a form of afterlife akin to the one sustained by the dead, by waiflike wraiths. Whereas *The Woman Warrior* concludes, after many detours into ancestral and composite selves, with a fifth chapter that moves beyond psychic splintering to promise a translated Asian-American reconciliation, *Gangster* concludes with its fifth chapter reflecting the narrator's Asian-Americanness off the mirror of a lost Asianness turned spectral double. And while Kingston's final line in *The Woman Warrior*—"It translated well"— is subtly alluded to in lê's final chapter title —*nu'ó'c*, a foreign word in need of translation to arrive back at its own meaning as "home" in the English text — in light of the brother's failed traversal across the multiple meanings of this word, his unsuccessful crossing through water and homeland, the girl's own traversal can only be characterized as half-complete, half-fulfilled. Indeed, Kingston's hopeful last line cannot but resonate with an unexpected melancholy in lê's novel, for not only is lê's "translation" of Asian to American haunted by the brother's drowning, but Kingston's adverbial "well" reverberates here not as abstract praise or judgment but, with paradoxical concreteness, as the structure through which one can plunge into a watery death — for Kingston's no-name woman as much as for lê's phantom brother, except that the latter ends rather than inaugurates the narrative.

Names and Afterlife

The body of lê's novel itself has an afterlife. In the "author's note" that trails the fictional portion of the text, the narrator's first-person voice flows into lê's own "I": "When I was a child, I was given the formal name Trang. I had an older sister whose formal name was Thúy. At home, we were only called by our familiar nicknames: Big Girl and Little Girl. Though it must have occurred, I have no memory of having ever been called Trang in Vietnam." This original familiarity and homeliness of the name, however, is literally lost in translation when, after leaving Vietnam by boat and arriving in the U.S. with her father, he "incorrectly filled out the paperwork" and listed her name as Thúy rather than Trang. We are then made aware of the personal origins of lê's Gothic themes: "My older sister, the original Thúy, had drowned at a refugee camp in Malaysia. My mother saw my father's mistake as propitious; it allowed a part of my older sister to come to this country with us.

And so I kept my sister's name and wore it like a borrowed garment, one in which my mother crowded two daughters, one dead and one living" (159–160).

In this autobiographical continuation of the novel's narrative, we are given the prior life of the text, the pre-fictional account of an oceanic crossing from which is born not only the ghost (a sibling dying at sea) but also the double (two siblings in one name). Both tropes are saturated with associations with water, and by linguistic transference, with dissociations from country and homeland. The fluidity between the two tropes highlights how, on lê's handling, they have become one. What lê hands us, in effect, is an Asian-American Gothic on which the ghost and the double, by their very immateriality, become paradigmatic metaphors for diaspora's post-migration afterlife. Just as her narrator concludes the novel with an image of herself running, "like a dog unleashed," along the beach (158), so lê transfers this action over to the afterword as a metaphor of her own name's translation. As she explains, she has chosen to publish under her full name, as in the Vietnamese fashion, but all in lowercase because she prefers "the way it runs," so that she may "break the name down, rebuild it and reclaim it" as her own (160). It would seem that lê wants us to read her new hybrid name, not as a frantic animal running between English and Vietnamese as opposite poles, but rather as an interlinear translation that runs alongside both as though they were parallel lines, mirror shores.

One more biographical aspect interests us here, a detail that lê intriguingly omits from her authorial note: the fact of her real-life older brother's drowning in Vietnam.[6] While it may seem at first that lê has taken creative liberties with her own life by fraternalizing her drowned sister and hence converting the common motif of same-sex doubles into a rarer one of male-female doubles, this extratextual piece of information complicates the matter. We can certainly interpret lê's text along such feminist lines as laid down separately by Charlotte Goodman (1983) and Joanne Blum (1988), who both explicate male-female doubling as a strategy adopted by women writers to dramatize and critique patriarchy's gender inequalities. That lê fictionally resurrects her brother but not her sister lends support to this reading. What I want to amplify here, though, is another dimension of lê's creative move, particularly as it relates to my discussion of diasporic afterlife. If lê suggests to us that the fortunate mistake of her father's misnaming of her bestows a partial resurrection to the drowned sister — the sibling and almost-twin in real life who also made a partial cross-national passage through water, between Vietnam and Malaysia, thus also partly sharing the hyphen of a geographic displacement — the brother, by contrast, remains undiasporic, unnamed. Lê's spectral reincarnation of him therefore inverts her recalling of the sister in the coda: while the latter's name is recollected and resounds back onto the fictional body of the text, the former's name is never uttered, as though never having been given, as though always already denied of familiarity and homeliness.[7] Unlike the mysterious Ramone whose embalmed name on the dark, riverlike sidewalk reminds us of those etched into the reflective granite surface of the Vietnam Wall, that ever securely anchored and domesticated monument of Americans' crossings into Asia, lê's brother is a nameless memorial to the un-reconstituted Asian half in the reverse westward voyage, a memory that does not stay put but haunts the refugee's hyphen restlessly, intimately.

Contrary to Kingston's Gothic partitions, then, lê integrates the two tropes of the ghost and the double into this one figure of the also-unnamed twin-like brother. On lê's Gothic economy, the brother's Asianness signals neither a form of absolute cultural alterity nor one of simple cultural ancestry, for her collapse of metaphysical otherness onto projected selfhood compels us to read her Asian-American narrative as enfolding an internal Asian uncanny. That Kingston's book is published in 1976 and lê's in 2003 alerts us to the dramatic shift in Asian-American cultural politics and self-representation in the last three decades. Aligning these two female bildungsromans, we perceive how Asian-American identity is no longer defined primarily through nativity in America, nor America through an othering of Asia. In the more recent and expanded phase of Asian-American literature that lê exemplifies, the hyphen is read backward as much as forward, with the Asian-American subject's gaze turned in retrospection toward Asia as much as outward toward America. While an earlier model of Asian-American identity such as the one put forward by *The Woman Warrior* tends to cast the (Asian) ghost and the (Asian-American) double as oppositional categories, *Gangster* recasts the parallel life of the double left behind — the potential protagonist who fails to carry out the self-definitional journey from "Asian" to "Asian-American" — as a spectral shadow that cannot be exorcised from the hyphen. Instead of the hyphen's disintegration, lê illustrates the hyphen's overstretching: a continuity beyond displacement, an incomplete traversal that nonetheless safeguards the link between origin and diaspora, if in waterlogged, phantom form. Still, for both Kingston and lê, the task of hyphenated self-fashioning ultimately overflows the measure of a strictly Asian or American Gothic, whether it is by yearning to learn the outlawed, blinding knot of origin (Kingston 1976, 163) that some have called "the forbidden stitch" (Lim et al. 1989) or by donning the borrowed, oversized garment of a dead sibling's name — metaphors, finally, for Asian-America's own internal strangers.

Notes

1. The cultural offense connoted by *guei/kuei* returns unassuaged in Kingston's next book, *China Men* (1980), in which she retranslates the "white ghosts" of *Woman Warrior* as "white demons" — because, as she explains in an interview, "the [Chinese-American] men actually worked with white men, they had a relationship with them that was harsh, whereas the women hardly ever saw any, and so they're ghostly" (1998a, 152).

2. Wong's and Li's readings, however, are not without theoretical precedence, for we may trace their mode of argument to W.E.B. DuBois's well-known concept of "double consciousness," which outlines precisely this psychological complex of viewing oneself through the eyes of an "other world [...] that looks on in amused contempt and pity" ([1903] 1919, 11). DuBois explicitly adopts the language of psychic doubling to characterize racialized life in America, and to insert Kingston's double within this wider lineage of American race psychology and politics may have its advantages. It is quite another matter, however, for critics to take this complex as the inevitable premise of character psychology and textual analysis.

3. Kingston relates the origin of her memoir's title in one interview: "my original title was *Gold Mountain Stories*. The publishers didn't like a title that sounds like a collection of short stories; they never like to publish collections of short stories. I wasn't that happy with either of those titles, I think that calling that book *The Woman Warrior* emphasizes 'warrior.' I'm not really telling the story of war, I want to be a pacifist. So I keep hoping we will all take the woman warrior in another sense, that there are other ways to fight wars than with swords" (1998b, 48).

4. The theme of writing a literature of peace is already introduced by Kingston at the end of *Tripmaster Monkey*: "Whatever there is when there isn't war has to be invented. What do people do in peace? Peace has barely been thought" (1989, 306). By the time of *The Fifth Book of Peace* (2003), this project of peacemaking through language has become a pervasive one for Kingston, as she argues for a metaphysical link between disparate experiences of devastation, such as the first Iraqi war and the Oakland fire, that can facilitate intracultural healing as well as intercultural empathy.

5. I want to acknowledge my Introduction to Asian-American Literature class in fall of 2006 at Bowdoin College for helping me arrive at these insights.

6. lê alludes to this biographical detail in her e-essay "Tear the Pages Out" (no date).

7. The brother's name is not entirely unwritten in lê's corpus, however. In her "Electronic Chapbook" on *The Drunken Boat* (2001), an untitled poem names him: "tuan / i rarely write your name / almost never speak it / and when i dream you / closer to me / i call you / brother."

Works Cited

Blum, Joanne. 1988. *Transcending Gender: The Male/Female Double in Women's Fiction*. Ann Arbor: MI Research Press.

Botting, Fred. 1996. *Gothic*. London: Routledge.

DuBois, W.E.B. 1999. *The Souls of Black Folk* (1903). London: W.W. Norton.

Freud, Sigmund. 1990. "The Uncanny (1919)." *Art and Literature*. Ed. A. Dickson, vol. 14. London: Penguin, 335–76.

Goodman, Charlotte. 1983. "The Lost Brother, the Twin: Women Novelists and the Male-Female Double *Bildungsroman*." *Novel: A Forum on Fiction* 17, 1: 28–43.

Kim, Elaine H. 1981. "Visions and Fierce Dreams: A Commentary on the Works of Maxine Hong Kingston." *Amerasia Journal* 8, 2: 145–161.

Kingston, Maxine Hong. 1976. *The Woman Warrior: Memoirs of a Girlhood Among Ghosts*. New York: Vintage.

_____. 1980. *China Men*. New York: Knopf.

_____. 1989. *Tripmaster Monkey: His Fake Book*. New York: Knopf.

_____. 1998a. "Kingston at the University: Paul Skenazy / 1989," Interview in *Conversations with Maxine Hong Kingston*. Eds. P. Skenazy and T. Martin. Jackson: University Press of Mississippi, 118–158.

_____. 1998b. "To Be Able to See the Tao: Jody Hoy / 1986." Interview in *Conversations with Maxine Hong Kingston*. Eds. P. Skenazy and T. Martin. Jackson: University Press of Mississippi, 47–66.

_____. 2003. *The Fifth Book of Peace*. New York: Vintage.

Kristeva, Julia. 1991. *Strangers to Ourselves*. New York: Columbia University Press.

lê, thi diem thúy. 2001. *The Drunken Boat*. <http://www.thedrunkenboat.com/thuy.htm> (Accessed 31/03/ 2007).
_____. 2003. *The Gangster We Are All Looking For*. New York: Anchor.
_____. (no date). "Tear the Pages Out: Fragments from the *Gangster* Tour." *Powells.com*. <http://www.powells.com/essays/thuy.html> (Accessed 31/03/2007).
Li, David Leiwei. 1988. "The Naming of a Chinese American 'I': Cross-Cultural Sign/ifications in *The Woman Warrior*." *Criticism: A Quarterly for Literature and the Arts* 30, 4: 497–515.
Lim, Shirley, et al. (eds.). 1989. *The Forbidden Stitch: An Asian-American Women's Anthology*. Oregon: Calyx Books, Corvallis.
Melville, Herman. 1949 (1853). "Bartleby the Scrivener: A Story of Wall Street" (1853). *The Complete Stories of Herman Melville*. Ed. J. Leyda. New York: Random House, 3–47.
Poe, Edgar Allen. 1977 (1839). "William Wilson." *The Portable Poe*. Ed. P.V.D. Stern. New York: Penguin, 57–82.
Rogers, Robert. 1970. *A Psychoanalytic Study of the Double in Literature*. Detroit: Wayne State University Press.
Wong, Cynthia Sau-ling. 1993, *Reading Asian-American Literature: From Necessity to Extravagance*. New Jersey: Princeton University Press.

9

Gothic Aesthetics of Entanglement and Endangerment in David Henry Hwang's *The Sound of a Voice* and *The House of Sleeping Beauties*

Kimberly Jew

Given Asian American theatre's traditional preference for dramatic models that promote mimetic self-representation, the Asian American playwright seeking to experiment with Gothic fantasy faces numerous challenges. As will be discussed, David Henry Hwang's two short plays, *The Sound of a Voice* and *The House of Sleeping Beauties* (1983), illustrate the complexities of presenting Gothic processes of otherness and endangerment on the American stage.[1] Typically performed as a single bill, these minimalist dramas present twin images of a malevolent Asian landscape, one peopled by the mysterious figures of a witch, a warrior, a brothel madam, and a writer. As these isolated, socially-marginalized characters struggle against the inevitable forces of aging and death, they find themselves destroyed by entangling relationships.

At first glance, Gothic aesthetics of magnified otherness lie in direct contrast to the traditional imperative of Asian American theatre, a movement challenged to counter the historic deformation and objectification of Asian and

Asian American figures. While Asian American realism may seek to remedy historic otherness by initiating audience identification with the "real" figures on stage, Gothic aesthetics rely heavily on binary systems and oppositional difference, a discourse rooted in the open celebration of otherness. After all, Gothic otherness subverts the Enlightenment's hegemonic construction of Self, a Cartesian subject that is "dependent on excluding the Other in order to determine its own position" (Smith and Hughes 2). Through the exploration of the eschewed elements of consciousness — what Anne Williams refers to as absence or the "inexpressible other" (Williams 66) — Gothic narration challenges established systems of language, meaning and reality.

Gothic othering becomes even more intense when integrated with Orientalist perspectives, a process suggested by Hwang's creation of a mystical Japanese world in which to nurture his dark tales. The presence of an Eastern underworld fueled by chaos and menace allows for the reinforcement of the Western viewer's pre-conceived notions of the Orient. As Andrew Smith and William Hughes note in *Empire and The Gothic*, Gothic literature embraced a "complex set of views on the East [...] in order to consolidate rather than to question the kind of Orientalism identified by Edward Said" (Smith and Hughes 3). In other words, typical forms of Gothic othering such as monsters, inhuman oppressors and haunted spaces are energized by the Orientalist discourse on the "foreignness" of race and culture.

The Sound of a Voice and *The House of Sleeping Beauties* demonstrate a provocative perspective on a mysterious Japan, one that is informed by Gothic and Orientalist tropes. In *The Sound of a Voice*, a samurai travels through a forest to visit the home of a reputed witch, a lonely figure who tends mysterious flowers and plays the *shakuhatchi*.[2] Though the aging warrior's intention appears to be murder, he quickly falls under her spell and finds himself paralyzed, unable to act or to leave her home. Similarly *The House of Sleeping Beauties*, based in part on the novella of the same name by Japanese writer, Yasunari Kawabata (1899–1972), features an aging writer who visits a brothel run by an all-powerful madam. In this secret house, elderly men pay to sleep beside young sleeping virgins, women who are drugged into a state of lifelessness so as to preserve the anonymity of the encounter. Within this claustrophobic and symbolic space, the writer undergoes a regressive journey in which he realizes the futility of his existence.

Hwang's nightmarish presentation of sex and death in a distant, morally ambivalent Asian landscape of aging men, dangerous women, wandering samurai, prostitutes, trickery, sleeping potions, virgin fetishes and aging sexuality both stereotypes and estranges the Asian characters. The spatial metaphors of the inescapable woods and the confining brothel further suggest frightening spaces of liminality and disempowerment: the Asian figures on stage are caught in a topsy-turvy and oppressive world, one from which they cannot escape. This collapsing of Gothic and Orientalist constructions in an Asian American play potentially suggests an acceptance of a discourse that both objectifies Asian figures in an overdone Western fantasy and blurs the historic lines of distinction between diverse Asian and Asian American cultures.

Hwang complicates the presence of the eschewed other in these two plays, offering his audience members both a sense of safety from the foreign world on stage and a discomforting quality of Gothic presence and endangerment. In effect, Hwang first lures spectators into an aesthetically distant relationship, allowing them to feel pleasurably excluded from the actions played out in front of them. However, through subtle shifts in the narrative apparatus, he allows the dramas to shift into more invasive modes, small movements that begin to question the solidity of the fourth wall that separates audience and performance. This dual presentation of rigid and porous divisions is at the heart of a destabilizing Gothic narrative; as MaryBeth Inverso in *The Gothic Impulse in Contemporary Drama* explains, barriers in Gothic narrative "are maintained in order that they may be transgressed" (Inverso 4). By pulling at the edges of the established narrative frameworks of these plays, Hwang creates performances that endanger the audience's rejection of the inexpressible other.

Self-Destructive Entanglements

In many ways, *The Sound of a Voice* and *The House of Sleeping Beauties* are plays that revel in othering. The setting of dark fantasy narrative in a faraway Asian dreamscape clearly signals a desire to explore the underside of rationalism within the scope of the "not here." However, Hwang intensifies this project by establishing rigid gender binaries and triple-othering his female characters. As evidenced by the dramatic actions of these works, the four figures are strictly determined by abstract male-female trajectories: while the female figures are the empowered hosts who draw their guests into their feminine realms of experience, physicality and emotion, the male figures are wanderers and observers, who struggle against their female counterparts' overtures to disable their agency.

For a greater part in his plays, Hwang seems to echo the Gothic tradition of male to female projection, a narrative scheme in which a male character projects otherness onto his female antagonist. In *Our Ladies of Darkness*,

Female Daemonology in Male Gothic Fiction, a Jungian-inspired study of such gendered Gothic processes, Joseph Adriano grounds this male to female projection in the male subject's fear of his feminine self:

> What these men fear most is their crossing of gender boundaries. The haunting is an incursion into the male ego's dominion: the female demon is seen as a usurper; she inhabits and insidiously attempts to exert her influence, to feminize the male [Adriano 5].

To some degree Hanako, the witch with the magical ability to transform reality, and Michiko, the brothel madam empowered as the phallic mother figure, represent the eschewed elements of their male counterparts' consciousnesses. Hanako and Michiko are thus triple-othered: they serve as the "inexpressible other" through the lenses of Gothic, Orientalist and gendered perspectives.

By rooting dramatic action in the processes of gendered binary conflicts and female otherness, Hwang not only emphasizes an essentialist approach to gender, but also creates a dominating inclusiveness in his dramatic worlds. The heightened one-to-one focus between Hanako, Michiko and their male counterparts creates a dynamic introversion, one that tends to exclude social thematics, historical contextualization and the sphere of spectator. This process of "looking inwards" is dictated in part by the self-destructive nature of the relationships of the characters: each of the pairs is caught in an entangling web in which they simultaneously feed upon and destroy their counterparts. Like vampires, they deplete the very life force they thrive on, creating an environment in which nothing productive can be sustained. Hwang's absurdist vision of a bleak and deteriorating Asian underworld, one shaped by introversion and self-destruction, solidifies the apparent strength of the fourth wall, keeping the spectator safe from a close encounter with its performed other.

In *The Sound of a Voice,* Hanako, the witch living alone in the forest, and the Man, the aging samurai on a mission to murder her, play out conflictive gender symmetry through their journey towards mutual destruction. Two distinct patterns emerge that define this entangled relationship: first, in contrast to the Man, Hanako possesses an "unreal" multiplicity of persona. She can change her outward identity, alter time and transform into a younger and more beautiful version of herself. While the Man hides his intention to kill her, Hanako's complexity goes beyond masking her motivations; she simply functions by the rules of a different reality. The second pattern that emerges in this encounter in the woods is the inevitable condition of depletion. As the Man succumbs to Hanako's oppressive care, he finds himself emptied of his sense of agency. Likewise Hanako, who has fed on the living presence of the Man, finds that his resistance to her consuming love depletes her will to live.

Hanako's seduction of the Man is characterized by her feminine multiplicity of character: while she lures him into her realm through emotional neediness, she also overwhelms him with aggressive overtures. This gendering of the multiplicitous personality is not new in the Western literary tradition; as Williams notes, "in Aristotle's paradigm, unity is associated with the male, duality or multiplicity with the female. Such duality is typical of the female 'other' in patriarchal myth" (Williams 144). Thus Hanako's predisposition towards metamorphosis is part of a discourse on essentialized and binary gender differences developed in both of Hwang's plays.

Hanako's multiplicity is evinced as soon as the Man arrives at her home seeking a place to sleep. Immediately she places herself in an openly dependent position, bolstering his centrality to her well being: in this home, the guest rules over the host. After deflecting the Man's compliments on the food she has offered him, she says that "You are reckless in your flattery. But anything you say, I will enjoy hearing. It's not even the words. It's the sound of a voice, the way it moves through the air" (Hwang 188).

Haunted by the silence of the forest and her lack of companionship, Hanako depicts herself as being in great need of the life breath that humans carry within themselves; silence and loneliness have collapsed together into a condition of personal despair. A few lines later, she reiterates her emotional needs in more direct terms: "I'll lie down in the next room, and hear your breathing through the wall, and fall asleep shamelessly. There will be no silence" (189).

Hanako's emotional desperation reflects not only the Gothic's "primacy of feeling" (Inverso 11), but also an intense emotional hunger, a longing that shapes her feminine identity into a vampire that feeds on male companionship. Though Gothic vampires typically long for the life-sustaining element of blood, Hanako's need for the sounds of human life reflects the same emotional pain seen in the vampire narrative. As Dani Cavallaro in *The Gothic Vision* notes, "Vampires are frequently represented as not only physically vulnerable but also emotionally vulnerable — the repository for sorrow which humans have become too callous to comprehend" (Cavallaro 187).

Like a vampire that cannot die, Hanako appears cursed to live her existence in a lonely exile. Her condition causes her to invest in inanimate objects, psychically etching her loneliness onto the walls of her home and finding protection in the human-like sounds of the *shakuhatchi*. As she explains to the Man, "The *shakuhatchi* became my weapon. It kept me from choking on many a silent evening" (Hwang 196).

Hanako's self-portrayal as a retiring and isolated figure is countered by her overt seductive acts, a shift in persona that foreshadows greater revelations of her "unreal" multiplicity. Her first aggressive move occurs the morning after the Man's arrival. As he chops wood without his shirt on, Hanako stares at his body. When the Man demurs, surprised by her interest in his aging form, he begins to joke about his potbelly, calling it a "great horseman" (193). A moment later Hanako, who has complimented his body's strength and flirtatiously suggested that he "learn[s] to love it" (193), declares her undying faith to him, a visitor who just arrived last night:

> MAN: (still to his belly) You're also faithful. You'll never leave me for another man.
> WOMAN: No.
> MAN: What do you want me to say?
> (WOMAN leans over to MAN. She touches his belly with her hand) [194].

A similarly overt seductive act occurs when the Man inquires about the *shakuhatchi* music he had heard coming from her bedroom. In response to his question, Hanako promises to play for him every night — so that she can shape his dreams.

Hanako's shifts between emotional neediness and confident seduction reflect deeper elements of her multiplicitous persona. While the Man observes his female other's behavior, looking for clues of witchcraft, Hanako quietly demonstrates her ability to stop time, ultimately transforming into a younger, more beautiful version of herself right before his eyes. Her power to stop time is first hinted at in her tending of a group of mysterious cut flowers. Though the cut flowers were given to her by past visitors, they remain perennially fresh and in bloom; when the Man inquires about her secret methods of care, she acknowledges the space that separates them, "I create a world which is outside of the realm of what you know" and where "words become irrelevant" (191).

Hanako's transformation into her alternate self signals the beginning of their mutual destruction and ensures the deterioration of the bizarre fantasy world on stage. For as Hanako feeds on the presence of her male visitor and blossoms into her more beautiful self, she consumes his energy, leaving him paralyzed and unable to act. Most importantly, Hanako's feminine multiplicity directly attacks the Man's masculinity. This is seen most clearly in her metamorphosis into an adept fighter, a change that occurs while they practice swordplay. The stage directions read: "WOMAN executes a series of movements. Her whole manner is transformed. MAN watches with increased amazement. Her movements end. She regains her submissive manner" (200).

Hanako's unexpected effectiveness in sword fighting proves a double-edged blade to the Man's predicament: first, he recognizes that he cannot use his male-identified swordsman skills to overcome her, and second, he realizes that the woman with whom he has fallen in love is indeed a witch and must be killed. And although he later tries to murder Hanako and himself by means of his sword, he finds that he simply cannot act: "Weakness. All weakness. Too weak to kill you. Too weak to kill myself" (207).

This crisis of action leads to his realization that he has been caught in an entangling relationship with Hanako. While he has found solace in the loving oppression of her care — suggesting to her that he has become one of her contentedly imprisoned flowers — he also languishes in the depletion of his energies. Towards the end of the play, after having been caught sneaking away, he explains in highly gendered, militaristic terms that he cannot live with someone who has defeated him. Though Hanako initially appeared subservient to his needs, offering him the perfect balance to his masculine entitlement, she has now disempowered him ultimately:

> MAN: I came here with a purpose. The world was clear. You changed the shape of your face, the shape of my heart — rearranged everything — created a world where I could do nothing.
> WOMAN: I only tried to care for you.
> MAN: I guess that was all it took [207].

Hanako, too, finds herself entangled in a self-destructive relationship, an inescapable pattern that has been repeated to the point where she is now ready to end her life. Although she has fed on the presence of her past guests, blossoming into her beautiful self as she cares for them, she has also exhausted their energies and forced them into debilitating states that they resist. And while her metamorphoses are a natural part of her multiplicitous persona, they frighten her guests, increasing their desire to escape:

> And one day, inevitably, you step outside of the lines. The visitor knows. You don't. You didn't know that you did anything different. You thought it was just another part of you. The visitor sneaks away. The next day you learn that you had stepped outside of his heart [201].

Hanako's repeated rejections by visitors have increased her sense of loneliness; like her captive guests, she finds her energies whittled away by contact with her gendered opposite. As she repeatedly says to the Man in their final conversations, she would prefer to die than to suffer another loss. In death, she would still find a level of intimacy to sustain her: "Kill me but don't leave me. Even in death, my spirit would be comforted by your presence" (208). Hanako, who longs for the Man to kill her, has consumed so much of his energy that all that remains is his weakened impulse to leave. By the end of the play, both characters have exhausted each other: while Hanako kills herself, the Man discovers that he is too weak to leave her home.

A sense of anti–Hegelian self-annihilation characterizes this Gothic world; as these two aging figures approach one another, their gendered trajectories link them in a doomed battle over power and identity. The result is a mixture of impotence and emptiness that promises the narrative and performative death of the spectator's other. For as the drama peters out on a note of depletion — the Man's feeble attempt to play Hanako's flute in front of her hanging body — the living moment of the performance ends.

In *The House of Sleeping Beauties*, Michiko, the brothel madam, and Kawabata, the writer, play out a similar pattern of a conflictive gender binarism, female otherness and destructive entanglement, as that of *The Sound of a Voice*. In this case, however, when the male subject encounters his own abject primordial feminine self, a period of creativity emerges; he writes the novella on which the play is centered. *The House of Sleeping Beauties* is based in part on the novella by Yasunari Kawabata. In Kawabata's novella, a man named Eguchi visits a house of sex-less prostitution where elderly men sleep beside young women. In Hwang's play, it is "Kawabata" himself who visits the brothel, a life-changing event that inspires him to write his novella. Hwang not only significantly increases the role of the brothel madam but he introduces a conflictive relationship between her and Kawabata.

Like the pair in *The Sound of a Voice*, Kawabata and Michiko are engaged in a gendered power struggle over identity, one that is represented by yet another imbalanced host-guest relationship. While Kawabata insists that he is not a guest, but rather a visitor seeking information about the "parade of corpses" (154) that enters her home each night, Michiko insists that he plays the role of guest to her empowered position as host. From the moment they meet, their worlds are doomed to clash. For instance, as a defiant outsider to Michiko's realm, Kawabata views their first encounter on merely practical terms, referring to her guests as "customers" and offering her money in exchange for information:

> KAWABATA: Listen, I know you're a woman of business — may I offer you some fee for what you know?
> WOMAN: Money?
> KAWABATA: Don't worry. I'm not with the police or anything.
> WOMAN: Don't be ridiculous. What do you take me for? ... You might as well pay me to tell you how one falls in love [155].

Michiko's response, much like Hanako's explanation of her flowers, suggest that language (both medium and message) has gendered proclivities which can sometimes lead to manipulation and misunderstanding. For instance, Ruth Bienstock Anolik believes that the female language is "more literal than men's, more grounded in literal presence" (Anolik 26). This linguistic ludicity is capitalized by Hwang. During the course of the play, Michiko, who refuses to verbally describe the mysterious events that occur within her home, and who insists that Kawabata *experiences* sleeping with her women, is occasionally seen chronicling her guests' visits in her record book. Later in the play, her repeated references to Kawabata's novella as a "report" pointedly reflect on Kawabata's references to her guests as "customers." Language, its acquisition and use, separate these two figures; true union may be found before language begins.

In a strategic maneuver, Michiko promises to answer Kawabata's questions *only* if he undergoes her guest interview, the highlight of which is a game of tiles. The object of this game is to remove individual pieces from a house of tiles until the house falls down. While Kawabata schemes to win by jiggling the table and blaming the fallen tiles on Michiko, Michiko tricks Kawabata into accepting his role as a guest in her establishment: after the game has ended, she announces that she has accepted him as her guest and that his room is ready. Having been distracted by the game, a disoriented Kawabata allows Michiko to undress him and directs him towards the room where a young woman sleeps. Thus in a moment that captures their future entanglement, Michiko and Kawabata are intertwined in a game of mutual destruction, a model of ruin that will affect them equally.

As evidenced by Michiko's powerful position as host, her personality dominates the space. Michiko, who grew up in the country, spent her life maintaining this secret urban house, protecting her women from both abusive clients and the law while earning a meager living on the margins of society. As she later explains to Kawabata, this home is her life — without the brothel, she has nothing. The physical space of the brothel is also, however, an image of her feminine power. Michiko's supremacy within the brothel lies in the symbology of interiority that she orchestrates: secrecy, female sexuality and reproduction, imprisonment.

The setting of the play exclusively at night, in a brothel where sleeping is the primary activity, emphasizes the pervasive element of darkness in Michiko's home. Darkness reinforces the femininity of the space, suggesting the pre–Oedipal phallic mother, a fantasy body that proposes "the seductive totalization" of identity, physicality and sexuality (Ian 20). In this maternal world, the male child may imagine that his mother is one with him, sharing in the possession of the phallus. As Cavallaro notes, darkness does not always signify evil in Gothic literature, it may also reflect "primordial chaos and its

powers," the image of the embryo growing in the dark womb (Cavallaro 23)..
Michiko's brothel. where young women and old men sleep side by side, each
drugged into varying states of passivity, is highly suggestive of the primordial
womb incubating half-conscious beings. Michiko suggests this image of the
womb in her explanation that her guests enjoy sleeping in her home due to
its warmth; they are not afraid of darkness.

Not surprisingly, Kawabata is afraid of the dark. His discomfort towards
his first encounter is later demonstrated by an angry response and a petty act
of destruction. Having returned in Scene Two to burn the record of his visit,
he proudly announces, "I'm a writer" (Hwang 160). His threat to write a story
about her brothel portends the mutual self-destruction to come. Despite
Michiko's protestations that his story will end her means of survival, he
remains adamant about producing a story based on her home:

> WOMAN: What is this story to you?
> KAWABATA: I want to write a story. I can do it, I know. I haven't written a
>   story in ...in...
> WOMAN: That's just one story to you. This is my life.
> KAWABATA: Better if you were rid of it [163].

Kawabata describes his first experience as claustrophobic — he felt smothered
by the "mother" lying beside him. Rejecting his role as guest, he says, "I certainly have no desire to repeat last night's experience. It's been so many years
since I've had to share a bed. No room to stretch" (161). Though Kawabata
is confident that he has "outgrown the womb," his mind has in fact returned
to the memory of a past, maternal-like lover, whose hair he would nestle in
as he did with Michiko's sleeping woman. When Michiko asks if he worried
about suffocating if he did that, he jokingly dismisses her fears. But what is
implied is that his actions belie a gradual engulfment by the womb and the
phallic mother. Despite Kawabata's apparent rejection, Michiko easily guides
him back to the bedroom by offering him a second night for free, an offer he
cannot refuse.

During the next five months, Kawabata visits regularly and continues to
experience his regressive state. This journey is one of absence, both in terms
of Kawabata's encounter with his abject Mother and also the play's direction:
Hwang refuses to dramatize Kawabata's "return to the womb." Only after
Kawabata's regressive journey has ended is the audience allowed to view its
outcome. Thus in Scene Three, the spectator learns about Kawabata's experience exclusively through his narration in his by then completed novella. As
he sleeps beside the young female bodies, he remembers pleasurable elements
of emotion, experience and sexuality; images of his lovers, daughters and

deceased wife buoy his sense of loneliness and despair. As he explains to Michiko, "I'd lie awake at nights, too, but I'd love it, because I'd remember..." (168). Most notably during this period, Kawabata severs his ties with writing, an activity that not only marks his livelihood but also aligns him to the Symbolic realm of the Father. As he declares, "I stopped writing — even exercises — it all seemed so pointless" (168).

After five months, however, a radical shift occurs; his retreat to the primordial womb begins to destabilize. Increasingly, as he tells Michiko, images of suicide are haunting him, such as the *hara-kiri* of one his male friends. The female bodies lying beside no longer provide a sense of security but has renewed in him feelings of horror and repulsion: "I smell their skin, run my fingers between their toes — there's nothing but skin and bones" (169). He also now experiences claustrophobia, feeling like a prisoner in their beds. Psychoanalytically speaking, these feelings of horror, his fear of physical and tangible elements, may indicate a growing apprehension over the pre–Oedipal state; as Williams argues, horror, in contrast to terror, suggests the "earliest stirring of the pre-self's separation from the mother" (Williams 74), and represents the initial efforts of the male pre-subject to separate its identity from the mother, who must now become abjected. After abiding for a few months in the maternal imaginary and re-experiencing his earlier existence in the womb, Kawabata suddenly desires to reclaim his male subjectivity once more.

Kawabata's rejection of his female other piques in Scene Three. Michiko offers him two women for "twice the warmth" (172), but he later emerges from the bedroom in a panic: one of the sleeping women has died. The presence of the corpse in Kawabata's bed complicates his past engagement with the half-living female bodies, because it brings to consciousness his own collusion with "death" all this while. After all, these deeply inebriated women remind us of the undead, Gothic configurations that challenge the binary neatness of "living" versus "dead." In Julia Kristeva's theory of abjection, the corpse is the most extreme vehicle of abject waste, which Elizabeth Grosz terms a "contamination of the living," an entity that demonstrates the "body's recalcitrance to consciousness, reason or will" (Grosz 92). The horror of lying next to a dead female body has poignantly brought home the realization that for the last five months, he has been existing on the border of life and death, of the womb and the tomb, and he now recognizes that what he has done "is inhuman [...] not human" (172). Michiko commands him to return to bed, but he declares that he would rather die outside than become one of her half-living (or half-dead) visitors. But as Kawabata is under the influence of his sleeping potion, Michiko easily guides him back to the bedroom for one last night in her home.

Through their contentious relationship, Michiko and Kawabata play out a symbolic gender symmetry, one that presumes essentialized gender attributes, female othering and Symbolic privileges of male subjectivity. As developed in Hwang's previous work, such tightly focused, introverted binary systems are doomed to self-destruct with each side feeding on and destroying the other. This repeated paradigm also ensures the deterioration of the abject world on stage, suggesting that the "dark fantasy, foreign and female" other will be easily contained by the fourth wall. In *The House of Sleeping Beauties*, Hwang emphasizes this imagery of entangling destruction by inventing the double suicide of Kawabata and Michiko. In the original novella, the story ends abruptly as the dead girl's body is removed; Eguchi is caught in a moment of confusion as he returns to his bed. But in Hwang's play, both Michiko and Kawabata participate in their dangerous game to a chilling finish.

In Scene Four, Kawabata returns to the brothel to destroy both Michiko's home and himself. He has completed his manuscript in a feverish rush, a novella that will expose her secret practices and his encounter with the dead body. Without a doubt, Kawabata has emerged from Michiko's maternal realm rejuvenated, his creative processes re-energized. "It came out of me like a wild animal, my hands cramping at the pen" (178). Knowing that the publication of his novella will lead to the destruction of Michiko's life's efforts, he offers her all of the money left in his life, calling it "an even trade" (177).

In addition to his life savings, Kawabata also brings Michiko a kimono and a bottle of poison. Having fed on her nurturing maternal power, only to then destroy her world with the fruits of his re-birth, he now insists that Michiko aid him in his suicide. Requesting that Michiko wears the kimono, he directs her to pour the poison into the tea that she will serve him; together they are to re-play the guest's interview from their first meeting. In this manner, Kawabata implicates Michiko in her own cycle of destruction; though he has picked the last tile, the house falls down on both of them. Just as she lured Kawabata into her maternal realm and thrived on his disempowerment, she must now destroy the "infant" that she has incubated, a being who recognizes the futility of his existence within the confines of her warmth and darkness. Ultimately, it is Kawabata's encounter with his other that leads him to end his life. The aged Michiko, too, sees only a bleak and deteriorating future for herself, and as Kawabata dies peacefully in her lap, caressed by her motherly strokes of his head, she drinks the poisoned tea as well.

Gestures of Endangerment

According to Inverso, contemporary neoGothic drama can be identified by the original Gothic aesthetics of moral ambiguity, the celebration of riot and the endangerment of the spectator (Inverso, see chapters one and five). While *The Sound of a Voice* and *The House of Sleeping Beauties* appear ambiguous in their avoidance of moral judgments and equal distribution of depletive effects, elements of riot are more difficult to identify. These two plays appear to dampen riotous impulses through their reliance on highly controlled patterns of ruin: that which is othered — undesirable, inexpressible, eschewed — annihilates itself with cool restraint. In effect, the entangling relationships of mutual destruction as demonstrated by Hanako and the Man, and Michiko and Kawabata privilege Gothic moral ambiguity — a feature that suggests elements of Theatre of the Absurd — over that of the riotous. Indeed, when considering the age and expired condition of the characters, the bleak and infertile environments and the aura of oppressive stagnation that marks both plays, Hwang appears to have found a compelling link between Gothic narrative and theatrical absurdism in his experimental "Asian American Gothic plays."

One of the most intriguing explorations of Gothic aesthetics, however, lies in Hwang's use of threatening theatrical motions that endanger the audience. Gestures of endangerment, or tactics that "would imperil audience voyeurism, or at least jeopardize the inviolability of the spectator" are subtle but present in both works (Inverso 17). Through shifts in the established narrative framework, Hwang begins to acknowledge the presence of the audience and suggests the porous nature of the barriers he has created. In this way, he counters the rigid application of gendered binarism, female otherness and patterns of self-destruction analyzed in this essay. Ultimately these moments of danger suggest that the audience's other cannot be fully contained but "hovers," like the abject, "at the border of the subject's identity" (Grosz 87).

In *The Sound of a Voice*, Hwang suggests a crack in the fourth wall through the changing illumination of Hanako's bedroom. As clarified by the stage directions, Hanako's bedroom, located beyond the central room where Hanako and the Man interact, is illuminated twice during the play; the solid wall facing the audience becomes transparent when the lights are raised. In the first illumination, the Man has awakened to the sounds of the *shakuhatchi* emanating from her room. As he opens her bedroom door, Hanako's room illuminates and the wall becomes transparent. In an overt expressionist gesture, Hwang allows the audience to see Hanako's metamorphosis through the Man's eyes: a transformed Hanako now walks gracefully with her flowers, unaware of his gaze. While this narrative device privileges the perspective of the Man — after all, Hanako is his female other — it also draws attention to the presence of the witnessing audience, one whose visual process has shifted with the use of expressionist aesthetics.

In the second illumination, however, Hwang alters the source of light, confounding the narrative technique established in the previous transition. In the final moments of the play, Hanako escapes to her bedroom to kill herself. The Man, who has temporarily exited the central space, returns and slides open her bedroom door. When he peers into her bedroom, however, the room does not illuminate; the audience is no longer allowed to see through his eyes. Having witnessed an "unseen" horror, he returns to the central space where he sits and attempts to play the *shakuhatchi*. After a moment, Hanako's room lights up behind him and only the audience sees her illuminated dead body hanging amidst floating flower petals.

As suggested by the play's ending, Hanako's presence comes unexpectedly closer to the audience, offering one last tap against the fourth wall. In her last lines to the Man, she begs him to kill her, stating that "Even in death, my spirit would rest here and be comforted by your presence" (Hwang 208). These lines prove prophetic for not only does the Man remain in her home, her "comforted" response to his playing of the *shakuhatchi*— a moment shared *only* with the audience — may be inferred from the delayed illumination of her hanging body as well. Thus Hanako slowly emerges as the controlling voice of the theatrical event; even through death, she directs the plot and staging towards herself, making a momentary but threatening visual connection with the spectator, one that announces "I am still here."

Like *The Sound of a Voice*, the endangering shifts in narrative apparatus occur towards the end of *The House of Sleeping Beauties*. In Scene Four, the last scene of the play, two specific changes occur: first, the introduction of theatrical self-reference, and second, the intrusion of Kawabata's maternal regression into the playing space. In an intriguing theatrical gesture, Hwang introduces a pointed comparison between the original novella and his own dramatization, a dramaturgical choice that openly implies a reality external to that of the world on stage. Here Michiko challenges Kawabata on the "facts" of his novella: his use of Eguchi instead of himself, the inclusion of electric blankets, the death of a man at the brothel, and her portrayal as a cold-hearted woman. Speaking of Michiko's novella character in the third person, Kawabata responds with the defense, "The story's not about her" (174), a comment that draws attention to the real differences between the novella and the play. While the novella focuses exclusively on Kawabata, Hwang's play — the world on stage — offers an equal view of both characters, empowering the role of Michiko to a greater degree. This moment of self-conscious theatricalism not only implicates the fictive processes of Kawabata's novella and Hwang's play, but also the presence of a witnessing audience that may support Michiko's point of view.[3]

By Scene Four, the audience has become accustomed to the staged absence of Kawabata's regressive experiences; the processes of the primordial womb have occurred exclusively off-stage, left completely to the spectator's imagination. In the enactment of Kawabata's suicide, however, the spectator becomes privy to his final intimate moments with the maternal. In short, his regression escapes from the unseen bedroom and intrudes into the playing space. As Inverso notes, motions of intrusion and invasion are central to NeoGothic drama, suggesting an animated environment that threatens characters and spectators alike (Inverso, chapter five). From this perspective, Kawabata's once hidden maternal regression is brought dangerously forward, closer to the audience, revealing the full presence of Kawabata's other. In this final enactment, Kawabata performs the ritual of his private regressive activities: he drinks his "sleeping potion" and nestles into Michiko's body, kissing her hands and putting his head in her lap. Choosing Michiko for this ritual doubly emphasizes his desire to return to the phallic mother. In terms of a spatial metaphor, it also proves significant that Kawabata, who has access to the outside of the brothel, now returns to Michiko, who is associated primarily with the living room, to die. This suggests that he has finally completed his regressive journey after a brief interlude of symbolic awakening.

By offering gestures of endangerment in these two "Asian American Gothic plays," Hwang suggests that the spectator may not be completely safe from the othered world on stage. Though the Gothic and Orientalist tropes appear solidified by a system determined by gendered binarism, female otherness and self-destructive entanglement, the subversive shifting of the narrative apparatus implies a degree of instability. This changeability in structure — narrative device, the fourth wall, and spatial configuration — allows the dramatic action to shift and move forward in an invasive manner, challenging the spectator to feel its own presence and to make contact with its own dark side.

Notes

1. David Henry Hwang is an American-born Chinese American who grew up in an English-speaking, Christian fundamentalist household.
2. A *shakuhatchi* is a Japanese bamboo flute.
3. Of course, the audience will soon be able to verify that a man does die in her brothel. In other words, the Kawabata figure in the play has written his death into the novella.

Works Cited

Adriano, Joseph. 1993. *Our Ladies of Darkness. Feminine Daemonology in Male Gothic Fiction.* Pennsylvania: Penn State University Press.

Anolik, Ruth Bienstock. 2003. "The Missing Mother: The Meaning of Maternal Absence in the Gothic Mode." *Modern Language Studies* 33, vol., no. 1/2: 24–43.

Cavallaro, Dani. 2002. *The Gothic Vision: Three Centuries of Horror, Terror and Fear.* London/New York: Continuum.

Grosz, Elizabeth. 1990. "The Body of Signification." *Abjection, Melancholia and Love: The Work of Julia Kristeva.* Eds. John Fletcher and Andrew Benjamin. New York/London: Routledge, 80–103.

Hwang, David Henry. 1990. *FOB and Other Plays.* New York: Penguin.

Ian, Marcia. 1993. *Remembering the Phallic Mother: Psychoanalysis, Modernism and the Fetish.* Ithaca/London: Cornell University Press.

Inverso, Mary Beth. 1990. *The Gothic Impulse in Contemporary Drama.* Ann Arbor: UMI Research Press.

Smith, Andrew, and William Hughes. 2003. "Introduction: Enlightenment Gothic and Postcolonialism." *Empire and the Gothic: The Politics of Genre.* Eds. Andrew Smith and William Hughes. Basingstoke: Palgrave, 1–12.

Williams, Anne. 1995. *Art of Darkness: A Poetics of Gothic.* London/Chicago: The University of Chicago Press.

Part III

The Gothic Tradition in Chinese, Japanese, Korean and Turkish Literature

10

Reading Shi Zhecun's "Yaksha" against the Shanghai Modern[*]

Hongbing Zhang

The historian of the strange comments: A yaksha wife is indeed rarely heard of, but on a thorough second thought it is not so rare, for on every bedside there is a yaksha.
— Pu Songling, "The Yaksha Kingdom" (379)[1]

The fact that I have said that the effect of interpretation is to isolate in the subject a kernel, a *kern* to use Freud's own term, of non-sense, does not mean that interpretation is in itself nonsense.
— Jacques Lacan, "The Field of the Other and Back to the Transference" (1992: 250)

An essential dimension of the metropolitan "I," the narrator in Shi Zhecun's 1932 story "Yecha" (Yaksha), is his distrust and doubt. To the German doctor's diagnosis and the nurse's description of the symptoms of his friend's illness as those of a mental disorder, resulting from some setback in love, the Chinese narrator's response is: "But I doubted very much this kind of explanation, because I knew my friend had not had any love affairs before." According to the doctor and nurses, however, his friend would sometimes act

[*]This article was first published under the title of "Writing 'the Strange' of the Chinese Modern: Sutured Body, Naturalized Beauty and Shi Zhecun's 'Yaksha'" in the *Journal of Modern Literature in Chinese* 5.2 (2002): 29–54. It was revised when included in this volume. I would like to thank Xiaobing Tang, Jason McGrath, Ling-hon Lam and Andrew Ng for their comments and suggestions at various moments.

strangely, as if he were pushing someone away with his two out-stretched hands. He would talk nonsense in his delirium: "Horrible woman! Strange woman! Don't come close to me!" (Shi 1991, 323).

The distrust and doubt of the narrator, a fictional urban dweller in the 1920s and 1930s Shanghai, resonate well with what Georg Simmel has diagnosed as a "reserved" attitude of most people living in a modern metropolis (Simmel 414). But the intensification of nervous stimulation that would generate such a protective psychological mechanism among people living in Shanghai came not just from the metropolitan life in the Simmelian sense of a universalized modernity but also from the Chinese city's "cultural and historical crisis vis-à-vis the West" that created "severe psychological pressures" at the historical moment (Link 198). One indication of such historical crisis — and quotidian contradictions — was that, during the late 1920s and early 1930s when the Western medicine was already widely practiced in Shanghai, the Chinese people there still "held a 'belief' in the Chinese medicine over the Western medicine" (Lei 59, 103–18). Another such manifestation was the controversy over "science" and "metaphysics" in the early 1920s. Some Chinese "metaphysics ghosts" (*xuanxue gui*— a term used by the participant of the debate Ding Wenjiang) took the Western civilization to be essentially a "material civilization achieved by science" and believed that "China should value her own spiritual civilization," as the Western material civilization had been doubted and detested by Europeans themselves since World War I (Chow 334).

The story "Yaksha," like some of Shi Zhecun's other modernist stories, presents a psychological exploration of the reaction of metropolitan inhabitants in Shanghai to the contradictions and conflicts in their everyday life. In the story, Bian Shiming, the friend of the narrator Lao Shi, falls strangely ill at the sight of the narrator's female cousin and is thus sent to a Western-styled hospital. Three weeks after Bian is hospitalized, the narrator, as we have seen, distrusting the German doctor's diagnosis, visits his friend at the hospital. As an explanation for the cause of his sudden illness, Bian tells the narrator his own adventure in the countryside near Hangzhou, where he believes he met a female yaksha and then, mistaking a mute country woman for the yaksha, he killed her. Even after he comes back to Shanghai, Bian believes that the yaksha or the spirit of the murdered woman continues to haunt him.

Strange as it is, the story forces us to look into the production of "the strange" in a modern time and space. The traditional Chinese narrative of "the strange," appropriated here by Shi Zhecun to structure the modern experience in Shanghai as a pathological and cultural symptom and to interpret the same experience as an aetiological and semiotic object, touches upon some larger problems about Chinese modernity: What is the relationship between the nonsense and the Shanghai modern? Will the desire to be a modern Chinese person inevitably lead to the desire to totalize? If not, how should these two be distinguished and separated in the formation of modern Chinese subjectivity? What kind of role should women play in the effort to achieve Chinese modernity? To these questions, the story offers us some "strange" phenomena, together with symptomatic descriptions rather than aetiological diagnoses, but even these "strange" phenomena and enigmatic symptoms concerning the Shanghai modern are worth examining in our reconsideration of Chinese modernity, especially literary modernity, in the twentieth century.

"It Figures There as the Element Which Is Lacking"

While questioning the German doctor's diagnosis, the narrator Lao Shi comes to the hospital in the hope of finding out the real cause for his friend Bian Shiming's sudden illness, a cause that he suspects the Western medical narrative may have failed to represent truthfully. But to see in the relationship between the doctor and the narrator only the latter's distrust of the former, as well as the latter's suspicion of a possible Western misrepresentation, is incomplete and misleading. For, at the very beginning of the story, the narrator tells us that he decides to visit his friend three weeks later simply because "I obeyed the doctor's instructions" (Shi 1991, 323). Placed at the very beginning of the story, the narrator's abiding by the doctor's "instructions" (*dingzhu*), though overshadowed by his subsequent compulsion to seek some alternative explanation for the illness, functions to control the way the story develops and the way readers read it.

The narrator's observance of the doctor's instructions registers an implicit distancing from Bian. Although the narrator believes that the doctor does not really know Bian from the vantage point of an insider like him, he himself does not know much about Bian's personal life, either. He only knows that Bian is an "innocent middle-aged man" (323) working in an office and practicing fencing after work. Another thing he knows is that Bian likes to make fun of other people being frustrated in love. But, for Bian's own subjective, emotional life, especially his love affair, the narrator does not know anything. He merely surmises that, even if it had something to do with women, Bian would not be suffering from any mental disorder, as the doctor asserts. In his eyes, Bian is a typical modern man who would by no means be afflicted by love. Yet Bian's strange behavior, his sudden illness at the sight of the narrator's female cousin, suggests that there is something that lies beyond the narrator's knowledge.

The distance from his friend Bian leads the narrator not only to see Bian's behavior as "really strange" (323) but also to frame within the narrative of "the strange" what his friend tells him. This method also allows him to see Bian as a patient, a man who may now be suffering from a mental disorder. However, his illusion that he is in a position to better understand Bian functions, in his mind at least, to shorten the distance between the two of them, while it increases the distance between himself and the German doctor. Though the narrator has had to obey the doctor from the very beginning, he can distrust and doubt him as much as he wishes. In the narrator's relationship to Bian and the German doctor we see his double yet dislocated identification with both the symbolic and the imaginary. If in imaginary identification, to use Slavoj Žižek's words, "we identify ourselves with the image of the other inasmuch as we are 'like him,'" while in symbolic identification we identify ourselves with the other precisely at a point at which he is inimitable, at the point which eludes resemblance" (Žižek 1989, 109), what we see in the narrator here is a quotidian battle of split identification with both the symbolic and the imaginary. He has an imaginary identification with his friend, who is "like him" and whom he believes he knows well as his co-national, and a symbolic identification with the German doctor as the dubious other, a foreigner whose instruction he has obeyed but who does not bear any resemblance to his friend and himself.

It is no wonder that, with this split identification with both the symbolic and the imaginary, the narrator feels that something is missing in his communication with the German doctor. For this, he blames it on the doctor's poor English: "Doctor Liszt (*Lie Xide*), other than saying in his clumsy and awkward English that [my friend] was suffering from a mental disorder as a consequence of his being exposed to some great horror, said nothing about the cause [of the illness]" (323). This split identification also finds the narrator in confusion in the Western-styled hospital:

> I stood in front of the door of Room 437. The white wall and the white door gave me a sense of horror. These should be black, but the white color in the hospital — not only the white wall and door, but also the white beds, white bedding, white instruments, white operating table — made me feel as if I had walked into a house full of mourning arrangements for the recently deceased, and it made me so nervous that I had to hold my breath. I took out my handkerchief and, thanks to the blue squares on it, I felt a little relieved. Then I bent my index finger and knocked at the door slightly. I could not imagine what I would see when the door was opened [323–24].

As if intent on avoiding the inadequacy of language that he has detected in the German doctor's bad English, the narrator not only dutifully records everything he sees but, more importantly, transcribes truthfully his own sense reactions. The narrator's sense reaction to the white color is revealing here. Although it has become normal today, especially in the West, for this color to be used in a hospital, it was not so self-evidently "normal" in China in the 1920s and 1930s. In traditional Chinese cultural practice, whiteness is mostly connected with death and funerals, where relatives and friends wear white clothes or scarves to see the deceased off to his "eternal home" in the other world. This is why the narrator believes everything in the hospital should be black, and he associates almost instinctively the whiteness with "the mourning arrangements for the recently deceased." He feels nervous and terrified, and becomes grateful and relieved at the sight of the "blue squares" on his handkerchief. The handkerchief, whose significance in modern metropolitan life Shi Zhecun defines in another context as "helping you accomplish your natural gesture" when you feel nervous or insecure in public (Shi 1996b, 113), saves the narrator from his disorientation. It also returns him, at least momentarily, to a state of equilibrium among the pigmentary forces and to his calmness as he walks on inside this Western-styled hospital.

Yet, the cultural difference as reflected in the color, as well as the nervous feeling generated in the narrator, can hardly be covered up by a blue handkerchief. The white color is so pervasive that the narrator cannot divert attention from it. After the door of the ward is opened, the narrator first sees two black eyes, then a lovable red mouth, and finally the white face of a nurse. However, against the whiteness of the wall, the face and the bonnet, the nurse's two black eyes and red mouth appear, in his eyes, like "two longans and a water chestnut" left on a white towel (Shi 1991, 324). This description of a nurse's face against the white background further reinforces the narrator's fear of whiteness in the hospital. Indeed, the constant recourse to sense reaction as a register of cultural shock in the narration demonstrates a characteristic that Lou Shiyi observed in his 1931 article about Shi Zhecun's writings; he notes in them a "New Sensationalism" (*xin ganjue zhuyi*), a designation that has now become widely accepted as a description of the modernist style of Shi Zhecun and his like-minded writer-friends. Tracing the source of influence to French surrealism, Japanese New Sensationalism and the "Nonsense" school, Lou regards Shi's New Sensationalist writing, nevertheless, as a direct product of a particular social class living off bank interest in a capitalist society. He asserts that the fictional characters representing this class, since they are alienated from social production, understand life only in terms of consumption and enjoyment. Although they are well-educated and have felt the disintegration of old society deeply, they do not entertain any personal fear at all. They only "search for new and strange beauty amidst the disintegration," Lou remarks, "and use this new and strange beauty to cover up their own inner emptiness" (Lou 305–306).

What Lou Shiyi says about the use of sensoria (especially when obtained through seeing) as a primary means in Shi's writings is an appropriate characterization of how the narrator in "Yaksha" narrates his experience in the Western-styled hospital. In the story, the narrator's fear of whiteness registers, by means of a complicated sensorium indeed, how a personal fear arises as a result of the disintegration of the traditional Chinese symbolic system, as a consequence of the invasion of Western cultures. It may also have arisen from his realization of the threat of a mental disorder in himself not so dissimilar to that diagnosed by the German doctor with regard to Bian.

In recording the cultural difference and its related anxiety by means of his own sensorium, the narrator also articulates his own desire. In his depiction of the nurse, he first presents her eyes, mouth and face as fragmented by the pervasive whiteness and then sutures them onto her body. In doing so, he manages to first direct his desire to eat against the nurse's fragmented facial features, which become for him fruits such as longans and chestnuts. Then he transforms it into the desire for love, for the narrator tells us that "we talked as if we were a couple of secret lovers in a tryst" (Shi 1991, 324). The swift narrative transition from the fear of whiteness to the sweet feeling of lovers in a tryst shows, in a vivid manner, the ideological and existential function of writing for metropolitan people in Shanghai, a function which Lou Shiyi has called "using a new and strange beauty to cover up their own inner emptiness." But, in order to displace the "inner emptiness," or the lurking anxiety over the threat of some mental disorder, writing as a transparent description of social reality has to be transformed into a transcription of one's sense reactions to the surrounding reality. For Shi Zhecun, such a sensorial turn is required not only because (as Lou Shiyi suggested) the metropolitans have undergone a shrinking of experience due to their alienation from social production and are overwhelmed by the consumer culture in the reified life of financial capitalism, but mainly because the social reality in Shanghai has already been so fragmented and dislocated that it does not leave much room for the construction of an unalienated, ideal life. The narrator here uses the senses "as the medium through which reality became image, the terms into which the broken data and reified fragments of a quantified world were libidinally transcoded and utopianly transfigured" (Jameson 239).

The narrator's eye, just like that of a camera, moves along as he walks down inside the hospital, and the description of the nurse's face is indeed a final close-up shot.[2] The series of shots here is, however, constantly intercut to a series of reverse shots of the narrator's sense reactions; these shots and reverse shots are organized and edited by Shi Zhecun, using the technique of suture. This technique allows Shi Zhecun, in Jacques-Alain Miller's words, to "name the relation of the subject to the chain of its discourse" and "it figures there as the element which is lacking, in the form of a stand-in" (Miller 25–26). For the narrator, the technique enables him, in his effort to turn the metropolitan world into a narrative-image, to suture such colors as blue, black, red and white in the hospital. More importantly, it figures there in the form of a stand-in for his fear of whiteness and for his otherwise disembodied desire arising from his dislocated, double identification.

However, the narrator's desire here ought to be better understood as the desire to gain access to the sensorial surface — the true face — of contradictions and ambiguities in metropolitan life or, in Lacan's words, as "the metonymy of our being" (Lacan 1992, 321), as it is caught up in a fragmented urban existence. Even though suture as a technique of writing helps the narrator transcode libidinally the fragmented world into a narrative-image, it does not succeed, however, in displacing his anxiety and moving him into a linguistic utopia where an idealized harmonious totality can be found. It manages, rather, to transfigure them into an awareness of an insufficiency in the narration. Here, after the description of the nurse's face, seen as a "strip" through the narrowly opened door, the narrator immediately adds: "When I said a strip of a face, I meant the part of her face in the narrow gap between the door and its frame, which was not so easily seen" (Shi 1991, 324). These words, supposed to perfect the previous description, betray the narrator's anxiety over the inadequacy and inaccuracy of his language.

The narrator's self-conscious attitude toward his own narration prompts him to pay all the more attention to the description of what he sees, hears, touches and feels; the more exact and detailed, the better. After he enters the ward, the narrator zooms in on almost every detail that comes his way: the movements of his friend Bian's head and lips, their eye contact, the slightly audible groan coming from Bian, Bian's outstretched hands and their handshake. From the dutiful transcription of all these physical appearances and activities, the narrator concludes that Bian has lost the strong and healthy physique that he used to have. In order to see if Bian has recovered from the mental disorder as the German doctor has diagnosed it, he asks Bian time and again, "Do you recognize me?" (325). This repeated question seems to show that he will "have peace of mind" (*xin'an*) if Bian is able to recognize him. He feels, however, that Bian is still shrouded in an "air of derangement" (325). But Bian recognizes him immediately and tells him that he is going to leave the hospital in two or three days. At Bian's words, he seems to feel relieved and starts to ask Bian what really happened the other day when he saw his cousin. Here, it seems that, with the obvious successful verbal exchange between them, the narrator's distance from Bian becomes shortened and his anxiety about language is gone. In fact, Bian not only recognizes him but also welcomes him as a trustworthy person, perhaps also as a prospective Freudian psychoanalyst equipped with the "talking-cure" method who is to be admitted into the fortress of derangement to hear the unspeakable horror: "This was a horrible event, which I should not speak about. But, if I do not tell you, soon I will really go mad" (325).

"I Wanted to Seek Some Natural Beauty out of the Unnatural Event"

With Bian Shiming coming down center stage to tell his own story about what has led to his sudden illness, the setting of the whole story shifts from the Western-styled hospital in Shanghai to the countryside near Hangzhou. The narrator's narration of his experience in the hospital recedes into the background, serving as a distant but powerful frame for Bian Shiming's story. The significance of the location of the story in a rural environment outside of Shanghai will become obvious as we follow Bian in his journey into the countryside.

Bian travels to the countryside because he has to take his grandma's dead body to their home-village for burial. Such a move is a traditional Chinese practice, because a dead person is always expected to "go home," to join other deceased members in the family. It also indicates that, for most metropolitan dwellers, the emerging modern metropolis is still a temporary dwelling place and only the countryside is an "eternal home." This is why Bian wants to stay for some more time when the funeral is over. For him, the countryside "was really a good place for a hermitage"; there is a lot of bamboo, an ancient pond and a creek, the sound of whose running water "gave [him] more pleasure than anything else" (Shi 1991, 325–26).

After the funeral, Bian writes a letter back to Shanghai, requesting an extension of his leave for another ten days. He wants to take a good rest, to "cultivate the mind and heart," and make full use of this opportunity to "enjoy the natural scenery" (326). It is apparent that, in his mind, the best cure for the fragmented and alienated metropolitan life he lives is the countryside, where people can not only derive pleasure from nature but, more importantly, live a harmonious life. However, for Bian, the countryside is more than merely a natural environment for such a primitive, organic life; it is also the repository for a tradition exiled from its central position in China. As he tells us,

"From the Pine Logging Ground to Liu Xia Village, about eighteen *li* long, on both banks of the Creek Xi, there were all kinds of unknown, wonderful historical relics and sites for us to explore" (326).

In such a frame of mind, Bian Shiming checks out from the West Lake Library many books on "the old anecdotes and stories" (*zhanggu*) about the place. He also rents a boat to go and visit the local temple, where he sees paintings by such painters as Ni Yunlin (Yuan dynasty) and Tang Yin (Ming dynasty). The short stay in the countryside allows him to recall some classical poems such as Du Fu's "The spring water has just grown four to five feet / The wild boat could allow only three to four men" (326). It also revives his own poetic sensibility, and he manages to narrate this part of his story in a beautiful poetic language. The countryside and inland towns, according to Perry Link in his sociological study of Chinese popular fiction in the early twentieth century, not only represent the values of a life of the past from the perspective of Shanghai; they have even become "ontologically prior," coming before the modern city and yet in some sense still lying beneath it. "A person could rise and fall and be hurtled about in the city, and the city itself might entirely collapse, but the countryside would always be there" and "one could count on it" (Link 202). In light of this, to stay and travel in the countryside means, for Bian, not only to live a hermit's serene and meditative life, but also to recover and revive a marginalized and repressed tradition (as an ontological prior) in China at that historical moment.

But, during the trip to the local temple, Bian encounters the "woman in white" (Shi 1991, 326). She haunts him all the time, from the moment he happens to cast an eye at her in a small boat next to his. For him, "a shadow glittering with a brilliant white light would forever dance before my eyes, just like a speck of dandruff on the lens of my eye-glasses" (327). He cannot concentrate on the paintings, because the white woman would go inside them; she would distract and disturb him by emerging from behind the temple buildings or the bamboo forest in the paintings. This "bewitching woman" appears not only in the paintings but also wherever he goes and her dancing image "made [him] feel an irresistible melancholy" (327). She blocks his view of the natural scenery, the paintings and other "wonderful historical relics and sites"; she makes him stumble in his imaginary effort to approach and revive the marginalized tradition as an ontological prior. It is this blocking of access, visual or otherwise, to the nexus of countryside-nature-tradition that marks Bian's irresistible melancholy.

The erotic dimension of this melancholy is obvious here, though in the beginning Bian denies that he indulges in any erotic fantasy, since both his mind and his physique are strong and he has not been moved by hundreds of similar prostitute-like women he met in Shanghai. Then, he acknowledges the presence in his mind of some "wicked ideas" (*xienian*) about her, for her crouching posture in the small boat has an "unseen, sweet charm" (327). Bian feels confused: "In Shanghai, no woman would seduce me like this, but here I could hardly control myself. Does it have anything to do with me or with the place?" (327). Unable and perhaps also unwilling to come up with a satisfactory answer, he then proceeds to "impute all the blame to [his] unhealthy eyes" (327). Unlike his friend, the narrator Lao Shi, who would single out his sense apparatus, the eye in particular, as more reliable than his use of language in grappling with the surrounding world, Bian considers his sensory apparatus as the least dependable tool in his approaching the external environment. Instead of questioning the adequacy of language, he embraces its magic power: "the power of written words could penetrate the insulation of time and space" (328).

It is apparent that, by faulting his unhealthy eyes, Bian chooses to blame himself, rather than the place, for his erotically disastrous encounter with the woman in white. But he tells the narrator, "I do not believe that my nerves would rebel against my nature all of a sudden" (327). Though he later suspects he is suffering from neurasthenia (a disease that many Chinese at the time believed had something to do with excessive nervous stimulation), it is the eye that he believes to be the arch-criminal rebelling against his own "nature" (*benzhi*). Positioned in the liminal space between the somatic-psychological economy, within which an individual's "nature" is supposed to reside, and the external world, the eye poses a challenge to any claim concerning the autonomy of the individual's deep-seated "nature." But, as we are already told, in his daily life in Shanghai, Bian defends such an autonomy by doing frequent exercise, laughing at those involved too much in love affairs, reminding himself not to allow his rationality to be carried away by his sentiments. In a Simmelian sense, he is indeed a normal metropolitan in the city, who would do anything possible to protect the autonomy of his subjective life, though his autonomy is based upon a well-defined and well-defended division between the inside and outside of his psycho-somatic territory, between the self and the other.[3]

The woman in white is, to be sure, the *unheimlich*, the uncanny or unhomely, that "ought to have remained ... secret and hidden but has come to light" (Freud 225). The exploration of the unhomely or uncanny experience of the metropolitan reveals in a most conspicuous manner Shi Zhecun's touch of Freudianism in the text. Despite all his effort to build a home for his subjective life (his "nature"), however, Bian fails to prevent the uncanny from intruding into his subjective territory once he comes out to the countryside. From an orthodox Freudian perspective, this irrepressible force is essentially an illicit sexual desire for one's parent or even grandparent, which Bian has endeavored to push away but which has managed to come back through the woman in white after the death of his grandmother. His grandmother's death might well mean the permanent loss of a love object for Bian and the appearance of a bottomless abyss where an "irresistible melancholy" is located. However, shifting the focus from sexual desire to the order of the Real, a Lacanian perspective would regard the uncanny as "the gaze as such, in its pulsatile, dazzling and spread out function," a gaze of "the anamorphic ghost" (Lacan 1977, 89) that looks back perhaps from the grave of Bian's grandmother, blots the idyllic scene of the countryside, embodies itself in the woman in white, and remains meaningless like a filthy stain on his eye-glasses. It renders everything suspicious, thus "opening up the abyss in the search for a meaning — nothing is what it seems to be, everything is to be interpreted, everything is supposed to possess some supplementary meaning" (Žižek 1991, 91). Such a psychoanalytical interpretation certainly helps us understand the apparition of the woman and the "non-sense" of Bian's "wicked ideas" about her. But, by calling the woman a "yaksha" and engaging subsequently in a passionate, heroic pursuit of her in the countryside, Bian also forces us to examine Shi Zhecun's Freudianism in a broader social context and stake out the historical conditions for his "psychologizing [of] the fantastic" (Liu 133).

In reading a book about the history of the countryside where he is staying, Bian finds a record of some yaksha haunting the area. According to the record, about one hundred years ago, a yaksha appeared in the mountain; it often transformed itself into a beautiful woman, seducing passers-by and eating them after capturing them. At one time almost every night there would be one person missing from the nearby village. It was believed that he had been eaten by the yaksha. Then the villagers burnt down all the trees in the mountain and the yaksha disappeared. But Bian suspects that the yaksha has not died and the woman in white is just its latest incarnation. The yaksha that the villagers burnt is a hideous and dangerous intruder into the peaceful life of the countryside.

The woman in white, now suspected to be an incarnation of the yaksha, becomes a dangerous figure both "alien" and "unnatural" to the native community, unhomely to "the home," and exactly what the whiteness in the Western-styled hospital signifies for the narrator Lao Shi. But, as a yaksha and an other, she is meant to embody here, as in the tradition of writing, reading and retelling of yaksha stories, a desire for a homogenized, purified life, a life without the disturbing presence of the other.[4] As Theodor Adorno has said, "The archaic is appropriated as the experience of what is not experiential. The boundary of experientiality, however, requires that the starting point of any such appropriation be the modern" (Adorno 349). In the fragmented and reified metropolitan life of semi-colonial Shanghai, what is archaic and what is not experiential is the very homogenized, purified life of the Chinese self. The woman in white, a survivor from the past in the countryside, seems to articulate, however, just such an otherwise impossible desire for a homogenized life. To make her forever alien and strange, so as to sustain his own desire forever, Bian refuses to see the true face of the yaksha woman, no matter whether it is hideous or beautiful: "No, I hoped to see neither of them, for I knew, whichever of the two was realized, it would still be dangerous" (Shi 1991, 331).

Bian Shiming's decision to tarry with ambiguity and indeterminacy, as well as his adherence to an "ambiguous vision," which Tzvetan Todorov sees as the necessary condition for the production of "the fantastic" (Todorov 33) or of "the strange" in traditional Chinese literary terms,[5] marks a significant change in his attitude to the woman in white. In the beginning she is a "horror" that makes him irresistibly melancholic because she blocks his access to the nexus of countryside-nature-tradition, but after she has been appropriated as a yaksha, as a tool to articulate his desire, she becomes a welcome love object. "I knew loving a female yaksha means I would have to sacrifice myself," he tells us. "But before the arrival of the final punishment, what strange delights I would have!" (331). These strange delights are certainly attractive for him but what appeals to him even more is the opportunity to make a heroic move toward his utopia — his ultimate home — of naturalized beauty and totalized harmony. Therefore, we hear him proclaim ecstatically, "I wanted to seek some natural beauty out of the unnatural event. I had really completely taken leave of my senses. I had fallen in love with this beautiful yaksha who was forever before me, seducing me with her graceful gait" (332).

The female yaksha therefore leads Bian forward, moving so fast that he sometimes feels that he keeps lagging behind: "My heart was burning with a strange desire [...]. I wanted to expand the realm of love for all human beings" (331–32). But, no matter how closely he follows her, he never manages to catch up with her. The moment when he thinks he is embracing her with his two hands, reality sets in with a pull that turns out to be deadly. The woman in white turns out to be a mute country woman. "How could I believe myself that I had come to this place to strangle and kill a country woman on her way to meeting her lover?" (334). This unexpected turn from the heroic pursuit of love to the gruesome crime of destroying a real love reveals the bankruptcy of the wish to return to the native tradition in the countryside, and it also puts an end to the escape from what is considered fragmented and dislocated modern metropolitan life. For a moment, it also halts the further production of "the strange" in the narrative. He suspects he has been bewitched by the yaksha or the spirit of the killed woman even after his hurried retreat back to Shanghai. The sense of being bewitched comes as "the final punishment" when Bian collapses at the sight of the narrator's cousin, newly arriving from the countryside. He mistakes her for the yaksha or the revengeful spirit of the murdered woman: "All my nerves became confused; horrors, worries and frightened haste assaulted me. So I came to this place [...]" (335).

"Horrible Woman! Strange Woman! Don't Come Close to Me!"

The place that Bian Shiming reluctantly comes to, at the end of his supposedly fantastic journey into the countryside, is the Western-styled hospital, where he has been staying for over three weeks. Shi Zhecun has his characters stay in a place they do not like, talking about a fantastic journey elsewhere, in order to convey an unmistakable sense of irony, but the primary irony is to be found in the imagined relationship between an urban dweller and the countryside. In regarding the countryside as a good place for a hermitage where one could cultivate the mind and heart, Bian identifies with it both physically and metaphorically. His trip there signals a physical identification with it, though not one as thorough as his grandmother's, since death literally removes any possible insulation between herself and the "eternal home" of the countryside. Metaphorically, Bian identifies also with the countryside as an ontological prior, in contrast to the city as a phenomenological posterior — and with it as a repository of marginalized Chinese culture in a context of the disturbing presence of Western cultural influence in the city.

This kind of relationship to the countryside is closely linked to a view of metropolitan life, as experienced by Shanghai inhabitants like Bian Shiming and Lao Shi in the 1920s and 1930s, as an essentially fragmented and *unhomely* existence, so that they are stricken with the desire to "go home." But, Bian Shiming and the narrator Lao Shi have different attitudes. Bian's pursuit of the female yaksha in the countryside could be taken as his change from a reserved attitude, embodied in his self-controlled, rational life style, to what can be called an "exposé" attitude whereby, for the yaksha's sake, he would throw away all the rational and intellectual constraints that are supposed, à la Simmel, to protect the "personal core" of a metropolitan subject.

The acting-out of this metropolitan exposé attitude and the discharge of welled-up anxiety in the countryside serve, however, to effectively highlight his totalizing desire to construct a purified space for the self, an absolute autonomy beyond the pale of the fragmented, quotidian life in Shanghai. The woman in white, named and appropriated as a yaksha, embodies Bian's desire to go beyond the uncanny or unhomely metropolitan experience, a desire for a *beyond* of naturalized beauty and totalized harmony. But, this has proven to be historically impossible, as exemplified in his bloody murder of the mute country woman.

The narrator Lao Shi, on the other hand, accepts the unhomely existence and his split identification with both the Chinese and the Western, embracing these two as a series of living ambiguities and contradictions. He packages up and unleashes his anxiety in the act of suturing, the everyday practice of a modernist aesthetic in the city, *here and now*. Even in his libidinal aestheticization of metropolitan life, he is not prepared to construct a linguistic home for a naturalized beauty and totalized harmony; rather, by acknowledging the inadequacy of his language and the "element that is lacking," he leaves open a space for ambivalence.

However, Bian Shiming's account of his encounter with the yaksha in the countryside, as a "strange" explanation of the cause of his mental disorder and as a sort of talking-cure for it, leaves the narrator in even greater confusion. After Bian finishes his story, the narrator comes out of the ward and gives his wife a call, asking her and his cousin, who are supposed to come to the hospital in an hour, not to make the trip. This is an ambiguous gesture, and can be related to his own view of whether Bian is still suffering from a mental disorder, or whether he has really recovered from it. If he believes what Bian says and no longer sees him as a deranged person, the arrival of his wife and his cousin (especially the latter, whom Bian once mistook for the female yaksha or the spirit of the murdered mute woman) ought not to be a problem for Bian any longer. If he accepts the German doctor's diagnosis and thinks that Bian is still insane, then what Bian has just told him about the female yaksha and the murdered mute woman should not be taken as true. Maybe the narrator has stopped his wife and his cousin from coming to the hospital out of fear that there might be some other problems besides what the German doctor and Bian have suggested. However, no matter what the reasons are, the narrator here betrays his suspicious attitude toward both Bian and the German doctor, perhaps due to his split identification with both the symbolic and the imaginary. This also closes the door on any further effort to verify Bian's account. But, with his suspicion uncorroborated and the true-or-false question unanswered for the readers, the narrator finally manages to achieve a closure for his narrative of Bian's account of "the strange," an account that remains essentially in the ambiguous and indefinable "changing zone between history and fiction, reality and illusion" (Zeitlin 10).

This way of ending the narrative of "the strange," with the narrator preventing the two women from coming to the hospital, is, however, just one example in the story of the price paid in writing "the strange" of the Shanghai modern at the expense of Chinese women. In the hospital where whiteness is all-pervasive, the nurse becomes a sutured body, rescuing the narrator from his fear of whiteness and embodying his otherwise disembodied and "unhomely" desire. In the countryside, the woman in white becomes either a filthy stain on Bian's eye-glasses or a seductive yaksha who inaugurates the strange experience that he would like to have so as to create his desired natural beauty. And the mute woman becomes a direct victim of his fantasy,[6] while her death serves to intrude into the fantastic world of his pursuit and send him back to the reality of metropolitan life. In all these cases, women are employed just as a vehicle for the narration, as "the symptom of man"[7] who lives an unhomely metropolitan life and writes about his own anxiety and desire. For the sake of unity and closure of the narrative, women are presented as fragmented, mute, ambiguous or dead, not given any chance to speak out as a subject.

This is a debt that the Chinese modernist writing owes to Chinese women.[8] In his retreat back to Shanghai, Bian senses the inevitable need to repay the debt: "My life has become a debt that has to be paid back, and now the creditor is coming" (Shi 1991, 335). The potential of woman to become an active subject is (mis)recognized here to be a powerful, uncanny and unhomely force, coming to settle accounts with the man caught in an unhomely existence yet desiring to "go home," and threatening to break through the forged closure of the narrative of "the strange." This is perhaps one of the reasons why, in the beginning of the story, Bian behaves as if he is pushing someone away with his two hands stretched out, and speaks of a frightening truth like someone talking nonsense in his delirium: "Horrible woman! Strange woman! Don't come close to me!"

Notes

1. All translations from Chinese texts in this paper are mine, unless indicated otherwise.
2. In her study of film culture and vernacular experience in modern China before 1937, Zhen Zhang points out that Shi Zhecun's writing, together with the writings of others of the New Sensationalist school, can be viewed as "cinematic writing," writing that derives a lot of its techniques from the cinema, such as montage, mobile points of view, the screenplay-like form, and rhythmic editing (Zhang 72).

3. Simmel asserts, because of the swift change of outer and inner stimuli in metropolitan life, most people living in a metropolis rely increasingly on their intellect and rationality to preserve their subjective life. Consequently, the split in their mental life between rationality and emotion renders urban life more and more impersonal. However, if the external stimulation is too intense and rapid, a metropolitan will lose his or her intellectual capacity to react to new sensations appropriately. The essence of this behavior, which Simmel calls the "blasé" attitude, lies in "the blunting of discrimination" and an inability to perceive "the meaning and differing values of things" (Simmel 414).

4. For instance, Pu Songling, the historian of the strange in the eighteenth century, records a story called "The Yaksha Kingdom" (Pu 1994) in which a Chinese merchant, because of a shipwreck, lands on a yaksha island. He marries a female yaksha there, who gives birth to two children. Later, the merchant manages to bring his yaksha wife and children to China. One child grows up to be a famous general, and the other, an excellent scholar. Though Pu's story tells how the yakshas (the minority) are "assimilated" and "civilized" into the Chinese culture, it registers the same mechanism of desire to homogenize and purify the space, and also to expand that space, for the self.

5. In her study of Chinese classical tales of "the strange," Judith Zeitlin argues that it is problematic to apply Todorov's schema of the fantastic, the marvelous and the uncanny to the Chinese literature of "the strange" in general and to *Liaozhai zhiyi* in particular. She believes that we cannot assume the same "laws of post–Enlightenment scientific common sense" in the Chinese context. Also, Todorov's chosen narratives are, according to Zeitlin, based on clear-cut distinctions between realism and fantasy, whereas in Chinese literature the boundary between the strange and the normal is never fixed but is constantly altered, blurred, erased, multiplied or redefined (Zeitlin 6–7). Zeitlin's argument is convincing in the case of classical tales of the strange in Chinese literature. In twentieth-century China, as the thinking of Chinese people and their literary writings were undeniably influenced by Western cultures on a large scale, I believe it is possible to use Todorov's theories to analyze modern Chinese narratives of "the strange." In the case of Shi Zhecun, the use of Western theories will be fruitful, as Shi acknowledges his writing has been greatly influenced by Western writers such as Arthur Schnitzler (Lee 166–68) and Western theories such as Freudian psychoanalysis (Yan 140–42).

6. For a discussion of violence in Shi Zhecun's literary texts, see Jones (1994).

7. For a discussion of this Lacanian notion, see Žižek (1992, 154–156).

8. Although I do not want to generalize about all of Shi Zhecun's stories, this debt can be found in many of his modernist stories collected in *Jiangju de tou* and *Meyu zhixi* [On a rainy evening]. Even in his *Shan nüren xingpin* [Exemplary conduct of virtuous women], it is still debatable if women occupy a subject position, for as Leo Lee has pointed out, "none of the heroines has an identity of her own apart from her man, and Shi's probing of their minds reveals no feminist consciousness" (Lee 172).

Works Cited

Adorno, Theodor. 1997. *Aesthetic Theory.* Trans. Robert Hullot-Kentor. Minneapolis: University of Minnesota Press.

Chow, Tse-tsung. 1960. *The May Fourth Movement: Intellectual Revolution in Modern China.* Stanford: Stanford University Press.

Freud, Sigmund. 1955. "The Uncanny," in *The Standard Edition of the Complete Psychological Works of Sigmund Freud,* vol. 17. Ed. James Strachey. London: The Hogarth Press, 218–56.

Jameson, Fredric. 1981. *The Political Unconscious: Narrative as a Socially Symbolic Act.* Ithaca: Cornell University Press.

Jones, Andrew F. 1994. "The Violence of the Text: Reading Yu Hua and Shi Zhecun." *Positions: East Asia Cultures Critique,* 2.3: 570–602.

Lacan, Jacques. 1977. *The Four Fundamental Concepts of Psychoanalysis.* Ed. Jacques-Allan Miller, trans. Alan Sheridan. London: The Hogarth Press.

_____. 1992. *The Ethics of Psychoanalysis 1959–1960.* Trans. Dennis Porter. New York: W.W. Norton & Company.

Lee, Leo Ou-fan. 1999. *Shanghai Modern: The Flowering of a New Urban Culture in China, 1930–1945.* Cambridge, Massachusetts: Harvard University Press.

Lei, Sean Hsiang-lin. 1999. "When Chinese Medicine Encountered the State: 1910–1949." The University of Chicago. Ph.D. dissertation.

Link, Perry. 1981. *Mandarin Ducks and Butterflies: Popular Fiction in Early Twentieth-Century Chinese Cities.* Berkeley: University of California Press.

Liu, Lydia H. 1995. *Translingual Practice: Literature, National Culture, and Translated Modernity—China, 1900–1937*. Stanford, California: Stanford University Press.

Lou Shiyi. 1988. "Shi Zhecun de xin ganjue zhuyi" [Shi Zhecun's neo-sensationalism]. *Shi Zhecun.* Ed. Ying Guojing. Hong Kong: Sanlian shudian, 305–307.

Miller, Jacques-Allan. 1977–78. "Suture (Elements of the Logic of the Signifier)," *Screen* 18.4: 24–34.

Pu Songling. 1994. "Yecha guo" [The yaksha kingdom]. *Liaozhai zhiyi* [*Liaozhai's record of the strange*]. Eds. Yuan Jian and Xuan Sheng. Jinan: Qilu shushe, 374–79.

Shi Zhecun. 1991. "Yecha" [Yaksha]. In *Shi Xiu zhi lian* [*The Love of Shi Xiu*]. Beijing: Renmin wenxue chubanshe, 323–36.

Shi Zhecun. 1996a. "*Jiangjun de tou* zixu" [A preface to *The General's Head*], in *Shi Zhecun qishi nian wenxuan* [*A collection of Shi Zhecun's writings over seventy years*]. Ed. Chen Zishan and Xu Ruqi. Shanghai: Shanghai wenyi chubanshe, 804–805.

Shi Zhecun. 1996b. "Shoupa" [The handkerchief], in *Shi Zhecun qishi nian wenxuan*, 112–15.

Shi Zhecun. 1996c. "Wo de chuangzuo shenghuo zhi licheng" [My writing career], in. *Shi Zhecun qishi nian wenxuan*, 51–58.

Simmel, Georg. 1950. "The Metropolis and Mental Life." *The Sociology of Georg Simmel.* Ed. Kurt H. Wolff. Glencoe, Illinois: The Free Press, 409–24.

Todorov, Tzvetan. 1975. *The Fantastic: A Structural Approach to a Literary Genre.* Trans. Richard Howard. Ithaca: Cornell University Press.

Zhang, Zhen. 1998. "'An Amorous History of the Silver Screen': Film Culture, Urban Modernity, and the Vernacular Experience in China, 1896–1937." The University of Chicago. Ph.D. dissertation.

Zeitlin, Judith. 1993. *Historian of the Strange: Pu Songling and the Chinese Classical Tale.* Stanford: Stanford University Press.

Žižek, Slavoj. 1989. *The Sublime Object of Ideology.* London: Verso.

_____. 1991. *Looking Awry: An Introduction to Jacques Lacan through Popular Culture.* Cambridge, Massachusetts: The MIT Press.

_____. 1992. *Enjoy Your Symptom!: Jacques Lacan In Hollywood and Out.* London: Routledge.

11

"Disappearing with the Double": Xu Xi's "The Stone Window"

Amy Lai

Xu Xi (1954–), one of the very few Hong Kong authors who write in English,[1] is a Chinese-Indonesian native of the city, which was home to her until she went to the United States for her education, and thereafter led a peripatetic existence around Europe, America and Asia. The *New York Times* (Dec 25, 2001) calls her a pioneer English-language writer from Asia, and according to *Singapore Business Times* (Jan 11, 2002), her works portray "Asia as it is today — gritty, modern and confused."[2] It therefore comes as a surprise that there has been little scholarship on her. By studying "The Stone Window," one of the stories collected in *Daughters of Hui* (1996), I wish to contribute to a critical evaluation of Xu Xi's writings. There are obvious "Gothic" elements in this tale — especially the split self — which prompts me to examine how the Gothic tradition, developed in the West and predominantly deployed in the study of Western texts, is being reconfigured in her work. And because the Gothic has a strong affinity with psychoanalysis as both explore the ostensibly irrational, idiosyncratic and excessive, and hence, share a mutually influential relationship throughout literary history (Masse 230), it is useful that my theoretical framework adopts a psychoanalytical approach in the study of the Gothic double in Xu Xi's story. Using a predominately deconstructive methodology, I aim to illuminate how the Gothic is transposed into an Asian literary context that at once enriches the understanding of both discourses (Gothic and Asian literature). One of my main interests in this story is its "feminist" agenda. Through a close reading of the narrative, I want to demonstrate the way in which Xu Xi deploys — as I see it — Gothic devices to raise issues of repression, feminine resistance and empowerment.

Xu Xi's "The Stone Window" foregrounds the motif of the double quite prominently, and it is useful that I briefly rehearse the importance of this motif in the Gothic and in psychoanalytical traditions at this juncture. According to Fred Botting (1996), doubles, alter egos, mirrors and animated representations of the disturbing parts of identity are stock devices in gothic literature, signifying the alienation of the subject from the culture and language in which s/he was located (12). Sigmund Freud, in "The Uncanny" (1919), suggests that the double arises out of "an unfulfilled but possible future to which we still like to cling" in our fantasy, or "all those strivings of the ego which adverse external circumstances have crushed" (163). Otto Rank (1941), another psychoanalyst, traces this literary motif back to the concept of the soul (71); for Rank, the double is initially acknowledged as a guardian angel that assures the immortality of the self, but which later becomes this self's antithesis; in this latter capacity, the double reveals the mortality of the self, even serving as the harbinger of death (76). Interestingly, both Rank and Freud rely on the works of E.T.A Hoffman, a German Gothicist, to illustrate their theories. While Rank pays homage to *The Student of Prague* (1913), a film based on E.T. A. Hoffman's story, Freud turns to stories like *Elixire des Teufels* (*The Devil's Elixir*) and "The Sandman" to illustrate the doubling, dividing and interchanging selves, whereby mental processes are dialectically shared between the "host" and the "double," so much so that the two possess common knowledge, feelings and experiences to the extent that they become indistinguishable.[3] Andrew J. Webber's *The Doppelganger* (1996) similarly describes the double as the "performative character of the subject" after selfhood which, as a metaphysical unit, is abandoned and is now shackled to "a process of enactments of identity always mediated by the other self." (3)

One obvious disadvantage in the theories outlined above is that they tend to be male-centered. In other words, the double seems to be a "male" problem. This is perhaps inevitable in view of the fact that most traditional Gothic narratives tend to foreground ruptured male characters (Frankenstein, Jekyll, William Wilson and Dorian Gray). What is more, such men — by virtue of their ruptured experience — become feminized, thus suggesting that the double is, if not female, is always feminine, and therefore emasculated, version of the troubled male. Xu Xi's story is interesting because it uses the double motif in a way that is clearly "feminist." In Western literature, female doubles typically appear in the service of male fantasies of the other, corresponding to the polarization of the Madonna and whore, the sexless and the over-sexed, the vamp and the virgin (Webber 20–21). True enough, this echoes the antithetical configurations of the good woman and the bad woman as argued in *The Madwoman in the Attic* (1971) by Gilbert and Gubar, although both these theorists fundamentally see the double as an active strategy deployed by women writers. They contend that British women writers, conforming to patriarchal literary standards and denied the right to create their own images of femaleness, sought a roundabout way to attain literary authority by creating a dark double of the passive, docile and selfless angel — the duplicitous "monster," whose consciousness is opaque to man, who has a story to tell, but may choose not to tell it (73). It is through this "mad double" that they manage to come to terms with their keen sense of discrepancies between what they are and what they are supposed to be (78).

Xu Xi's "The Stone Window," in significant ways, corresponds to such a framework as well. By focusing on the tale's two main female characters, this essay not only demonstrates how the double can possibly problematize one's secret, unrealizable desires, but also examines how Gilbert and Gubar's polarity of the angel and the monster are applicable to the analysis of this story. But Xu Xi's narrative does more: "The Stone Window" revolves around men who become confused by a mysterious woman and *her* double. The inability to distinguish the two women brings about a mistrust in the men's ability to rationalize and categorize the women, thus prompting their emasculation.

"The Stone Window" is divided into four sections. The first part, entitled "Benefactor," introduces the reader to Ralph, a Boston-based architect, and his encounter with the mysterious Philomena, a painter of Hong Kong Chinese descent living on Kea, a Greek Island; two years later, Ralph buys a watercolor painting by Philomena at a London art gallery for his Boston flat. The second part, "A Gambler in Athens and a Girl from Hong Kong," is set in Athens and describes how Constantin, a Greek divorcee, tries to befriend Hui Sai Yee, a thirty-year-old Chinese writer from Boston. Constantin too, as the reader is informed, was acquainted and infatuated with Philomena, and his story prompts an intrigued Sai Yee to buy a charcoal portrait by the painter at the same London gallery. In part three, "An Aegean Box," the story makes a temporal leap to the future when Ralph is married to Sai Yee, whom he met three months ago. They honeymoon in Hydra, a Greek island where, according to Constantin, Philomena resides. The couple also finds a huge box, washed up to the shore by the Aegean (I will discuss its significance later in the essay). The last part of the story, "Philomena," is again set in Hydra. Sai Yee has mysteriously disappeared, and Ralph frantically searches for her. A final male character, Roach, an old Greek, is introduced at this juncture, and like Constantin, he too claims that he knew Philomena (and even once lived with her). In the tale's non-conclusive denouement, Ralph remains deeply confused as to Sai Yee's whereabouts and identity, largely because she seems — in Ralph's mind — to have "merged" with Philomena.

Structurally, Xu Xi's complex tale corresponds to the kind of "tortuous, fragmented narratives" which are characteristic of Gothic stories (Botting 3). Scott Brewster (2000) observes that the gothic story does not merely transcribe disturbed, perverse or horrifying worlds, but its narrative structures and voices are interwoven with and intensify the madness they represent (218). Indeed, the strategy of doubling in "The Stone Window" is attained precisely through such a narrative structure with, among other things, its abrupt shifts in time frame, its unexpected and unexplained affinities among characters, and its textual ambiguities. For example, although Philomena's "aggressiveness" is not quite found in Sai Yee, unlike the various female characters in the other stories collected in *Daughters of Hui*,[4] that they share the same surname already signals a doubling strategy that will eventually complicate, even obscure both women's identities. When Constantin meets Sai Yee for the first and only time, he remarks that she looks "just like" Philomena: "The same long, black hair, and those sloped eyes. You are small too, like her" (234–235). Constantin even insists that she *is* the painter, although Sai Yee stresses that she is "not related" to Philomena (235). But later however, Sai Yee begins to feel a keen sense of kinship with the painter. She tells the proprietor of the gallery: "I think she might be a relative of mine whom I've never met. You see, we have the same surname, and I'm also from Hong Kong" (240). It is also during this time that Sai Yee encounters Ralph at an exhibition of Philomena Hui's "Stone Window And Other Works" in London (242). One particular episode in the third part of the story attenuates the mysterious relationship between the two women. As Sai Yee rests on the beach of Hydra, she hears a twig snapping and leaves rustling just behind her; turning to look, she (thinks she) catches the glimpse of "a flag of long black hair disappear further up the slope" (244). The story makes an equivocal hint that this might be Philomena. Immediately following this episode, the narrative suggests that Sai Yee is behaving increasingly like Philomena, almost as if she has become "possessed." When Ralph proposes to marry her in order to "free" her up to write, she rejects his offer and explains why "she couldn't have some man support her" (245). This reply is strongly reminiscent of Philomena's reaction to Constantin's proposal when he too offered marriage in order to enable the painter to pursue her work (236). Sai Yee's behavior increasingly resembles Philomena, which perplexes her lover. By the end of the tale, having heard Roach's account of the Philomena, Ralph becomes so confused as to the identity of Sai Yee, and his memories so muddled, that he begins to "remember" the two women as interchangeable (254).

Meta-critically, the doubling of the two women is mirrored by the narrative's doubling of parts as well. In part two, the title "a Girl from Hong Kong" can refer to either/both Sai Yee (who used to live in Hong Kong) or/and the painter, who was originally from Hong Kong. This ambiguity is further reinforced in the title of part four, "Philomena," which, although appearing to be highly specific, can also point to Sai Yee who, by this time, has become indistinguishable from Philomena, at least to Ralph.

Perhaps not as extreme a configuration as Brontë's Bertha Mason in *Jane Eyre*, Philomena nevertheless reminds us of the "madwoman" who dares defy male (in this story, this term also encompasses Western and Orientalists) imperatives which would otherwise confine her to a submissive Asian hyperfeminine imaginary. Like Bertha, she is intemperate and unchaste, the embodiment of levels of sexual energy unacceptable and frightening to men. Gubar and Gilbert contend that Bertha propels and protects Jane until her literal and symbolic death "frees her from the furies that torment her and makes possible a marriage of equality — makes possible, that is, wholeness within herself" (361–62). Although it can be argued that in the same way, Philomena too "protects" Sai Yee, the narrative clearly places agency on Sai Yee's side. It is the writer who deliberately seeks to identify with the painter, suggesting that as much as Philomena is her double, the painter is also an inspirational model for emulation *imagined into power* by Sai Yee. Here, the "angel" of the story — Sai Yee — draws on the "imagined" strength and mystery of the "monster" — Philomena — to gain self-presence and independence from a man who allegedly wants to take care of her.

Indeed, such prototypes of the angel and the monster, and their mutual sisterhood, are not uncommon in contemporary Chinese literature. For example, in Wei Hui's recent novel *The Shriek of the Butterfly* (1999), the wild woman, Judy, is instrumental in helping the "angelic" protagonist achieve a certain measure of socially acceptable living, after which she disappears. Considered by some critics as "avant-garde," Wei Hui's story foregrounds alternative lifestyles which are possible for Chinese women, and criticizes social hypocrisy and women's persistent marginalization. Unlike Wei Hui's story however, even the "angel" in Xu Xi's narrative disappears without explanation, leaving her husband — and the reader — completely bewildered. Sai Yee not only, in Freud's description of the double, plays out her desire for an independent, unfettered life through an identification with Philomena, she goes so far as to disappear with her double altogether.[5]

Xu Xi's capitalizing on the stock characters of the angel and the monster for a novel purpose underlies her feminist agenda, one which is — in my view — in direct contrast to the one outlined by Gilbert and Gubar. If the two feminists' literary project aims at "recreat[ing] a lost female unity," and the re(dis)covery of the female other "whom patriarchal poetics dismembered and whom we have tried to remember" (101), Xu Xi's feminist aim, at least as suggested in the mysterious ending of "The Stone Window," is to clearly frustrate any attempt at the reconstruction of female "wholeness." As such, Sai Yee's disappearance should not be construed as a form of narrative suicide, but as a strategy of resistance against the male imperative.

One of the ways in which the male imperative insinuates its insidious presence in the narrative is through the instrument of the "gaze." But each time this gaze is activated, the narrative directly subverts it with the very "object" upon which the gaze attempts an imposition. Philomena is one such "object." When Ralph first meets her, he immediately fetishizes her, as implied by the text: "Her lean, brown legs stretched out under his gaze.... Ralph found his gaze fixated on her bare legs. Her skin was smooth and completely unmarked. Even her feet, clad only in sandals, seemed delicate and untouched by the roughness of the landscape around her. Like a child's" (231). Ralph's fetishistic gaze not only reduces Philomena to eroticized body parts, but positively infantilizes her as well. Yet this fetishistic gaze is quickly undermined in at least four ways in the story, all of which directly emasculating Ralph. First, when Ralph accepts Philomena's invitation to pose for her, he becomes the "looked-at" instead. Philomena even declares his body as less than "ideal" (231) but is nevertheless acceptable to her. Here, it is the female gaze that confers value to the male body, and not *vice versa*. Second, Xu Xi employs a spatial metaphor to challenge the male imperative to "see" by foregrounding Philomena's home as finally inaccessible to Ralph (236). Ralph discovers that her house is structured like a fortress made of "large, roughly hewn blocks" (232), which makes penetrability impossible. Third, Ralph is perhaps also drugged by Philomena with retsina,[6] thereby losing consciousness only to awake later naked on the patio but for a blanket carelessly thrown on him (232). Once again, the male body becomes subjected to the feminine gaze — this time even without conscious knowledge of his subjection — and is declared, by his being left unattended and uncomfortable in the patio, ineffectual and of little worth to her. Finally, Ralph's fetishistic desire also suffers an overdue reprisal through the very painting by Philomena that he buys to grace his home. When he first bought the painting (part one), the picture depicted a "building with faces ... the colors seemed limited to grey and scarlet, although he was sure some hint of green or blue washed the scene"

(234). But in part four, upon closer inspection, the painting has now acquired a chilling, uncanny quality:

> He stared at the picture. Chinese faces on buildings. The skyline of Hong Kong, of Philomena's city village. The scarlet and grey swath of color captured him long before the buildings and faces. Sai Yee asked, the first time she saw it, is that perhaps her face on the center building, it's the only woman.... What else had Sai Yee said? Ralph thought his head would burst [254].

What is more, the picture seems to be undergoing a metamorphosis as well: "[Ralph] watched the picture change in hue from scarlet and gray to blue and green. It changed quickly today, like an automatic remote flicking between television channels. Soon, the moving colors would settle into a mixture of oils thick on the canvas. Like a stone window" (254). The Chinese faces staring back at him, and the gradual transformation of the painting to the impenetrable wall of Philomena's home, both imply the reversal of the Orientalist, male gaze back to the fetishist himself. In the end, what Ralph is allowed recognition is his own lack of understanding and confusion. His desire to prescribe certain signification to Philomena's (Asian, female) identity completely backfires. That Sai Yee soon leaves him is merely a logical culmination to his already increasing state of (Western, male) emasculation. Philomena's painting, unlike Dorian Gray's portrait which, according to Kenneth Womack, functions as Gray's "ethical doppelganger, his willful sacrifice for a decadent lifestyle and the means via which he will preserve his youth" (176), is another "double" in the narrative that testifies to its host's resistance against the male gaze and retaliation against preexisting gendered categories.

According to Andrew Webber, stories of the double are rife with the effect of mise-en-abyme, in which figures or structures are reflected within each other (6). I have already noted one meta-critical aspect of Xu Xi's story in which this effect occurs. Another mise-en-abyme that is evident is the way "The Stone Window" is intertextuality related to a Greek mythology which features a character whose name almost resembles Philomena's. This intertextual imbrication that suggests a strategy of doubling is most pronounced at the end of Xu Xi's story, when Roach calls Philomena "Philomela" instead. This mispronunciation, which slightly bothers Ralph, nevertheless causes him to recollect the tragic story of Philomela, with which he soon becomes obsessed. The intertextuality between both stories is clearly evident here when Philomela's story is henceforth also textually embedded within the main narrative.[7]

In the Greek myth, Philomela and her sister Procne are daughters of Pandion, King of Athens. They are both violated by Tereus, who imprisons

Philomela after severing her tongue, but marries Procne. Procne does not know of her sister's predicament, but Philomela nonetheless manages to weave a tapestry depicting the narrative of her imprisonment and sends it to Procne.[8] In this way, the two sisters manage to find a way to "speak" to each other without Tereus's knowledge. In my view, this "unspeaking" method of communication is subversive because of its resistive and secret qualities which are outside patriarchal apprehension. The weaving is both the unfolding of an otherwise denied voice as well as a powerful criticism against the perpetrator of her marginalization and suffering. The reference to this Greek myth has interesting significance in "The Stone Window." Like Philomela, Philomena too resists and criticizes the male imperative through an aesthetic activity — this time, painting. It is evident that her art finally "speaks" to her intended "hearer" — Sai Yee — who takes a lesson from her "monstrous" sister to defy Ralph's potential will-to-control that is, at the moment, disguised as innocent interest for her wellbeing. While Ralph feels discomforted by Philomena's painting because it resists his "understanding," Sai Yee finds enlightenment to her unspoken female plight, and chooses, like her predecessor, to disappear. As such, the two sisters — Philomela and Procne — becomes intertextually transcribed in Xu Xi's narrative as Philomena's and Sai Yee's double.

Another significant Greek mythology that is textually embedded in Xu Xi's story to suggest a further level of doubling is the tale of Pandora and her box. In part three of "The Stone Window," Sai Yee and Ralph find a box washed ashore by the Aegean while honeymooning in Hydra. The couple jokingly refers to it as Pandora's box, which, in the Greek myth, encloses all evil, and if opened, would bring dire consequences to the world. Sai Yee however, makes an interesting quip: she thinks that the box is "just like a Philomena Hui.... Because you see it but can't see into it" (241). There is no attempt made at opening the box because it is so tightly attached to the coast that no manner of pulling could detach it. The box, in this case, like the painting, is another instance of doubling that suggests Philomena's impenetrability to the male gaze. Like Pandora's box, Philomena invites both dread and desire from those who wishes to identify her mystery, but unlike the box, she remains intractably "lidded," frustrating whatever attempts at exposing her. It is also interesting that Sai Yee acknowledges this quality in Philomena, almost as if she has intuited her predecessor's power over men, and one she will eventually come to emulate.

It should be quite evident that the motif of the double in "The Stone Window" is not pertinent to the female characters only. Doubling also occurs among the male characters through textual parallels and mirroring effects.

For instance, Constantin's face, "badly scarred by pockmarks" (235), echoes Roach's "pockmarked cheek"; more intriguing however, is Roach's description of himself as "fat and ugly" (248) — as is Constantin — when he is actually "thin and bony" (248–9). This is probably, as the story suggests, because he is too accustomed to his old appearance when his body is actually being ravaged by cancer. Despite this allegedly "rational" explanation, the interchange of physical attributes, coupled with such curious descriptions, tempt us to consider the two men as textual parallels of each other, especially since they were both once infatuated with the painter and tormented by the loss of her. In fact, it becomes unclear as the narrative progresses if the two men are not actually a single person. A firm friendship is also forged between Constantin/Roach and Ralph after Sai Yee disappears, and the tortuous state of mind suffered by the Greek man/men is now transferred also to Ralph, thus making all two/three men mirror images of each other in the end. As such, while the female doubles in the story, who both disappear in the end, are suggestive of a resistance to patriarchal imperatives, and to frustrate the potential for reading a unified female selfhood, the doubling of male characters indicates their fragmentation and confusion. In this way, Xu Xi's deployment of the double with a clear gendered agenda suggests not only the story's feminist proclivity, but deliberately provides this Gothic motif with a new twist.

The diverse concerns reflected in Gothic literature — from political revolution, industrialization and urbanization, to the shifts in sexual and domestic organizations, and scientific discovery — articulates socio-ideological anxieties during periods of change. If this view is tenable to "The Stone Window," it could be said that this contemporary Asian story reflects the shifting image of Chinese women within a culture that has long practiced the suppression of women. This newfound image is both empowering and fearful, resulting in the tale's ambiguous tone. Through the motif of the double which occurs on various levels — characters, meta-critical, intertextual — Xu Xi's tale achieves, to a laudable point, the textual instability characteristic of the Gothic that proliferates interpretation and refuses closure. In the end, the Gothic significance of "The Stone Window" echoes what Fred Botting sees of contemporary Gothic, in which "identity, reality, truth and meaning are subject to a dispersion and multiplication of meanings, realities and identities that obliterates the possibility of imagining any ... order and unity" (157).

Notes

1. The other English-language writers include poets Agnes Lam and Louise Ho, and novelist Timothy Mo, who now resides in London.

2. She first attracted media attention by winning the RTHK/SCMP Short Story *Competition* 1992, and later became well-known in Hong Kong and abroad with her six books of fiction and essays. *The Unwalled City* was named by the 15 anniversary issue of *Hong Kong Magazine* as one of the top fifteen books about Hong Kong to appear in the last fifteen years (see author's official website, cited in *Hong Kong Magazine*, June16, 2006). Her short story "Famine" earned her the 2005 Ploughshares Cohen Award for Fiction and was nominated for an O. Henry 2006 prize.

3. In "The Stone Window," there is a passing reference to dolls. Philomena's Greek benefactor addresses her as "my little doll" ("Philomena, kalaki-moo") (233); the implications of female objectification and masculine will-to-control are, of course, unmistakable. But dolls, as Freud demonstrates in "The Uncanny," are objects that can emasculate simply because its lifelikeness troubles the certainty of its inanimate status (Freud 157). In Xu Xi's story, Philomena "the doll" is certainly not the passive, willing object, but the dangerous automata that strikes back and emasculates the men who try to subdue her.

4. The other stories collected in *Daughters of Hui* are "Danny's Snake," "Loving Graham" and "Valediction." The protagonists in these stories share the same surname.

5. That Philomena is the Gothic double, and hence the "monster" of the story is implied through metaphors of bestiality as well. "The Stone Window" makes oblique references to bestiality, implying a kind of mysterious affinity between women and animals. Barbara Creed, whose bases her work on the Julia Kristeva's psychoanalytical model, suggests that such an affinity is an exemplification of female abjection and her body's disrespect for "borders, positions, rules," thus directly "disturb[ing]" identity, system, order" (Kristeva 4; cited in Creed 8). This liminal state of being—half human, half animal—challenges patriarchal injunctions for strict divisions of categories, order, and guardedness against contamination by alien presences. Of course, there are no actual transformations in Xu Xi's story, but bestiality remains a crucial metaphor nevertheless. Once more, it is Philomena that powerfully suggests bestial qualities. To Ralph, she is a cat with her agile-like and quick movements (230). To Roach, she is reminiscent of a bird (251). On one level, that Philomena is cast in such "pet-like" configurations reveals the men's desire to domesticate her. I want to posit, however, that her bestial affinities indicate her power and the flexibility with which Philomena's body can "twist" (230) and adapt to different men and situations. Philomena's animal ways are, of course, precursors to her figuratively "monstrous" identity. According to Andrew Ng (drawing from Timothy Beal), a textual "monster" usually occupies "a position of indefatigable power as long as it remains unseen or partially seen, or doubtfully recognized," and that in contemporary monster narratives, it has learned to manipulate visibility in order to remain unseen (12). I have already argued that Philomena, as a configuration of the Gothic double, is the story's "monstrous other"; as such, her hide-and-seek game with her various lovers (and the reader) merely reinforces this point. And unlike many monster narratives where the monster is, in the end, apprehended, that Philomena disappears maintains that the "monster" in Xu Xi's tale escapes, and directly frustrates, the male gaze.

6. A Greek region-flavored white wine.

7. A reader familiar with Gothic literature would know that such framing device is another recognizable Gothic characteristic.

8. The story of the two sisters is actually outlined in Xu Xi's narrative (252–53).

Works Cited

Botting, Fred. 1996. *The Gothic.* New York/London: Routledge.

Brewster, Scott. 2000. "Seeing Things: Gothic and the Madness of Interpretation." *A Companion to the Gothic.* Ed. David Punter. Malden, Mass.: Blackwell Publishers, 281–292.

Creed, Barbara. 1993. *The Monstrous-feminine: Film, Feminism, Psychoanalysis.* New York/London: Routledge.

Freud, Sigmund. 1998. "The Uncanny" (1917). *Literary Theory: An Anthology.* Eds. Julie Rivkin and Michael Ryan. Malden, Mass.: Blackwell Publishers.

Gilbert, Sandra M., and Susan Gubar. 1979. *The Madwoman in the Attic: The Woman Writer and the Nineteenth-century Literary Imagination.* New Haven: Yale University Press.

Masse, Michelle A. 2000. "Psychoanalysis and the Gothic." *A Companion to the Gothic.* Ed. David Punter. Oxford, UK; Malden, Mass.: Blackwell Publishers, 229–241.

Ng, Andrew Hock-Soon. 2004. *Dimensions of Monstrosity in Contemporary Narratives: Theory, Psychoanalysis, Postmodernism.* Basingstoke: Palgrave.

Rank, Otto. 1971. *Beyond Psychology* (1941). New York: Dover.

Webber, Andrew. 1996. *The Doppelgänger: Double Visions in German Literature*. Oxford: Oxford University Press.
Wei Hui. 2000. *The Shriek of the Butterfly*. Hong Kong: Cosmos Books Ltd.
Womack, Kenneth. 2000. "Withered, Wrinkled, and Loathsome of Visage: Reading the Ethics of the Soul and the Late-Victorian Gothic in *The Picture of Dorian Gray*." *Victorian Gothic: Literary and Cultural Manifestations in the Nineteenth Century*. Eds. Ruth Robbins and Julian Wolfreys. Basingstoke: Palgrave, 168–81.
Xu Xi. 2002. *Chinese Walls & Daughters of Hui* (1999). Hong Kong: Chameleon Press.

12

Asian Cell and Horror

Sheng-mei Ma

Cell

The human body is a cell, a prison-house, from which the voice, speaker of the mind, escapes through the invisible line of a cell phone, a computer, or a film reel. That umbilical cord to Western technology eases Asian subject's atomization, but paradoxically implicates the cell-, telephone-, and computer-user in a web of bondage, a pandemic of evil, as exemplified by Asian horror films and ghost stories, such as *Ringu* (1998), *The Eye* (*Gin Gwai* 2002), *Oldboy* (2003), *Ju-On* (2003) and many more. What connects such on-screen horror with Asian audience and, increasingly, global cinema is a malaise of disconnect. For if the human body is graphed by the coordinates of the x-axis of time and the y-axis of space, then the z-coordinate of the mind ranges far from the two-dimensional plane of daily existence. Among other things, the mind dreams of renewal, of transformation from old to new, hence reversing the flow of time and rejecting the confines of space, albeit temporarily. Transformation is but changes, the essence of life, speeded-up, which would otherwise progress in a gradual and slow-paced manner. In the frenzy of modernization, Asia desires to fast forward alteration. A case in point: many Chinese believe that China has completely bypassed in recent decades the phase of household telephones in Western history, moving directly from no household phones to cell phones.[1] Yet such leapfrogs are so gigantic and swift that one feels torn, as if leaving behind one's heart, the thin thread of attachment ripped. Nostalgia for what one has lost invariably shadows forward-looking, even futuristic, sentiments, except melodramatic tears are now replaced by horrified screams. While reveling in the new, the self secretly conjures up the old, either female ghosts (*Ringu* and *The Eye*) or buried memories (*Oldboy*). The horror genre thus returns to modernity's repression, or Asia's ghost. To cast in the metaphor of human dichotomy again, the millennial Asia in the precocity of modernization acquires a mature, full-grown body, while the mind dangles between a wayward child and a traditional patriarch, between what is to come and what refuses to pass on, between, in Jagdish Bhagwati's words, the PC (personal computer) and the C.P. (Communist Party).[2] Far from Asia-bashing, the figure of speech simply subscribes to the truism of the discrepancy between biological and psychological age. In such schizophrenic divide, China's meteoric rise as the twenty-first-century's factory is plagued by environmental devastation, disparity of rich and poor, human rights abuses, gender inequity, minority repression, and a mishmash of childish willfulness and moribundity. This disconnect is not unique to Asia: rarely is the infrastructure or hardware of a developed, postmodern society supported by comparable "software"; egotism and self-interest rather than altruism and compassion appear to drive civilization. In Asian horror genre, the disjunction finds a metonym in cell phone, which echoes E. M. Forster's plea: "Only connect!"[3]

The cell phone, in effect, becomes a surrogate or mirror image for the human body. The human body and mind contains a universe within, characterized by incalculable biochemical and biological linkages, which the Wachowski brothers visualize in *The Animatrix* (2003) in the image of transmission of points of light on computer's circuit board. Stephen King dubs it "organic circuitry" of the brain in his 2006 sci-fi thriller *Cell* (158), hence erasing the romantic separation of the organic from the mechanic. Placed as it is, the body is the thinnest of placenta, porous to boot, that separates the universe within from the universe without, until death, some say, releases the one inside the placenta to merge with the one outside. Ditto the cell phone, whose plastic shell holds a constellation of network whenever it reaches out to the cosmos beyond. Technology has indeed yoked infinity and infinitesimality: while its size continues to shrink, the cell dazzles in multitasking in telephone, text message, camera, internet access, daily planner, address book, calculator, timepiece and alarm clock, and whatnot, so much so that a cell-user develops a near-dependency. As a cell phone is misplaced, the user feels incapacitated without his or her familiar (soul?), stricken with grief. Consistent with Freud's insights in "Mourning and Melancholia" (1917), losing one's cell equals losing oneself, for the cell is the self, or dream-self, which, despite its smallness, does big things.

Such externalized dream-self claims a virtual, at least auditory, community. As a cinematic device in Korean television serial dramas or the Korean

Wave rippling throughout Asia and Asian diasporic communities, cell phones justify the ubiquity of shot-reverse shot editing. Wherever and whenever the characters happen to be, they are, by means of cells, perennially face-to-face, even intimate close-ups for each other and for the viewer. This no doubt reflects the wish-fulfillment of the millennial Asian diaspora where fans seek to reach characters, frequently, of another culture, another language, and another time. Yet this essentially global, diasporic dream suggests that the cell-user may shy from being alone with oneself, placing such calls to virtual voices in place of actual voices from actual bodies, a symptom of deep-seated neurosis. That the virtual community is flimsy at best is born out by the recurring "nadir" in the Korean Wave. The dramatic felicity courtesy of cell phones routinely vanishes at the heart-wrenching moment for lovers when the "heart" or memory chip of the cell phone is removed by one party in attempt to end the relationship. The "heartless" cell-user formulaically turns depressed and catatonic, whereas the other user, agitated beyond words with each thwarted call and unanswered message, tries frantically to give his or her heart. The former is resigned to solitary confinement; the latter strives to break it.

Largely following this pattern, Daniel H. Byun's 2004 thriller *The Scarlet Letter* features a memorable reversal: an egomaniac police officer talks to his lover, a blues singer played sultrily by Eun-ju Lee, on the cell as they thread past and greet guests at a reception in honor of the officer's cellist wife, who has just completed her solo performance. The cell's dubious nature emerges unequivocally with this brilliant scene. The cell places the user in two communities, simultaneously, with respect to reception guests and to a disembodied voice. Parallel communications take place in a mutually exclusive fashion, unless the cell-user chooses to relay the message. Yet this mediation is never transparent: in *The Scarlet Letter*, it is downright duplicitous. The officer's supposed dialogue may well be a monologue insofar as his wife is concerned, who is not privy to that low whispering in his ear. The suspicious wife wonders whether he responds to the "inner voice" oblivious to or because of the presence of the public.

Among other attractions, the cell intrigue is no doubt one of the selling points to garner international distribution. An adept cross-cultural communicator, Byun fashions a tie-in between a Korean product and the global market. The commercial aspect notwithstanding, the match between the Christian paradigm and the Korean psyche of crime and punishment is well-nigh perfect: the namesake of Nathaniel Hawthorne's Puritan allegory; the opening epigraph of the Original Sin; and the refrain of guilt, confession, and repentance. The plot twists are somewhat contrived, though, in the relentless sensationalism — passion, murder, mercy killing, liaison, and lesbianism. Unbeknownst to the officer, his lover and wife were once involved in a lesbian relationship; the triangular love is far more complicated than what he conceives. Straddling the genre of thriller with scenes portraying carnal desire and the genre of horror, particularly the two killings splattered with blood, Byun succeeds in flirting with the transgressive fringes of Korean sensibility.

One-and-one-half casualties, however, never return from his project of far-flung "overreaching." Eun-ju Lee received scathing criticism for the daring performance baring her body as well as the character's mental instability. Her troubles compounded by family debts and personal problems, the 25-year-old Lee hanged herself on February 22, 2005.[4] Serendipitously, the double entendre of Asian cell for cell phone and prison cell converges in her final moments on-screen. Her passionate lovemaking with the officer locks them in a car trunk, their death trap, perhaps a subconscious maneuver to possess him, even if it means twin suicide. As they wrestle in love and, subsequently, with death in the "coffin" of the trunk, his cell vibrates on the dashboard, his present wife and her ex-lover hoping in vain to reach them. Rather than an ascent to stardom, Lee's escape from Korean social roles into bluesy plumbing into eros and thanatos alienates her to the point that she parts from herself. Yet another casualty of sorts is Hyeon-a Seong, whose character beats her husband's head to a pulp with the statuette of Virgin Mary. Seong used to have a beautiful round face, yet her cheeks are now shaved off by cosmetic surgery, leaving a long, slender, and stylized Western face.[5] Seong's "old" body embodies a cocoon, from which she emerges a butterfly in the image of the West. Successful self-transformation for Byun, Lee, and Seong involves the trapping of Western modernity, from the glamorous, Hollywood-inspired surface of the film and of the half-face to the explosion of pent-up Korean libido. A tinge of unease, nevertheless, haunts this flight from the cell of Asianness: Western opera, classical music, and blues punctuate transgressions against social mores and law, all unfolding within chic upscale apartments, and the Virgin Mary, of course, is the weapon of choice. In particular, a panning shot from the back at the two nude lovers recalls the traditional Korean ritual of the bridegroom carrying the bride on his back, which has become almost an obligatory scene marking the climax of love in contemporary Korean television serials. (Instead of the traditional "sealed with a kiss," Koreans seal their vow with a portage.) Avoiding frontal nudity, Lee sits on the poolside, her right knee drawn up, leaning on the officer's back, who turns out to be standing in the pool and clipping her left toe nails. This tableau recreates, momentarily, the traditional ritual, which only accentuates the tragic trespasses of adultery and nudity. The longing to be one with the lover, with the West, and, paradoxically, with Koreanness is doomed from the start. The void left by Lee's nude body and Seong's round face is the true, Conradian "Horror! Horror!" which is aestheticized as and renamed the genre of horror for mass entertainment.

While cell phones and other vehicles of mobility or communication are designed to enable connectedness, alienation has always been a spell cast on modernization in the wake of the industrial revolution. For producers of modernity, Karl Marx theorizes that labor in the modern era reifies laborers. Charlie Chaplin's worker character bears out Marxist prophecy in lapsing into a mere cog in the assembly line of *Modern Times* (1936). For the masses, the machine in the garden, in Leo Marx's terms, causes a disturbance to pastoral ties to Nature and human nature. The engine to progress and the master narrative of modernity, reason and science ameliorate human life as much as estrange it, in part because they suppress alternative discourses, such as religion, belief in the supernatural, and other myth-making efforts. Peter Brooks' pioneering *The Melodramatic Imagination* (1976) has maintained that melodrama and the Gothic give voice to what is repressed during the Enlightenment. Amidst the rational and secular mid- to late-eighteenth century, the need for transcendence, for the supernatural, and for sentimental excesses is satisfied, Brooks asserts, by such genres. G. Richard Thompson agrees that "Gothic literature may be seen as expressive of an existential terror generated by a schism between a triumphantly secularized philosophy of evolving good and an abiding obsession with the Medieval conception of guilt-laden, sin-ridden man" (*The Gothic Imagination* 4–5). The Gothic tradition metamorphoses into horror and sci-fi in the modern West. Isabel Cristina Pinedo sees postmodern horror film as manifesting a general malaise, casting in doubt "temporal order and causal logic" (96). Almost nihilistic in its unremitting violence, horror films expose, maintains Pinedo, "the terror *implicit* in everyday life: the pain of loss, the enigma of death, the unpredictability of events" (Pinedo 106). Such logic sees horror as a working-out of modern and postmodern repressions. One figure associated with this angst is what Noel Carroll calls the "overreacher" or mad scientist, whose demise is invariably caused by the hubris of playing God. The scientist's will in this psychodrama within the West drives experiments, causing self-alienation in the end. Whereas science and technology inflate the ego unduly, infringing on the Creator's domain, they are seldom viewed as alien invasion from another part of the world. After all, the machine roaring across the idyllic countryside initiates the industrial revolution, part of the history of modern West. Likewise, the mad scientists — Drs. Faustus, Frankenstein, Jekyll, Moreau, Strangelove — are all part of "us." (The only doctor who is one of "them" is Dr. Fu Manchu, the archetype of the Yellow Peril, who, you will agree, does not belong here.) The ensuing colonialism of the East by the West comes about as a result of the differential pace of technological development. Accordingly, Asia is thrust into modernity, an awkward embrace even for Japan, perhaps the most successful of Asia's modernizing efforts. Japan, needless to say, is the only nation in the world with a bitter taste of atomic bombs, the "pinnacle" of modern science.

Ringu

Water exists in three states — solid ice, liquid water, or vaporized steam — and so does a telephone — transmitting, ringing, or dead. Any electronic device, for that matter, is either operating or not, with a brief moment of warm-up or wind-down between the two more durable states. In human terms, that sliver of space between living and dead is inhabited by shadows of ghosts. Even when humans are "solids," sixty percent of the human body consists of water. Even when humans are gone, they flow through the loved ones' memory like currents of water. Despite its elusiveness, water or ghost (watery ghost in *Ringu*) is the secret of life, the hidden passage that either end goes through before reincarnation. *Ringu* fully deploys such symbolism of water, from the film's rain-soaked aura to the genesis of life in the ocean and in the oceanic womb. However, as the ghost in *Ringu* resides in the well, the vagina or birth canal turns out to issue death from the earth's womb of subterranean water. The telephone calls to the hotel guests staying right above the well in *Ringu* constitute a wicked umbilical cord from the ghost to her "stillborn." In such a grotesque reversal of life, the telephone ring symbolizes a Keatsian pregnant moment between connection and disconnection, or connection under erasure. In and of itself, every telephone connection is already a disconnection. While the telephone, especially the cell, demolishes all spatial and temporal prisons, it presupposes a dissociation of the physical body from its voice. Even on a Skype Web Cam, the split between the physical body and its image persists. The cell, pun intended, rarely captures a whole person — body and mind — as we would like it to, only parts, which, fetishistically, metamorphose into that person. Given that face-to-face communication often involves less than a whole person as well, since one may be distracted and not all there, the cell comes to encapsulate the wish to connect and the ultimate failure of doing so. This argument based on a hypothetical "whole" person begs the question of what a person is. In point of fact, one may well contend that only fragments of self exist at any given moment, not unlike water under the proverbial bridge. That the bridge is fixed does not mean water or thoughts ever are. Short of an ontological thesis refuting the self altogether, I merely submit that the cell and other communication tools serve to highlight the limitation of contact.

The futility of "only connect" haunts even Walter Benjamin's utopian mechanical reproduction, the lynchpin of modernity. Benjamin celebrates the emancipatory potential of machine use, which evolves into Jean Baudrillard's postmodern simulacra, copies without an original. Benjamin and Baudrillard dispense with the question of the machine-maker or of the original, relishing instead in the horizontal or rhizome network. Their playful, quasi-apocalyptic stance posits, nevertheless, an originary absence, a void schizophrenically displaced onto popular culture, from Gothic monsters centuries ago to specters in contemporary horror. Rather than retracing human origin back to the Creator, as medieval predecessors used to do, horror films constitute a genealogy of evil parallel to the lost lineage. Yet horror hinges on the void of good, which evokes, like memory, mental images rendered powerful by virtue of their absence. For instance, the female ghost Sada (short for Sadako) at the core of *Ringu* comes from a mysterious origin, while her name (chastity, virginity, or virtue) implies an immaculate conception from the devil. Commercially, such a pan-Christian motif lends itself to Western remakes and global cinema. Conceptually, the perversion only comes into being vis-à-vis the existing Christian and Japanese orthodoxies. The failure to unite with a missing God prompts reaching back to origin of another kind. That Sada's story is told over and over again — from Koji Suzuki's 1991 misogynist, paranoid novel to Hideo Nakata's 1998 more politically correct *Ringu* to Gore Verbinski's 2002 remake *The Ring* to Nakata's Hollywood debut of the 2005 *The Ring Two* and to more — suggests the global audience's need to revisit primal fears, each remake harking back to antecedents, ultimately to the mystery of Sada or death. Similar to the symbiosis of good and evil, the mystery of death links inextricably with that of life, each deriving its meaning from the other.

Into this stormy marriage also go East and West. Since the Meiji Restoration of 1868, Japan has succeeded in mastering Western technology. For the modern West, its identity is constructed on the basis of science and technology. Even technological glitches in Western horror films, such as those perpetrated by mad scientists, rarely discredit technology as a whole. In fact, technology often provides redemption for humanity in sci-fi postnuclear holocaust. (What Neo and Trinity need in order to rescue Morpheus are "Guns! Lots of guns!") On the contrary in modern Japan, technology acquires a duality standing for, on the one hand, the essence of modernity of the self-anointed "Robot Kingdom," and, on the other, for a part of the self that points ambivalently to the Western other. A classic example comes from Junichiro Tanizaki's "Terror" (1913), which presciently opens with the protagonist's "railroad phobia" that comes to infect even Nature itself, now transformed into industrial images of "blast furnace" and "movie screen." A doctor with a Western-styled moustache remains blind to the protagonist's inner malaise and perceives only his strong physique. About to be conscripted into the military and the machinery of expansionism after a near century of Westernization, the terrified protagonist escapes into whiskey, a Western import. Western technology is a net that interpellates modern life so seamlessly that the net is invisible to the protagonist. Tanizaki pinpoints the Japanese "conundrum," to borrow from *The Ring*, of a highly developed nation ill at ease with its own technology, of ancient Japanese myths (re)possessing ordinary modernity.

Contextualized by this ambiguous relationship with Western technology, the director Hideo Nakata adroitly combines technology of quotidian life with supernatural ghosts and ancient haunting. Before this point, the twins are usually separated. Alfred Hitchcock's *Dial M for Murder* (1954), for instance, features the telephone as a mere prop for malicious intent; the telephone does not embody, as in *Ringu*, malice itself. The other extreme manifests itself in *The Matrix* when old-fashioned telephone landlines offer the escape routes for freedom fighters. By contrast, *Ringu* manages to vest in modern technology the Japanese tradition of female ghosts and repression — with classic long black hair, white gossamer gowns, and the setting of a drowning well. All three characteristics derive from traditional ghost stories. The long black hair reflects not only the long hair worn by East Asian women of old but also the fact that one's hair "lives on" after one is dead. In 1769, Uyeda Akinari thus gives the ghost of a faithful wife "tousled hair tumbling down her back" in "Homecoming" (*Ugetsu Monogatari* 10), which inspires, together with Lafcadio Hearn's Orientalist *Kwaidan* (1904), "Black Hair" in Masaki Kobayash's avant-gardist film *Kwaidan* (1965). The white gossamer robe, on the other hand, has come to be a stylized feature of female ghosts, as Izumi Kyoka in "The Holy Man of Mount Koya" (1900) imagines one such waif in "gossamer gowns as sheer as butterfly wings" (59). Finally, drowning in the well and hanging account for most female suicides in traditional Asian texts.[6] Whereas the three attributes delineate sharply the image of ghost in stasis, motion picture requires movement. Sada and her spectral colleagues, consequently, move in an awkward and hopping gait, a stylization taken from the horror genre, especially Hollywood's slasher films and Hong Kong's zombie films of previous decades. More primeval and feral than the hopping ghosts, the animalistic phantom of *Ju-On* crawls exclusively.

Yet these female ghosts alone do not effect haunting; Sada, for one, is channeled through modern everyday amenities, such as playing a videotape and receiving a telephone call, screen image and lived experience no longer kept apart. The series of "passive" images in Sada's "home video" memorialize past suffering, yet they actively foretell the future. Past and future are bound in the present viewing. The ruthless spread of evil finds its perfect metaphor in virus, both as an epidemic and as a computer bug, once again a yoking of primitive life force and advanced technology. There is no way to resist the malevolence contained in the videotape; the only way to survive is to make a copy of the videotape and have someone else watch it. Part of the urban legend, Koji Suzuki's novel likens this to "chain letters," the reaching out from cells of anomie. In other words, the victim in *Ringu* survives by becoming the victimizer or at least the willing accomplice in a network of sin. The "ring" in the Japanese title and in Hollywood remakes refers to both the ever-expanding circle of "membership" of victim/victimizer and to the telephone call. The call arrives punctually at the end of the tape, delivering the ill tiding seven days hence, an inverse Genesis of horrid death marked by the silent scream from a mouth wide open and horrified eyes, always captured upside-down on a film negative, the antithesis to life's "positive." In Verbinski, the death mask resembles a "scrambled" face, jumbled dots and lines on TV when reception is denied. This death mask symbolizes as much the haunting of a traditional ghost as the wrath of a tape for not having been mass produced. When a viewer falls short of spreading the message of misery, that viewer is erased like film negatives or reformatted by the image on the television screen that materializes into the ghost. Watching a tape is now the other way around; each audience is being watched by the sun-eye on the tape, the first recognizable image after the static and electronic noise. The circular shape of the sun-eye is associated with the circle of the well; with Sada's inverse, bloated fisheye that kills with a single look; and with the hollow sockets of the death's head that the protagonist Asakawa retrieves at the bottom of the well and embraces in a trance.

This horror scenario is by no means original. Indeed, *Ringu* succeeds because it taps into not only modern mass hysteria but the horror formula of alien infection, as in David Cronenberg's *Videodrome* (1983) and *Shivers* (1975). The former focuses on a hallucinating TV producer with a slit in his stomach to play video cassettes; the latter features, in the words of Adam Lowenstein, "phallic/fecal-looking parasites that cause sexual dementia in their human hosts" (*Shocking Representation* 156). Nakata's relationship to the West is far more pervasive than the idiosyncratic and art-house Cronenberg. *Ringu* opens with a baseball game on TV, an American icon from the postwar occupation of Japan. The first casualty, a high schooler Tomoko, is taken unawares since her parents are out enjoying an extra inning of the baseball game, an eerie association between the game broadcast on TV and the real life of the characters. The TV screen and the viewer's life are already wedded by means of Western symbols. In addition, Tomoko's death must be traced back to her stay seven days ago at an Izu hotel's Western-styled log cabin, where Tomoko and other victims watch the tape. The interior design of the cabin includes Western skylights, sofa, fireplace, and, of course, television and VCR. Western food with knife and fork is served against a backdrop of tennis courts. Western sets complement body language and themes related to the West. At Tomoko's funeral, her cousin Yoichi keeps rubbing his forehead, evoking the cross on Ash Wednesday. Yoichi's mother, the journalist Asakawa, seeks help in solving the mystery from her ex-husband, Professor Ryuji Takayama, who is endowed with extrasensory perception, just like Sadako and her mother. The study of ESP is closely associated with the turn-of-the-century spiritualism in the West, a revival of religiosity and the supernatural amidst what was becoming the hegemony of science. Although Sada's powers come from ancient and unknown sources, the specific marker of ESP and science suggests an alliance with alien forces from outside Japan, accounting for Sada's wizardry in electronics.

Sada in *Ringu* places telephone calls only to the Izu hotel right above the well in which she is drowned. The phone line connects the two realms of existence of the living and the dead, although Sada remains silent on the phone except electronic noise, which is perhaps her voice after all. By contrast, the ghost Samara in Verbinski's *The Ring* can call a downtown Seattle apartment. Not only do her calls turn "mobile" in Western culture, but Samara becomes more vocal and whispers: "Seven Days!" Samara is so prone to dialogue in fact that she leaves a message on the answering machine. The fundamental difference in where to place the call has to do with the Asian concept of bones. Sada unfailingly rings the hotel because, as Asakawa conjectures, that is where her bones lie. The *Ring*'s phone call, consistent with the American myth of mobility, is not bound by the location of the bones. The cell service allows, so to speak, more *roaming* in the U.S. Asakawa's realization sets in motion the alleged "closure"—finding and burying Sadako's bones in the well, which turns out not to have appeased the angry spirit, contrary to Asian folk beliefs over burial of remains. As a consequence, Ryuji is killed when his "deadline" of seven days is up. Ryuji's tragic death arrives when he notices his female student's prank on the plus sign on his blackboard. He adds the vertical line to the minus to restore what is also the sign for crucifix, hence inadvertently hailing the coming of the "anti–Christ" Sada from the TV. That vertical line completing the crucifix connects God on top, human in the center, and ghost at the bottom of the well. Surely, Ryuji does not intend to bring on his horrid demise, but being an ESP expert, there may be an eerie kinship between himself and Sada. The human yearning for attachment, through the physical line of the telephone, the invisible thread of human memory, or the trinity of God-human-devil, results in his death.

Posthumously, Ryuji is able to warn Asakawa to save their son Yoichi, who has watched the tape at the urging of Tomoko in a failed attempt to save herself. Ryuji's affinity with Sada is confirmed when the viewer realizes, with the wisdom of hindsight, that Ryuji appears in Sada's video as a hooded figure pointing to "COPY," capital letters in English printed on the spine of the cassette. Western images help damn some characters, yet Yoichi is saved by a message in English. This duality of the West resonates with that of traditional Japanese family: the polarized East and West turn out to be alike in terms of the innate dualism within either one. The horror story stems from the erosion of traditional family: a Dr. Ikuma, whom some suspect to be Sadako's father, pushes Sadako into the well and seals the mouth with a slab of stone. The horror continues in the broken family of Asakawa, Ryuji, and Yoichi. Ryuji, at one point, bemoans that he with his abnormal ESP gift and his estranged family should perish together, hence putting an end to the curse. Ironically, the curse must be honored should family be preserved. At the end of the film, Asakawa drives into an ominous rainstorm gathering in the horizon, with her tender voice-over asking her father "for a favor." The tape and a spare VCR in the passenger's seat, Asakawa is sure to ask her father to watch the copy in order to lift the curse from his grandson, a perverse sharing of gifts from the devil. That Asakawa would ask suggests at least a glimmer of hope for humanity in that the grandfather is likely to sacrifice himself out of love. But unless he stamps the surge of evil with his own death, Sada's tape would never end, "She never sleeps!" as *The Ring* puts it: infection and pollution is one sure way to connect with fellow human beings.

Park Chanwook's Horror

Sada the Unmoved Mover dwells in the supernatural realm, contaminating the human world due to her insatiable wrath. That Unmoved Mover is in turn conjured up by the creators and fans of horror. We will Sada into existence because hate and revenge are fundamental, although unseemly, emotions, which are then projected outward. The motives of the ghost stem squarely from human psyche: vengeance evens the score between felt grievances in the past and violence in the present, seeking equilibrium between internal tension and the status quo. The lopsidedness within one's heart is cancelled out when transferred onto the society, particularly the torn bodies of the adversaries. Revenge is human contact of the most naked kind, feasting on each other's flesh and blood.[7]

Asian cell provides the set, literally and figuratively, for Park Chanwook's revenge trilogy — *Sympathy for Mr. Vengeance* (2002), *Oldboy* (2003), *Sympathy for Lady Vengeance* (2005) — and a short feature "Cut," one of three marketed in the U.S. as a packaged DVD entitled *Three Extremes* (2004), the other two shorts being Fruit Chan's "Dumplings" and Takashi Miike's "Box." Park's avengers suffer kidnapping and/or incarceration, ranging in length from one deadly evening in "Cut" to thirteen and half years in *Lady Vengeance* to fifteen years in *Oldboy* and to lifelong deafness and slavery in *Mr. Vengeance*, a period when the prisoners are secreted away, their lives ingested and cannibalized by enemies with overwhelming material resources linked to Western modernity. Nursed in hate, the avengers embark upon a cycle of violence so horrific and indiscriminate that it amounts to endocannibalism, the flesh-eating of one's own kind, and self-mutilation. The most tabooed form of this self-consumption is incest, which occurs in *Oldboy*, "Dumplings," and "Box."[8] The thread running through incarceration, ingestion, and incest follows, cinematographically, the line of cell phone, computer, photographs, film reel, and, ultimately, viewers' gaze, all modern conveniences that embody a primal loss. Like bodies in space and time, where Western modernity is, the Korean tradition is not. Postmodern and ethnic heterogeneity, hybridity, and multiplicity championed by Fredric Jameson, Lisa Lowe, and the like are intellectual theories that undo, in the hands of postmodernists, the myth of Classicism's Golden Age and, in the hands of ethnic scholars, of area studies' melancholia and nostalgia. Such theorizing focuses more on white and Asian American conditions than on Asian and Asian diasporic ones. Whether postmodern "universalist" affectlessness or Asian American "particularist" identity politics, their playful or activist insistence on hybridity subscribes to only one side of the Janus-faced Asian modernity, the side that laughs or rages, whereas suppressed tears and horrified screams are exorcized and find accommodation in the horror genre. Ghosts and victims of violence thus lurk in Park's elaborate prison-house of Western capitalism, framed by the lens of global cinema. On the other hand, reflecting the ambivalence vis-à-vis the other, avengers' nativist revolt proceeds under the auspices of Western, Chinese, or non–Korean tropes, most notably *Lady Vengeance*'s Virgin Mary and *Oldboy*'s Chinese fried dumplings, the "spiritual" food throughout their captivity and the key to their revenge. Jeeyoung Shin in "Globalisation and New Korean

Cinema" holds that "the hybrid nature of Korean cinema is a product of the localization of global media culture," echoing Jenny Kwok Wah Lau's idea of the new Asia in formation displaying "multiple modernities" (57). Rather than content with a depthless postmodernist heterogeneous grab-bag, I analyze inherent contradictions of Asian globalization, evidenced in Park Chan-wook.

The earliest of Park's horror oeuvre, *Mr. Vengeance* demonstrates the strongest ideological bent, whereas subsequent films turn increasingly stylish, self-conscious modernist visions of retribution. Yong-mi in *Mr. Vengeance* is a left-wing terrorist with lines such as "Movement of capital maximizes the value of money," "Dissolve the big business conglomerates," and "Expel the U.S. imperialist army" ever ready on her tongue. Despite or because of Yong-mi's role, the film critic Chong Song-il is reported to have accused *Mr. Vengeance* of "skulking Stalinism" (in Kyu Hyun 113). Kyu Hyun Kim goes on to defend the film as "less concerned with the evils of capitalist exploitation than with our refusal (or inability) to transcend our subjective perspectives and enter into communication with one another" (115). Nonetheless, the film balances its critique of social bondage and individual anomie. Yong-mi's boyfriend Ryu, a deaf and mute foundry worker, gives his own kidney to an organ-harvesting gang in exchange for the right kidney for his ill sister. With different blood types, Ryu's organ would be rejected by his sister. This and all the other schemes go awry: Ryu is not only locked forever in a soundless and voiceless world but robbed of one of his vital organs. Ryu's disabilities, inborn or imposed, epitomizes Marxist theory on how capitalism drains laborers' life like vampire. Alienated by labor, Ryu is one of many walking corpses on the dim, deafening, and dehumanizing plant floor. When they emerge into the sunlit outdoor after their shift, all look dazed, stumbling in exhaustion and half-asleep, reminiscent of underground workers slouching out of the lift in Fritz Lang's *Metropolis* (1927). Social injustice does not negate the customized cell-block each character is assigned. One striking scene shows four young males masturbating while eavesdropping on what they believe to be a woman's prolonged orgasm. The camera then moves through the thin partition between the cells to reveal Ryu's sister crying out in pain and Ryu in an extreme close-up to the left of the frame slurping ramen noodles. Depth of field is deliberately eschewed; the blurred image of the sister tossing and moaning emphasizes the siblings' separation, despite their devotion. The eavesdroppers are trapped by their sexual fantasy, the sister by her illness, and Ryu by disabilities.

Barred from one another, characters seek connection through revenge, a veiled devouring of one another, evoking the mythical union of Oedipal complex within one's digestive system postulated by Freud in *Totem and Taboo* (1913). Witnessing a laid-off worker begging, and then mutilating himself in front of two "captains of industry," Ryu decides to kidnap the capitalist Tong-jin's young daughter for ransom. Ryu's sister learns of the crime and commits suicide in shame. Burying her along a creek, the deaf Ryu is unaware of the young daughter's cries for help as she slowly drowns in the distance. Park's signature montage comes into play when the girl in the background splashes and howls, a blurred shot framed on the left by a close-up of Ryu. Despite following the kidnappers' instructions, transmitted through mail and text messages, in paying the ransom, Tong-jin is bereaved and avenges the death by electrocuting Yong-mi; slashing, drowning, and dismembering Ryu. The bloodbath is by no means cathartic, as Aristotle teaches us in *Poetics*; instead, it simply halts when all parties touched by the revenge perish. Tong-jin him-self is stabbed to death by Yong-mi's fellow terrorists. The knife thrust into Tong-jin's heart fixes in place a propaganda leaflet, and Tong-jin, in his dying gasps, cranes his neck and squints hard to read what is in effect his own death certificate. The fade-out is punctuated by Tong-jin's unintelligible mumbling, which appears to be a senseless, farcical reading aloud of the leaflet, but it may well be a deathbed confession or an obituary for himself.

This hauntingly grotesque "closure" bears out Park's style of Gothic comic or gallows humor. Unequivocally, Western scholarship on such genres sheds light on a Korean filmmaker since not only is Park's sensibility mod-ernist in its jarring incongruities but also his products are internationalist from conception to distribution. Avril Horner and Sue Zlosnik defines Gothic's comic turn as:

> a double remove, an inflection within an inflection since in the Gothic comic turn — as in the joke — terror is suspended and horror is held in abeyance. If, as Brooks suggests, melodrama and the gothic gesture theatrically towards a lost transcendence, then it could be argued that the comic within the Gothic offers a position of detachment and skepticism towards such cultural nostal-gia [...] the beginning of a deconstructionist turn inherent within modernity. Such a perspective breaks the twinning of the Gothic and the psychoanalyti-cal in a proto-deconstructive impulse [3].

They proceed to situate such comic turn in the tradition of "the grin of the skull beneath the skin. This aligns with graveyard or gallows humour and is expressed graphically by one of Gothic's famous characters, Van Helsing in *Dracula*, through the figure of 'King Laugh'" (15). As part of his Gothic comic, Park's stylish cinematography distances and frames violence in such a way that horror unfolds with clinical precision and ludic absurdity. As the massacre of kidney-harvesting gang proceeds with minimum soundtrack, viewers are offered a bizarre camera angle from under a steel staircase, inches above the ground, peeping in safety but threatened by the expanding pool of blood. Violence is doubly removed and rendered an aesthetic experience for the bodies in pain, observed voyeuristically, utter no sound. Earlier, one gangster's rape of an unconscious girl is interrupted by Ryu coming down the staircase. He turns and moves toward Ryu in baby steps, his pants wrapped around the ankles. The tracking shot of his plump shins in mincing steps tempers carnage with comic relief. Such montage-like incongruities are poised between laughter and terror. Still earlier in the film, Ryu wakes up naked, minus a kidney, gesticulating desperately on the roadside to hitchhike, a scene straight out of supermarket tabloids, erstwhile Candid Camera, or today's YouTube. Dehumanization, in Park's hands, turns chillingly funny.

Rather than the generic divisions between the Gothic and the melodramatic advanced by Peter Brooks, Horner and Zlosnik, and other Western scholars, Park illustrates perhaps the quintessentially Korean sensibility in yoking the two. This wedding seems strange to the West that keeps apart the literary form channeling repressed passions versus that channeling pathos/bathos. Put simply, the West see the Gothic as releasing excess blood, the melodramatic excess tears. The Korean Wave follows no such breakdown, giving rise to episodes confusing to Western viewers. When Ryu cleans and tickles his naked sister, the scene evokes tenderness instead of incestuous impulse. When Ryu horse plays with the kidnapped girl by lifting her skirt, this inappropriate act of sexual harassment is meant to maximize the child's play. When the kidnappers jump rope with the kidnapped to the tune of a patriotic song about North and South Korea, the innocent fun may look incredulous to Western audience paranoid about abductions and terrorism. But this scene set at the playground, which enjoys an eternal return to nearly every show in the Korean Wave, professes a deep-seated Korean melancholia over the loss of innocence, amplified by the litany of the division of Motherland. The urge to restore to oneness can be psychologically regressive, culminating in the Oedipal, incestuous complex.[9] In one fell swoop in *Oldboy*, Park compresses all these impulses by grafting the horror of incest to melodrama. After fifteen years of incarceration, the protagonist Dae-su enjoys a sweet moment with his lover Mi-do, gently blowing dry her hair. Dae-su is soon to discover, however, Mi-do's identity as his long-lost daughter. But the film most eloquent in this juxtaposition of melodrama and horror is *Lady Vengeance*, which, true to its title, is the next of kin to *Mr. Vengeance*.

The refrain of innocence lost is shared by both films in the kidnapping and death of children. The villain Mr. Baek in *Lady Vengeance* teaches schoolchildren English. At gunpoint, he even serves as the English-Korean translator between Lady Vengeance Lee Geum-ja and her daughter adopted by Australians. Western language provides the cover for the child killer, but the West is a sanctuary as well. In addition, Geum-ja specializes in European pastries and cakes, the counterweight to or reiteration of the film's cannibalistic motif. The overwhelming Christian metaphors bedeck this drama of sin and redemption. Geum-ja is both an angel of compassion and a hell's angel, spending over a decade in prison plotting against Baek. In his capacity as the English instructor at various schools, Baek has murdered five children, his victims' marble, Hello Kitty, and other "mementos" stringed on his cell phone. Cell phone chain alone does not reanimate the past crime; Baek's videotapes documenting crying children in bondage before they meet their ends so shock and outrage the victims' parents that they decide to take justice into their own hands. The videotapes unspool to strangle Baek in a collective reprisal. The butchering of Baek should logically conclude the film, yet a melodramatic "closure" drags on, balancing blood with, for lack of a better word, sweets. That bittersweet scene at the delicatessen completes, so to speak, the group therapy, butchering knives now replaced by knives and forks in a celebration of the victims' lost birthdays. When the chandelier tinkles in the breeze, one bereaved parent alludes to France, where people believe that an angel passes through in each crystal clink. The parents look up, as if to witness their children's souls ascending. This sentimental ending can barely contain the nausea over the suspicion that the apparently chocolate cake they partake in memory of their children is made with Baek's blood, collected in the previous scene and mysteriously unaccounted for. The strange looks when they taste the cake do little to dispel the doubt.

Based loosely on the Japanese comics by Garon Tsuchiya and Nobuaki Minegishi, *Oldboy* ups the ante on transgressiveness by way of double incests and self-mutilation. The victim-turned-avenger Oh Dae-su has been imprisoned for fifteen years for an unknown offense, during which time he had been repeatedly hypnotized and programmed to orchestrate his romance with Mi-do upon release. The confinement and incest are masterminded by Lee Woo-jin, whose own incestuous tryst with his sister Soo-ah at their Catholic high school, Evergreen, was witnessed by Dae-su. Dae-su blabbed the scene to his friend No Joo-hwan before moving away to Seoul. Haunted by gossips, Soo-ah drowned herself, after having taken a picture of herself for Woo-jin to remember her by. Grieved by the loss of his sister-lover and mother surrogate, Woo-jin returns from his study in the U.S. a millionaire to destroy Dae-su. Dae-su learns of Mi-do's true identity from the "family album" Woo-jin presents him, an album that strings together the two-year-old Mi-do and the adult Mi-do. To prevent Woo-jin from revealing the horror to Mi-do,

Dae-su cuts off his own tongue since he, as Woo-jin accuses, "talks too much," silencing himself forever to buy Woo-jin's silence.

This schematic sketch immediately brings to mind Greek tragedies where the Oedipal complex, cannibalism, and self-flagellation find early expression. Searching in the other direction, into futuristic science fiction, one sees resemblance between Dae-su's cutting of the tongue and Neo's losing of his mouth. When Neo in Agent Smith's custody in *The Matrix* demands the right of making a phone call, his mouth is magically sealed with skin-colored slime. Undoubtedly, Dae-su's action of raw, realistic brutality fits squarely into horror, whereas Neo's belongs to the fantastic, insulated as it is by the genre of science fiction. Neo's surreal, nightmarish experience continues when an electronic bug is planted through his navel and removed therefrom. By contrast, the schizophrenic Dae-su has the vision that ants troop out of his veins to cover his body. The bug in the sole of Dae-su's shoes may be more easily removed than Neo's internal bug, but the mind control is intact vis-à-vis a Neo "unplugged" and freed from the Matrix. That Dae-su's severed tongue is self-inflicted only accentuates his psychological turmoil, while Neo the Christ figure moves inexorably toward freedom. The tongueless Dae-su is no more prophetic than before, quite different from the sightless Neo with true insights in *The Matrix: Revolution* (2003).

Yet another key difference lies in the role of telephone in Neo's apocalypse and Dae-su's anti-apocalypse. Whenever cornered, Neo and the Zion underground flee through the telephone line, turned into atoms by the Zion "operator." Dae-su, on the other hand, remains in bondage, as Woo-jin says, "in the bigger prison." His isolation and anguish stem from telephone and other vehicles of communication. He is abducted near a phone booth during a lull in the conversation with his daughter. Severed from the human society, removed from the stream of time, Dae-su, for fifteen years, stares at the TV in his cell, a constant reminder of what he has lost. Upon his release, Dae-su is given a wallet full of money to tide him over in a capitalist society and a cell phone to "bond" with his captor. Dae-su pursues the villain with the aid of computer and instant messaging, getting so close that Woo-jin slashes his ally Joo-hwan's throat with a cracked CD, indeed a double-edged sword. Prior to cutting his own tongue, he calls Mi-do to forbid her from opening the gift box with the "family album," which is a thread to the past that can strangulate. All such tools of communication are designed to shorten spatial and temporal distance. But time seems too persistent to be erased. The film resembles a fugue on time: the opening credits of melted timepieces in the style of Salvador Dali's 1931 *The Persistence of Memory*; the clock secured on a cartload of belongings when Dae-su moves to Seoul; the "going-away" present of a wrist watch when Dae-su is released, a handcuff of time in the middle of tattooed lines all over his hands, one line for each year of incarceration; the five days from the first to the fifth of July for Dae-su to discover the truth; the subtle ticking of the clock in the background music.

Apparently, time lurches on without pause, mirrored in the ruthless stalking of the sinner. To exact punishment, Dae-su favors the hammer and his fists. When he engages the gang in his former prison-house, the fight unfolds, in a linear fashion, in the long, dimly-lit corridor like a side scroll videogame. Even the trajectory of his hammer aiming at a guard's forehead is diagrammed, cartoon-style, as a straight line, while it is bound to be an arch. Yet the flow of time is not unidirectional; it circles back, as if on a Mobius strip, around and around. Linearity bends backwards and cyclical. Thus, the film opens with a "twice-told" shot of Dae-su holding onto the necktie of a man about to fall off a highrise building. The refrain does little to lessen Dae-su's ambiguity: savior or murderer of the suicide in this scene; avenger or monster in the rest of the film. These lines of differences prop up the linear revenge plot, but the futility of revenge sabotages the forward thrust of human intention, inevitably turned inward against oneself. Woo-jin, despite his wealth, is a sick and twisted man, an "Evergreen" boy whose maturing and psychic growth are arrested by the trauma of losing the sister-mother. His infantile regressiveness evinces itself when he latches onto Soo-ah's nipple in a semblance of suckling. Moreover, the groping of her thighs and the removal of her panties connote the desire to return to the womb. The past revisits Dae-su in similar tropes of "homecoming" to the lost maternity, rendering him yet another oxymoronic Evergreen "oldboy." Sitting idly in a salon in green shower cap, Dae-su listens to a high school classmate reminiscing. He drops his gaze at the classmate's exposed knees, suddenly awakened by the ring of the salon's door bell. The proximity of knees and vagina, accompanied by the "thundering clap" from the past, evokes in grainy, almost yellowing images one particular scene from the Evergreen High School, when Soo-ah rings her bicycle bell, baring her knees and thighs in the wind. Memory rushing back, Dae-su ascends school staircases to peep at the tryst. A series of jump cuts reconnect the avenger monster with his high school self, both following Woo-jin up the stairs for the rendezvous of sin. As the voyeur peeks through broken glasses, Soo-ah is likewise mesmerized by the suckling she examines at various angles through her mirror. Layers of reflections and narcissistic mirror-images problematize demarcations of voyeur and sinners. Ambivalence arises as well in an extra pair of legs, which belongs to the hypnotist, once in Woo-jin's employ, brainwashing Dae-su. Thematically echoing the prison food of Chinese fried dumplings, she wears revealing Chinese cheongsam, and her legs summon him back to the oneness of incest. This hypnotist is fraught with the duality of the perpetrator and the redeemer. Her bell is initially used to trigger subliminal messages, leading step by step to incest. Moved by Dae-su's plea in the melodramatic finale, the same device of bell ring expurgates tabooed memory. Dae-su's dubious expression hovering between laughter and tears, however, calls into question the effectiveness of the catharsis.

Park Chanwook's short feature "Cut" distills the stylish horror of the latter two of his revenge trilogy rather than the raw butchery of *Mr. Vengeance*. Park's Gothic comic makes possible his film's idiosyncratic hipness: the gruesome violence is magnified by the comic relief of a clownish perpetrator, his romantic dance number, and his victim's pseudo-striptease and flatulence, an awkward attempt to buy time. The perpetrator's eccentric delivery of lines shuttles likewise between explosive, wrathful rhetoric and explosions of air or aspirated sounds, interspersed with drawn-out nasal whine. "Cut" revolves around mirror images and doppelgängers, which are tied together by means of sadomasochistic bondage, symbolic film reel, and viewers' gaze. The short opens with the filming of a vampiress sucking blood, playing piano into the cell phone for her "darling," and vomiting onto the chessboard floor. A receding shot as if retracing camera cable takes the audience from the set to the filmmaker's control room where he commands "Cut!" to conclude the day's work. Both vampiric and cannibalistic motifs serve to conjoin self and other, inside and outside, and Korea and West. In addition, thematic refrains counterpoint the have's fantasy world and the have-not's anthropophagic reality. The director's castle-mansion resembles the film set in its chessboard floor as well as his pianist wife or, as he calls her later, the thirty-three-year-old "Botox queen" filled with cosmetic silicon rather than blood. Right above the fireplace in the living room hangs a painting of a room with identical chessboard floor. Self-referentiality of sets makes the short as much about the deadly game played by a break-in murderer as about the director's own mind.

This murderer turns out to be an extra harboring psychotic rage against the affluent director and his Western lifestyle. The King and Queen in the chess of life are checkmated by a mere pawn, who cuts off the pianist's finger every few minutes should the director refuse to follow his command to strangle a girl also tied up and gagged. The roles are reversed: the extra now orchestrates the corruption of the apparently good Samaritan director. A series of jerky extreme close-ups from a hand-held camera, particularly when the cut-off fingers are smashed in the blender, exteriorize the jolts to the director's mental state, paving the way for his confessions of adulteries and resentment against his wife. Her fingers, sneers the director, are useless anyway and she is a "nothing," uttered in English. Harking back to the director's earlier identification of the "extra" in English, "nothing" erupts, once again, in a string of Korean, spewing forth his hate as deep as the extra's. Furthermore, the director's misogynist vitriol is a displacement of ambivalence over the West that lies behind the couples' accomplishment and South Korea's modernization. The director subconsciously duplicates the extra's fury against the social pyramid with the West at the very top. The director is not the only character who undergoes an identity shift to his doppelgänger. The most shocking reversal comes when the pianist bites her tormentor in the neck and hence becomes the vampiress. The multiple, elaborate, and radiating strings with which she is bound to the piano poses her in a precarious yet almost artistic tableau. A prey on the spider's web, she turns into the spider when the extra inadvertently entangles himself in the strings. In the first installment of his revenge trilogy, Park Chanwook has already inscribed on the body of the deaf and mute factory worker Karl Marx's classic indictment against capitalism: "Capital is dead labor, which, vampire-like, lives only by sucking living labor, and lives the more, the more labor it sucks." In "Cut," Park portrays a mutual consuming and blood-letting by the well-off and the dispossessed.

The cannibalistic transfusion accounts for the director's choking of his wife in the final dissolution of the mind. This homicide completes his morphing into the extra, who has earlier murdered his wife and disguised his own son as a girl to be sacrificed. The extra's sadism against the rich coexists with the masochism of bringing about his son's death, aggression targeting others now turned inward. As Freud hypothesizes in *Civilization and Its Discontents* (1930), internalized aggressiveness is imposed by the super-ego against the rest of the ego in the form of guilt, "express[ing] itself as a need for punishment" (70). Hence, the extra punishes himself by what amounts to a suicidal act of having his son strangled. The director manifests an identical psychic process when he, in a nauseously quaking extreme close-up, mentally switches the extra's son and his pianist wife. He then proceeds to suffocate his wife, believed to be the boy, while soothing the boy across the room, now taken to be his wife. The director may well be mad, but the killing fulfills his dream for a decade, while pretending, like the extra, the son is a female. The opportunity seems particularly ripe now that the façade of a happy union is no more. The son's last words "I will take revenge" foreshadows the perpetuity of violence, as the target of his hate is so ill-defined that it could aim at the director and masculinity who survive the game, at femininity since the pianist does away with the extra, or at the society at large that causes his family tragedy. The amorphousness of the son's revenge promises a repetition of his father's in that it turns inexorably against oneself.

Conceivably, any reflection on Asian horror can go on forever, with each nation contributing its nightmare, followed by the transnational flood of sequels and prequels. Between *Ringu*'s supernatural vengeance and Park Chanwook's human vengeance, many more filmmakers have tapped into the market of horror and reinscribed captivity within as well as escape from Western modernity. The Hong Kong Pang brothers' *The Eye* deploys the medical science of cornea transplantation as a bridge into the past and the dead, both hailing from Southeast Asia, postindustrial Hong Kong's primitive exotic other. Takashi Shimizu's *Ju-On* locates a cannibalistic female ghost at the heart of a metropolis, eating back at the capitalist patriarchy. Cell phones and various lines of contact carry on with their mission of (dis)connection. *The Eye 2*, for instance, opens with a suicide attempt in the wake of a failed cell phone call and ends with a successful suicide because of that same call. In between, floating spirits manage to wriggle into women's wombs at the moment of delivery. The dead and the newborn reconnect in the cycle of Buddhist reincarnation. Asian cell invariably weds Western technology with "Asianness," be it a traditional Japanese ghost who likes to keep in touch by phone, Korean Original Sin and repentance, or Buddhist reincarnation via levitation. The terrible beauty or beautiful monstrosity sired by that coupling shall chill our spines and warm our hearts for some time to come.

Notes

1. This claim of leapfrogging household phones in China is a widespread belief, but more statistics are needed to support anecdotal evidence. Lunita Mendoza's "China: Mobile Superpower" reports a more gradual change: It is said that by the end of October 2003, the number of telephone subscribers in China reached 512 million. Mobile phone subscribers exceeded fixed-line subscribers for the first time as well (374).

2. In Jagdish Bhagwati's provocative sound bite, "the PC (personal computer) is incompatible with the C.P. (Communist Party)" (25).

3. "Only connect the prose and the passion, and both will be exalted, And human love will be seen at its height. Live in fragments no longer. Only connect, and the beast and the monk, robbed of the isolation that is life to either, will die." (E.M. Forster's *Howards End* 214).

4. South Korea is plagued by a rash of celebrity suicides in recent years. The 26-year-old female singer U-Nee hanged herself on January 21, 2007. Her stage name is in English, as are to those of other Korean singers — Rain, SE7EN, and Sara. These English stage names join those of the sisters Da S (Big S) and Xiao S (Little S) from Taiwan; the Twins (who are not biologically related), Maggie Q, and Rosemary from Hong Kong; and many more. Even Asian films sport English titles — *Ringu* or *Oldboy*. If movies and movie stars embody the masses' collective dream, then Asians seem to dream in English. The discrepancy of the actual self and the dream-self paves the way for ultimate self-dissociation: suicide. In an Asia that idolizes things Western, many Asian American actors and actresses have their breakthrough in Asia. Those with looks that combine the "best" of East and West find instant success. A recent example is Daniel Henney who stars in the Korean TV drama *My Lovely Sam-soon*, despite being linguistically challenged. Henney cannot go anywhere in Korea or Koreatown, Los Angeles, without being mobbed by fans. Some performers can even make their way back to Hollywood, as does Maggie Q. These contemporary performers follow a trajectory somewhat different from those of the earlier generation of Bruce Lee and Jackie Chan. See Robert Ito's "Stuck

in Asia, Dreaming of Hollywood." Alas, the U.S. market that marginalizes Asian Americans is as biased and perverse as the Asian market that valorizes them.

5. Plastic surgery to acquire a more stylized Western look is widespread in South Korea and neighboring countries. See Chapter 7, "The O of *Han Ju*: Those Full, (Over)Painted Lips that dare to Confess," in Sheng-mei Ma's *East-West Montage* (2007).

6. The two methods of female suicide are uncannily connected in Zhang Yimou's *Raise the Red Lantern* (1991). Due to the location, Zhang changes the site of suicide from the family well in Su Tong's original story to a "hanging" room on the roof.

7. One thinks of Edward Albee's *Zoo Story* (1958) when a stabbing in the zoo constitutes human contact preferable to alienation within animal cages, reflected in the zoo setting.

8. As if endeavoring to live up to its English name of *Three Extremes*, the Korean, Hong Kong, and Japanese filmmakers probe into sadomasochism, cannibalism, incest, and other taboos at the margins of human sensibility.

9. See Chapter 8, "Tradition and/of Bastards in the Korean Wave," in Sheng-mei Ma's *East-West Montage* (2007).

Works Cited

Akinari, Uyeda. 1971. *Tales of Moonlight and Rain: Japanese Gothic Tales* (*Ugetsu Monogatari*) (1769). Trans. Kengi Hamada. Tokyo: University of Tokyo Press.

Bhagwati, Jagdish. 2007. "Made in China." Review of *The Writing on the Wall*, by Will Hutton. *New York Times Book Review*, Feb.18: 25

Benjamin, Walter. 1969. "The Work of Art in the Age of Mechanical Reproduction." *Illuminations*. Trans. Harry Zohn, ed. Hannah Arendt. New York: Schocken Books, 217–51.

Brooks, Peter. 1976. *The Melodramatic Imagination: Balzac, Henry James, and the Mode of Excess*. New Haven: Yale University Press.

Byun, Hyuk (Daniel H. Byun) (dir.). 2004. *Juhong geulshi* (*The Scarlet Letter*). Perf. Suk-kyu Han, Eun-ju Lee, Hyeon-a Seong, and Ji-won Uhm. L.J. Film.

Carroll, Noel. 1990. *The Philosophy of Horror, or, Paradoxes of the Heart*. New York: Routledge.

Chun, Oxide Pang, and Danny Pang (dirs.). 2002. *The Eye* (*Gin Gwai*). Perf. Angelica Lee. Metro Tartan Distribution Ltd.

Chun, Oxide Pang and Danny Pang (dirs.). 2004. *The Eye 2*. Perf. Qi Shu and Eugenia Yuan. Lions Gate Films Home Entertainment.

Chun, Oxide Pang and Danny Pang (dirs.). 2005. *The Eye 10*. Perf. Bo-lin Chen and Yu Gu. Tartan Video Ltd.

Forster, E.M. 1943. *Howards End* (1921). New York: Knopf.

Freud, Sigmund. 2005. *Civilization and Its Discontents* (1930). Trans. and ed. James Strachey. New York: Norton.

Freud, Sigmund 1950. *Totem and Taboo* (1950). Trans. James Strachey. New York: Norton.

Hearn, Lafcadio. 1904. *Kwaidan*. Boston: Houghton, Mifflin and Co.

Horner, Avril, and Sue Zlosnik. 2005. *Gothic and the Comic Turn*. Basingstoke: Palgrave.

Ito, Robert. 2007. "Stuck in Asia, Dreaming of Hollywood." *New York Times*. 11 Feb., AR15+.

Kim, Kyu Hyun. 2005. "Horror as Critique in *Tell Me Something* and *Sympathy for Mr. Vengeance*." *New Korean Cinema*. Eds. Chi-Yun Shin and Julian Stringer. New York: New York University Press, 106–16.

Kobayashi, Masaki (dir.). 2000. *Kwaidan* (1965). Perf. Michiyo Aratama, Misako Watanabe, Rentarō Mikuni. Criterion, 2000.

Kyoka, Izumi. 1996. "The Holy Man of Mount Koya," in *Japanese Gothic Tales*, trans. Charles Shiro Inouye. Honolulu: University of Hawaii Press, 21–72.

Lowenstein, Adam. 2005. *Shocking Representation: Historical Trauma, National Cinema, and the Modern Horror Film*. New York: Columbia University Press.

Ma, Sheng-mei. 2007. *East-West Montage: Reflections on Asian Bodies in Diaspora*. Honolulu: University of Hawaii Press.

Marx, Karl. 1967. *Capital: A Critique of Political Economy* (1867). New York: International Publishers.

Marx, Leo. 2000. *The Machine in the Garden: Technology and the Pastoral Ideal in America* (1964). New York: Oxford University Press.

Mendoza, Lunita. 2005. "China: Mobile Superpower," in *Asia Unplugged: The Wireless and the Mobile*

Media Boom in the Asia-Pacific, eds. Madanmohan Rao and Lunita Mendoza. London: Response, 373–83.
Nakata, Hideo. 1998. Dir. *Ringu*. Perf. Nanako Matsushima and Hiroyuki Sanada. Toho Company.
Park Chan-wook (dir.). 2004."Cut." *Three Extremes*. Tartan Video USA.
Park Chan-wook (dir.). 2003.*Oldboy*. Perf. Choi Min-sik and Kang Hye-jeong. Tartan Video USA.
Park Chan-wook (dir.). 2005. *Sympathy for Lady Vengeance*. Perf. Li Young-ae and Choi Min-sik. Tartan Video USA.
Park Chan-wook (dir.). 2002. *Sympathy for Mr. Vengeance*. Perf. Song Kang-ho and Shin Ha-kyun. Tartan Video USA.
Pinedo, Isabel Cristina. 2004. "Postmodern Elements of the Contemporary Horror Film," *The Horror Film*. Edited by Stephen Prince. New Brunswick, New Jersey: Rutgers University Press: 85–117.
Shimizu, Takashi (dir.). 2000. *Ju-On*. Perf. Yûrei Yanagi and Chiaki Kuriyama. Horizon Entertainment Ltd.
Shimizu, Takashi. 2004. Dir. *The Grudge*. Perf. Sarah Michelle Gellar and Jason Behr. Sony Pictures Entertainment.
Shin, Jeeyoung. 2005. "Globalisation and New Korean Cinema." *New Korean Cinema*. Edited by Chi-Yun Shin and Julian Stringer. New York: New York University Press, 51–62.
Zhang Yimou. 1991. Dir. *Raise the Red Lantern*. Perf. Gong Li. Orion Classics.

13

The Western Eastern:
De-Coding Hybridity
and CyberZen Gothic in
Vampire Hunter D (1985)[1]

Wayne Stein and *John Edgar Browning*

If you do not fear death, there is nothing you cannot do.
— Yamamoto Tsunetomo from *The Hagakure*

...by being Japanese I cannot help but feel a strong sense of crisis.
— Kenzaburo Oe, Conference at Duke University (1986)

Introduction: The Hunter Roams the Frontier Gothic

According to Fred Botting, with the dissemination of Gothic(ness) over national boundaries and genres comes the increasing difficulty in attempting to encapsulate the homogeneous parts and sub-parts of the Gothic (2–3). Shadowing the progression of these macabre narratives and their migration have been many (un)familiar monsters, one of which is the vampire, a long-time member of the Gothic. Buried and nearly forgotten under the surge of science, technology, and medical advancement that arose out of the Enlightenment, the vampire was suddenly (re)exhumed by Romantic and Victorian writers and then later rediscovered and reinvented by American writers of the frontier trying to cope with the contradicting realities prevalent in the West. In the case of the latter:

In forging a native style nineteenth century American writers were responding to European literary influences, but many of them also grappled with the most fundamental conflict shaping American experience, the battle between civilization and nature, between mental landscape of European consciousness and the physical landscape of the New World [Mogen, Sanders and Karpinski 14–15].

The rich symbolism and cultural malleability shared by (un)invited Gothic figures have helped to erect particular socially-constructed teratologies (studies of the "monstrous"). In the case of the vampire, different cultures have transplanted this trans/national figure across a network of venues simultaneously to represent social unrest during periods of transition and "crises."

In contemporary Japan, the vampire has found not only a new ethnic identity, but an innovative medium to manifest as well: the anime. Conceived in the tradition of the American frontier Gothic,[2] the 1985 Japanese anime *Vampire Hunter D* (*Bampaia hantâ D*), originally a novel (1983) by Hideyuki Kikuchi, has today become a global cult text amalgamating various genres (action/horror/fantasy/sci-fi/western/animation). This hybrid anime is set some ten thousand years into the post-apocalyptic future where vampires have come to rule over humans like feudal land barons. Overseeing these barons (and iconic of the outdated, patriarchal and otherworldly authority figures who typify traditional Gothic narratives) is Count Magnus Lee, referred to in the film as the "noble one," which we are left to infer as meaning the "ancient one" or "one who is of ancient nobility." Within this animated and highly contested world, a strange hybridity on many levels is engendered, producing a sense of postmodern frontier Gothic(ness) that oscillates between civilization and nature, while juxtaposing the syncretic tensions of the Old and New Worlds onto a Third World mind-/land-/culturescape. Just as D, the protagonist in the film, is a hunter, we too, as viewers, are involved in a sort of hunt (or journey) as we attempt to define the sense of the Japanese embedded in *Vampire Hunter D*. More importantly, this hybrid text uncovers or extends our understanding of a *Gothic* that is at once American frontier-defined and also uniquely Japanese.

There is a greater sense within the East Asian Gothic of a complex multiplicity or East Asianicity of merging and interrelated cultural, political, and social resonances that helps create the construct called the "individual." This has to do with an intermixing of Taoism (animism and nature), Confucianism (politics, the ethical and the social) and Buddhism (spiritual and psychological). What this essay proposes is to appropriate this generalized system in order to make lucid the (inter-)complexities of what we call Japanicity — with its rooted practices in Shintoism (which has grown out of Taoism and Zen),

Confucianism and Buddhism — in an attempt to arrive at definition of a Japanese Gothic as typified in *Vampire Hunter D*. As such, this essay traces the trajectory of the hunt for a Japanese Gothic: first, by examining the sublime setting in *Vampire Hunter D*, where the frontier Gothic merges with a cyberpunk aesthetic, and reveals in the process a Japanese dystopia; second, by peering into Japan's own hunt for a revised sense of human nature in the (anti-)hero (or "supahiro") who fights against the moral malaise — symbolized by a hunger for blood and identity — of a lost humanity (patriarchal/Confucian values); and finally, by decoding *Vampire Hunter D*'s Japanicity in order to cultivate a new form of spirituality that helps define what we call "CyberZen Gothic," a product that merges Eastern and Western Gothic constructs which transcends convention and identity, as well as the forces of hybridity that surface from such a union.

Hunting for the Gothic Identity: Ground Zero at Cyberpunk Aesthetics

Vampire Hunter D becomes a backdrop where competing forms of the Gothic come together. As the film starts, we catch the first shadowy glimpse of Count Lee's unsettling castle in the midst of what appears to be the aftermath of some great cataclysm. The castle's superstructure and ramparts ambiguously hint at European design while simultaneously eliciting a sense of Asianicity with the inclusion of temple-like spires protruding from all sides, supported by rocks and steel: a fusion of old and new that almost gestures towards a sort of "Tokyo Noir." Next, the film introduces Doris, the ambiguously gendered lead female character. Doris's skimpy attire and hyper-sexualized physical features contrast with her bayoneted laser rifle and electrified bull whip, the arsenal she uses to defend her farm and younger brother from trespassing creatures. Following a brief skirmish between Doris and one such creature, a werewolf (whose history and very namesake is of European origin[3]) suddenly appears and strips Doris of the cross (another Western symbol, and repellant of vampires) that hangs from her neck. Here, we are introduced to the obscured silhouette that is Count Lee, a Dracula-type character whose cape shrouds him in a way that ambiguously hints at the same bat/cape "form" first introduced by stage renditions of Dracula in the 1920s (and which is later carried over into motion pictures).[4] Count Lee (or simply "the Count" as he is often referred to in the film) and his attire mirror the visual trappings popularized by Universal and Hammer with actors like Bela Lugosi and Christopher Lee (in fact, that D's vampire is called Lee may also echo the latter). The film establishes a European Gothic dynamics very early on in the film: that Count Lee (an aristocrat) targets Doris (farmer) who is merely trying to defend her meager livelihood, echoes the traditional capitalist struggle that Franco Moretti has so amiably argued in his Marxist reading of *Dracula* in "Dialectics of Fear" (1983).[5] Also, in the vein of European Gothic, *Vampire Hunter D* also foregrounds an outmoded entity — a throwback — which nevertheless radically haunts and vexes the contemporary.

Indeed, *Vampire Hunter D*'s unique mixture of animated narrative style, vampire codes of honor, swordplay, eroticism, and a gamut of European and American Gothic staples distinguishes it from previous Dracula stage and filmic products. Also of interest is the film's setting, which is framed against a post-apocalyptic landscape. This essay therefore approaches the question of how situating the film in a decadent future reflects Japanese consciousness, and how this actually serves to culturally enrich, not problematize, the *Dracula* narrative.

The Gothic world of *Vampire Hunter D* parallels two Japanese mise-en-scènes: one filmic, the other historical. In the first instance, the film echoes traces of the Yakuza films that flourished in Japan in the sixties and seventies. These films represent the amoral or "post-moral" (*jingi naki*) society and became "increasingly linked to a dystopic mise-en-scene, providing the diegetic opposition against which the protagonists struggle, both legitimating and masking a spectacularization of the extremities of violence that is central to the genre and spectator pleasure" (Standish 330).[6] Such a morally empty, violent universe is indeed evident in the corruption and moral quagmire ruled by Count Lee. In the second instance, Count Lee's world, if viewed as a metaphor of wartime Japan, could also suggest the nation's capitalistic feudalism and its post-apocalyptic aftermath. Like the Emperor Hirohito (whom many Japanese people believed to be deity), Count Lee too is an outdated figure of an over-stretched economy who rules over a landscape that echoes Hiroshima and Nagasaki after their destruction. His legitimacy is now in question, and it is only through cruelty that he can maintain his resented authority. But there is another historical dimension to the Gothic landscape of *Vampire Hunter D* as well, one that reflects contemporary Japan, and which we will investigate shortly.

D is also a Dracula-type character, sporting a long flowing cape and a black cowboy-esque hat, as he wields a sword (instead of a gun). When we first meet him, he is "riding into town" on his cybernetic horse. It is clear from this representation that D, more than the count, is a vampiric construct that merges East and West. He literally embodies both Japanese and foreign significations. Coupled with this pairing is also his human/vampire dichotomy, and together they represent D's difficult struggle with two conflicting identities, both with which he is uncomfortable (Kotani 193). D, who suffers from a similar agony experienced by the *dampiel* (or *dhampir*), is the result of the union between a male vampire and a human female.[7] The novel clearly expresses this:

> With both the cruelly aristocratic blood of the Nobility and the brutally vulgar blood of the humans, *dhampirs* were tormented by the dual destinies of darkness and light; one side called them traitors while the other labeled them devils. Truly, the *dhampirs*—like the Flying Dutchman cursed to wander the seven seas for all eternity—led an abominable existence [Kikuchi 64].[8]

Hideyuki Kikuchi further notes that D's "personality constantly shifts between man and vampire" (in Martin). Met with contempt by both humans and vampires, D, the cowboy half-vampire, finds solace in neither race in his endless search for meaning to his life. This quest for meaning—a *bildungsroman* motif—that D exemplifies finds resonance in American Westerns as well. Here, the protagonist is often depicted as searching out adventures in an attempt to locate personal significance. Discussing a Western film, *The Searchers* (1954), critic James K. Folsom comments that in the film: "[T]he question of where one is "at home," and the metaphorical exploration of this problem, often falls into the predictable, if disturbing discovery that one does not have a single home at all, but rather two homes, mutually incompatible in their values. Exploration of this duality at the heart of human nature is central to gothic writing" (Folsom 36).

Appropriating this view to analyze *Vampire Hunter D* can yield interesting insights. In a sense, D's metaphorical search is a quest to heal the split to his personality. Desiring to be "at home" with himself, he nevertheless faces the rejection of both races which, in turn results in an inverted rejection of himself. He cannot, in the end, feel "at home" because his identity is always already rend and undercut by denial and loathing. For D, being at home in his corporeality is tantamount to experiencing the Freudian *unheimlich,* or unhomeliness.

On a macrocosmic scale, the experience of being discomfited by one's identity/home represented by D finds vital resonance in Japan of the 1980s. To further this argument, we want to draw a curious parallel between this anime and the genre known as cyberpunk to show not only the two categories' affinity, but the kind of socio-ideological assertions they make. Like the vampire hunter, the cyberpunk's console raider's quest to evade control by multinational corporations drives her to hack into systems to disrupt, and sometimes destroy, the flow of valuable information of the cyber frontier. Cyberpunk, a dystopic way to examine familiar social categories, questions how power and people are controlled and terrorized by a fear of reality and technology. As such, it lends itself to interesting deployments by genres that problematize such notions, for example, the frontier Gothic. As David Mogen writes: "contemporary American science fiction in particular adapts traditional frontier gothic conventions to modern circumstances. Because futuristic settings allow both for discovering New Frontiers and for recovering old ones" (102). In this curious space of the cyberpunk Western, hackers become the new postcolonial cowboys, trying to control the frontier of cyberspace, while attacking the technologies of oppression. Cyberpunk examines the future when cyberspace has relinquished its virtuality to become a more seductive reality where body and mind can be controlled. Humans acquire a new post-(in)humanity that implies a cyborg-like identity that is nevertheless interpellated by a highly intricate network of systems and machines (especially super-intelligent computers) which now manipulate them. In fact, the more "cyber-technologized" a human is, the more (in)human she becomes, prompting theorist David Mogen to deliberate that "computer-encoded personalities seem to see themselves as high-tech versions of the Undead, trapped in mechanical repetition of old patterns" (103). As such, cyberpunk foregrounds a realm where a new master narrative has metamorphosed out of the ashes of post-human history, a narrative which, interestingly, has also insidiously Gothic significances. Here, it is not so much that vampire-like automata thrive, but the dread of turning into such an automaton itself that plots the human into perpetual victim-coordinates within his or her own body. What theorists Mogen, Sanders and Karpinski iterate with regard to frontier Gothic may equally serve to explain this cyberpunk space: terror and horror, feelings of helpless victimization by forces from without that may after all be projected from within, a dread of annihilation more overwhelming than that induced by any merely physical threat (Mogen, Sanders and Karpinski 22).

This brief excursion to cyberpunk now paves way for a reading of *Vampire Hunter D* as a mirror of Japan in the 1980s, which forms another of the anime's ideological backdrop. Just as cyberpunk is less about some distant future and more about the political presence that helped to define the Reagan Era in the 1980s,[9] *Vampire Hunter D*, it seems, is less a warning about Japan's bleak future or a commentary about the problems of the past, than it is about a spiritual void that Japan came to experience in the eighties. Charles Inouye argues that contemporary Japan "suffers from [...] affluences and the insatiable contentment of consumer culture" (5) that have resulted in the sense of national *unheimlich*. In its race to become a highly modern and technologized country, what has been left behind, even forgotten, is a sense of originary Japanese-ness steeped in culture, tradition and religion. Rapid westernization has resulted in an identity crisis in modern Japan, compelling a constant "staging," according to Marilyn Ivy, of old customs, folklores and beliefs to paradoxically reinforce its own sense of identity and its loss thereof (Ivy 10). Read against this contemporary backdrop, *Vampire Hunter D* expresses some of the nation's unconscious fears of the Self becoming dissolved by an unchecked metamorphosis into Western otherness. As much as the anime is set in a post-apocalyptic temporality, there is also a sense of personal apocalypse — the denuding of the Japanese Self— that underlies the film's message. Perhaps unsurprisingly then that it is set in a frontier-like landscape of the West, for as David Mogen notes of frontier mythology, it "is still the vehicle which expresses an ambivalent sense of destiny, projected into dreadful apprehensions of personal or cosmic apocalypse, into visions depicting new forms of consciousness emerging from horror" (Mogen 102). In the frontier Gothic of *Vampire Hunter D*, the hunter's ambivalent destiny is not merely between his human and vampire halves, but between his Eastern (the samurai) and Western (the cowboy) ones as well.

Vampire Hunter D reverberates with symbolic spirituality of a lost era when demons, humans and deities intermingle on a similar existential plain. Very much like Ivy's notion of staging, both the novel and the anime are attempting to realize in the *present* something that is vanishing, if not already lost, and may perhaps return again in a distant future. Either way, it is a sense of longing that propels the narrative. In this possible world, the "human" is perpetually vexed by exterior forces which, upon closer scrutiny, may have arisen from somewhere interior in the first place. As Neocleous notes in a different Gothic context but reflective of *Vampire Hunter D*, "human appearance [...] helps to disguise the fact that the enemy is in fact — again contradictory — both superhuman and subhuman: it possesses superhuman powers enabling it to drive the world to perdition and yet is also a subhuman cause of degeneration, disease and disintegration" (136).[10] By prefixing "human" with "super" and "sub," it already suggests that the evil that humans encounter comes ultimately from within. Too much power and wealth, or too little, positions the human as either super or sub, reminiscent once again of the hyper-capitalist system which modern Japan has come to embody. This is further complicated by Japan's own wartime history: its "super human" and living God — Emperor Hirohito — became, overnight, a subhuman to the Allies which defeated him, and directly signaled the triumph of Western science over Eastern spirituality. This "defeat" has never been carefully negotiated, hitherto resulting in a schizophrenia that constitutes the Japanese identity crisis today.

Hunting for a Hero: Unleashing the "Supahiro"

During the 1980s in the "land of the rising sun," a land of seemingly endless bounty and economic prosperities also diffuses into contradicting values of corruption, consumerism, and depletion of cultural meaning, morals, and myths. Whereas Japanese businessmen find inspiration for their own capitalistic beliefs from *A Book of Five Rings* by Miyamoto Musashi, often called the greatest samurai in Japanese history, so too does *Vampire Hunter D* find its inspiration from samurai lore and philosophy, and from Gothic literary traditions. It seems that contemporary Japan's populace — both real and animated — communicates its need for heroes by recourse to a warrior figures of old who are also "essentially" Japanese.

Interestingly, both the samurai and the cowboy practice the virtue of loyalty. But while loyalty is an important part of the cowboy's and samurai's separate, but overlapping, codes of ethics, the latter takes it to the extreme in the form of deadly vengeances and suicides. The samurai code of loyalty is also later influenced by Confucianism, thus supplementing a dimension of filial piety as well to its already entrenched creed of retribution. According to Confucius, "one cannot live under the same sky as the man who killed one's father or brother" (Barrett 103), a principle that is profoundly advocated in one of the most popular samurai narratives which has also spawned endless cinematic remakes: the tale of *The Forty Seven Ronin* by Monzaemon Chikamatsu. Based on a true story, the lord of these forty-seven ronin commits an unforgivable deed and is sentenced by the Shogun to commit suicide. After his death, his samurai become ronin, or masterless samurai. Ideally, they should have committed suicide directly after his death, and inevitably, they do; but before doing so, they avenge the memory of their master by killing his enemy. Their sacrifice becomes the ultimate act of courage and sets itself apart as what it means to be Japanese.

In D, we see such qualities as well: D's unrivaled courage in the film, the memory of his father (Dracula) whom he secretly honors, and his "classical" sense of nobility (a sort of Japanese *noblesse oblige*) are all contrasted to Count Lee's feudal, capitalist and selfish mentality and disdain for "commoners."[11] That these qualities are infused within a half-vampire (a "monster") may be problematic for traditional European and American Gothic aesthetics which often rely on strict binaristic divisions (although this is also complicated by villains who are desirably depicted), but they seem to rest very well with a post-war Japanese consciousness, perhaps because the Japanese have acknowledged its own haunted-ness by an other that resides within the Self, as well as the fact that in Eastern religious systems, good and evil are not opposites but dialectically related. As Hughes posits, "the Eastern Gothic more often depicts not a mission against some perceived singular evil but the discover of an undivided world of good and evil" (60). *Vampire Hunter D* seems to do both: that there is a singular evil — Count Lee — which must be defeated signals the text's affinity with Western Gothic; but that the hero in the narrative is also an amalgamation between good and evil also points to Hughes's notion of Eastern Gothic concerns. Possibly due to his hybrid nature, D, despite the many dangerous situations in which he finds himself throughout his quest, remains *invincible*— a marked characteristic of a *"supahiro."* And like most *supahiros*, D also has a sidekick, Left Hand, which is literally his left hand, except that it can talk and act on its own volition. Interestingly D's *supahiro* qualities are the combination of his unique liminal identity. While his vampiric half allows him superhuman strengths and abilities, his human half renders him "very down to earth." Also, although he embodies characteristics of a Western superhero (demure, good-hearted, profound sense of justice and rightness, superhuman strength), that he is also in possession of "many of the characteristics of his samurai ancestors" (Schodt 78) evinces his unique, if unstable, Japanese identity as well.

The conclusion of the film fuses the various identities of D (*supahiro*, cowboy, samurai, Eastern, Western, human, vampire) into a celebration of an ambiguous, contradictory and heterogeneous whole. The viewer will learn of his past and the motivation for his actions: he is none other than the son of Count Dracula, which not only explains his noble ways, but exposes D's aristocratic background as well. The viewer will also discover, in a pivotal scene, that Doris has fallen in love with D, but that he must now choose between *giri* (duty) and *ninjo* (human emotions). D's human half lusts after Doris, but his vampire half gazes down at her neckline and desires her blood; in the end, however, his cowboy/samurai nature prompts his sense of *giri* to rise above both his lusts, thus preventing the "moment of the monster" (Ng 2) from becoming realized. Yet, despite D's ability to withstand his vampiric desires, it is not a certainty that he has conquered his vampiric blood. After all, the monster in him "cannot be definitively killed [because] the monster [...] is within the self" (Ng 5). And despite his defeat of the Count, D's real enemy is ultimately himself. He is both hero and monster — a duality embodied by many Gothic figures since Walpole's first Gothic novel in 1764.

Toward a Zen Gothic

The hero, in samurai terms, does not distinguish himself through great deeds, nor is he measured by the number of his enemies. The samurai is a selfless servant, and thus, the condition of being devoid of self is more important for one who has become masterless. This important trait, we argue, provides a unique perspective on the Gothic impulse in Japanese narratives, one which has been ably argued by Henry Hughes in a pioneering essay on Japanese Gothic. As he explains:

> Desire may cause self-division [...] but the Japanese solution is rarely found in the reaffirmation of the self. It is, instead, the emptying of the self that constitutes cosmic achievement. In addition, to the quest for an empty self, the Eastern Gothic more often depicts not a mission against some perceived singular evil but the discovery of an undivided world of good and evil. In translation, life is not a battle ground for God and the Devil — the two grow naturally together in the field of life [Hughes 59].

Thus, for a hero, desires of the self must be eschewed in order to render duty faithfully and impeccably; and in the absence of duty (because the samurai is masterless), then the relinquishment of desire must be performed through self-conscious acts of religious adherences, and more extremely, suicide. And because desire is often related to some future reward or gain, or some longing for what has past or has never been, one of the ways in which the samurai can cultivate a distancing from desire is to concentrate on the *immediate present*.

Such a view finds further resonance in Zen beliefs. Zen is about the power of immediacy and being *fully* aware of the here and now. As one Zen philosopher states, "If one fully understands the present moment, there will be nothing else to do, and nothing else to pursue. Live being true to the single purpose of the moment[...]. [Be] true to the thought of the moment [...] go to the extent of living single thought by single thought" (Yamamoto 68–69). The vampire D exemplifies this principle to a degree: a "man" of few words and emotions, he is also one who lives for the moment. In duels, D practices the art of *mushin* ("no mind"), which manipulates "no way" *as* the way, "no sword" *as* the sword. This is the samurai's discipline. The enemy cannot defeat the samurai using a sword or mere agility because the samurai has no presence, or self, for the enemy to attack. As such, there is nothing to defeat or kill, because the samurai, by virtue of his belief, is already (un)dead. If eyes are windows to the soul, then D's eyes, which are often shrouded, indicate an absence of such an essential part of his being. This mystery of presence that is absent is the Zen notion of *mushin*. Here, the self does not exist, only emptiness; "nothingness" becomes more powerful than "everythingness."[12]

That life and death are intricate aspects of existence and must be both equally embraced is vital to an understanding of what this essay refers to as

Zen Gothic. Every moment becomes a part of a natural cycle of rejuvenation and destruction, of cause and effect. Time is not so much a progressive march towards the future as it is a warping mechanism that results in either ennui or déjà vu. Such is the grandeur, the dread, and the paradox of *samsara* (the Buddhist cycle of death and rebirth). The hunter D shapes his existence in precisely this cyclic configuration: that he is always seeking new adventures suggest his never-ending quest for meaning. In fact, as part human and part vampire, his very embodiment already suggests a balanced embracement of death and life. Throughout the narrative, we see D at the point of death (such as his near-fatal battles with Reiginsei, the Snake Women of Midwich, and Count Lee), but he always overcomes his foes by either resurrecting himself or by invoking his (un)dead or vampire half. It is this blending of Eastern existential philosophy, and Western images of monstrosity that engenders an Asian genre that is at once uniquely Japanese and uniquely Gothic — or Zen Gothic, as we would term it.

Vampirism, Multiculturalism, Enlightenment

When Western audiences view Japanese anime characters in films like *Vampire Hunter D*, they may misunderstand these figures as merely imitating "Western features." But more than just imitations, *Vampire Hunter D* evinces how the Dracula myth can be wrested from its Western-centric parameters and be creatively deployed for multicultural purposes. This heterogeneous cult narrative enables us to recognize other ways in which the ideological intricacies (be it race, gender, class, traditions) of the Dracula cinematic myth are not isolated to Western usages and meanings only. It is in this sense that Caroline Picart has noted that *Vampire Hunter D* "reveals its tensions as a miscegenation fantasy, and shows how ambivalences reveal the struggle between conventional and progressive ideological elements in hybrid cinematic narratives of gender, race, power and technology" (18–19).

As a hybrid text, *D* carefully marries Eastern and Western images so that both are clearly and equally represented. For instance, in the scene when D faces the Snake Women of Midwich, Kabuki-like imagery of long, flowing black hair and pale facial features are foregrounded alongside the familiar Western vampire icon. Nuances of the noh plays are also carefully captured in the anime through its characters' mask-like demeanors and artistically calculated, stylized movements. And although, as mentioned, the dystopic frontier of the narrative inheres metaphors of the post-apocalyptic and the Gothic (Count Lee's castle is reminiscent of Usher's House), it is also at once subscribing to a Confucian principle that "the order of the universe [is] reflected [by] the moral conditions of a kingdom" (Prince 147). In other words, the world of Vampire D mirrors the evil nature of its ruler, Count Lee.

In Japan, hungry ghost scrolls (*gaki zoshi*) have become a popular Zen art (*zenga*). Creating and experiencing them have become a means to exorcising the demons that reside in our unconscious, which then leads to enlightenment (*satori*). Schodt explains that "the ultimate goal [in experiencing this art form] was not the creation of an image on paper but reinforcement of a state of mind" (30). One important feature of this Zen art is "an economy of line" (32). This aesthetical principle seems to manifest in *Vampire Hunter D* as well. By appropriating a minimalist style, the narrative perfects this haunting *zenga*'s special effect. For example in one of the opening sequences, despite the approaching of a dark, indefinite figure from mid-shot to close-up (it turns out to be D), this spatial unfolding is not translated by greater detail to the art work, unlike conventional animation. Throughout the film at various points, D's mask-like facial features are amplified by this minimalism through elimination of distinct facial features. Only his eyes are visualized, and nothing else. This replicates the use of masks in Noh dramas where "less is more." Such a minimalist style at once creates a dark, haunting pathos.

If the point of Zen art is to help its artist "arrive at a statement of quietude [...] when the agitations on the surface of actuality have reached an equilibrium and the essential form of object emerges in an aura of timelessness" (Ernst 4), then perhaps, for viewers of *Vampire Hunter D*, the aim should be an identification with the *supahiro* in his resistance against seductions (power, sexual) on various levels so that we too may come to a degree of enlightenment about our own divided nature and interpolated identities. Thereafter, we can perhaps also begin the next cycle of our journey: to seek transcendence beyond our ideological confinements. But that is another story.

Notes

1. We wish to thank the editor, Andrew Ng, for his insightful and incredibly helpful suggestions on earlier versions of this paper.

2. See David Morgen, Scott Sanders and Joanne Karpinski, *Frontier Gothic: Terror and Wonder at the Frontier in American Literature* (1993) for essays discussing this Gothic subspecies.

3. From the Latin, *vir* (man).

4. Dracula-type characters typically invoke one or several vampire stereotypes: clothing (cape, tuxedo, medallion), mannerism (Eastern European accent, suave), physical features (pale skinned) and engagements (moving into town and buying up real estate, searching for lost love) — all of which became instituted since Stoker's 1897 novel. For further analysis on the visual evolution of stage and screen Draculas, see John Browning "'Our Draculas tell us who we were': Shadows of Exotic, Ethnic, and Sexualized Self-Others" (2006).

5. In his *Signs Take for Wonders* (83–108).

6. Films like Fukasaku Kinji's *Battle Royal*, Miike Takashi *Triad Society* trilogy, and many post–1960s films in Japan are described as "post-moral" (*jingi naki*) narratives, according to film historian, Isolde Standish. Post-moral cinema has easily recognizable characteristics: "No one is saved and no apparent heroes exist; all are damaged individuals existing as global drifters lacking any geographical or emotional sense of connectedness. Violence and sex provide an alternative libidinal economy through which these characters negotiate their lives in alien cityscapes" (Standish 330).

7. The *dhampir* is a vampire of Gypsy folklore. Of *dhampirs*, J. Gordon Melton writes: "The product of such a union, usually a male, was called a *dhampir*. [It] had unusual powers for detecting and destroying the vampire. Some individuals believed to be dhampirs supplemented their income by hiring themselves out as vampire hunters" (196). For further discussion of "dhampirs," see Elwood. B. Trigg, *Gypsy Demons & Divinities* (1973) and T.P. Vukanovic, "The Vampire" (1976).

8. Another writer also notes the conflicting identity that these human-vampires experience: "At night, [*dhampirs*] often betray their vampire heritage by their red eyes which glow after sunset and their fangs. They are tragic creatures who spend their lives torn between two natures-that of a bloodthirsty creature of the night and that of an innocent who is horrified by a facet of his nature" (Rea 96).

9. Cyberpunk, whose birth and popularity are marked by two important works like William Gibson's novel *Neuromancer* (1984) and Ridley Scott's film *Blade Runner* (1982), was created at around the same time as *Vampire Hunter D*. In both *Neuromancer* and *Blade Runner*, the future—a noir, Gothic state—is a 1940s dystopian nightmare where East and West have merged. Both works are also allegorical commentaries on the Reagan years.

10. Neocleous is actually referring to Hitler's demonizing of the Jews by grafting vampirism onto Jewish identities.

11. *Vampire Hunter D* is also at heart a revenge narrative. Doris hires D to destroy Count Lee as a means to not only prevent her passage into the ranks of the undead, but to punish Count Lee for violating her flesh.

12. It is perhaps fascinating to note that one of the most well-known Spaghetti Westerns, John Sturges's *Magnificent Seven* (1960), is based on the *Seven Samurai* (1954). In fact, James Coburn, who plays the character Britt, studied and adopted the Zen-like acting style of Seiji Miyaguchi. In Japanese manga (comics), Golgo 13, an assassin for hire, is a perhaps one of the most popular heroes who exemplifies the zen spirit that less is more: "Golgo never smiled, and his typical response to any query has been a grunt, written in dialogue balloon as *mu*, or stony silence, represented by five vertical dots. Golgo is the embodiment of *mushin*, the Zen concept of the transcended, a moral state" (Schodt 79). Like Golgo, D too responds to situations with *mu*, a Zen "stony silence."

Words Cited

Barrett, Gregory. 1989. *Archetypes in Japanese Film: The Sociopolitical and Religious Significance of the Principal Heroes and Heroines*. London: Susquehanna University Press.

Browning, John Edgar. 2006. "'Our Draculas tell us who we were': Shadows of Exotic, Ethnic, and Sexualized Self-Others." *2004–2005 Film & History CD-ROM Annual*. Eds. Dr. Peter C. Rollins, John E. O'Connor, Deborah Carmichael, et al.

Ernst, Erle.1959. *Three Japanese Plays from the Traditional Theatre*, London: Oxford University Press.

Folsom, James K. 1993. "Gothicism in the Western World." *Frontier Gothic: Terror and Wonder at the Frontier in American Literature*. Eds. David Mogen, Scott Sanders and Joanne Karpinski. Madison: Fairleigh Dickinson University Press, 36.

Hughes, Henry J. 2000. "Familiarity of the Strange: Japan's Gothic Tradition." *Criticism*, 42.1: 59–89.

Inouye, Charles Shirō. 1996. "The Familiarity of Strange Places." Introduction to Izumi Kyoka, *Japanese Gothic Tales*. Honolulu: University of Hawaii Press, 1–10.

Ivy, Marilyn. 1995. *Discourses of the Vanishing: Modernity, Phantasm, Japan*. Chicago: University of Chicago Press.

Kotani, Mari. 1997. "Techno-Gothic Japan: From Seshi Yokomizo's *The Death's Head Stranger* to Mariko Ohara's *Ephemera the Vampire*." *Blood Read: The Vampire as Metaphor in Contemporary Culture*. Eds. Joan Gordon and Veronica Hollinger. Philadelphia: Pennsylvania University Press, 189–199.

Kikuchi, Hideyuki. 1995. *Vampire Hunter D*, vol. 1. Trans. Kevin Leahy. Milwaukee: Dark Horse, 64.

Martin, Richard, ed. 2006. "Vampire Hunter D Script & Notes." *The Vampire Hunter D Archives.* Trans. Marianne Symanowicz. http://www.altvampyres.net/vhd/vhdscr.txt/ Accessed at 10 April 2006.

Melton, J. Gordon. 1999. *The Vampire Book: The Encyclopedia of the Undead.* Farmington Hills, MI: Visible Ink Press.

Mogen, David. 1992. "Wilderness, Metamorphosis and Millennium: Gothic Apocalypse From the Puritans to the Cyborgs." *Frontier Gothic: Terror and Wonder at the Frontier in American Literature,* 94–108.

Mogen, David, Scott Sanders, and Joan Karpinski, eds. 1992. *Frontier Gothic: Terror and Wonder at the Frontier in American Literature.* Madison: Fairleigh Dickinson University Press.

Moretti, Franco. 1983. *Signs Taken for Wonders: Essays in the Sociology of Literary Forms.* Trans. Susan Fisher, David Miller and David Forgacs. London: Verso.

Neocleous, Mark. 2005. "Gothic Fascism." *Journal for Cultural Research,* 9.2: 133–49

Ng, Andrew Hock Soon. 2004. *Dimensions of the Monstrosity in Contemporary Narratives: Theory, Psychoanalysis, Postmodernism.* Basingstoke: Palgrave.

Picart, Caroline J.S. 2004. "The Third Shadow and Hybrid Genres: Horror, Humor, Gender and Race in *Alien Resurrection.*" *Communication and Critical/Cultural Studies,* 1.4: 18–19.

Prince, Stephen. 1999. *The Warrior's Camera: The Cinema of Akira Kurosawa.* Princeton: Princeton University Press.

Rea, Nicky. 1996. *Ravenloft: A Guide to Transylvania.* Lake Geneva, WI: TSR Inc.

Schodt, Frederik L. 1997. *Manga! Manga: The World of Japanese Comics.* Tokyo: Kodansha International.

Standish, Isolde. 2005. *A New History of Japanese Cinema: A Century of Narrative Film,* New York/London: Continuum.

Trigg, Elwood B. 1973. *Gypsy Demons and Divinities: The Magical and Supernatural Practices of the Gypsies.* New Jersey: Citadel Press.

Tsunetomo, Yamamoto. 2002. *Hagakure: The Book of the Samurai,* trans. William S. Wilson. Tokyo: Kodansha International.

Vukanovic, T.P. 1976. "The Vampire," in *Vampires of the Slav.* Ed. Jan L. Perkowski. Cambridge, M.A.: Slavica Publishers, 201–34.

14

Grotesque and Gothic Comedy in Turkish Shadow Plays

Ayse Didem Uslu

This essay studies the shadow plays of Asia Minor using a Gothic perspective. I argue that despite the celebration of the spirit of the carnivalesque in these plays, there is also a powerful element of the Gothic which imbues these plays with qualities of horror, and which renders the ideology of the plays ambiguous. Divided into three parts, this essay begins with a brief outline of the tradition of the Ottoman shadow plays, many of which feature two important characters, Karagöz and Hacivat. This section discusses the plays' history and provides a theoretical understanding of the grotesque-comic elements inherent in them. The second part of the essay considers the plots of two of the more famous Karagöz and Hacivat stories in order to draw out their Gothic dimensions, as well as the ideological underpinnings that could be elicited from such dimensions. In the last part, the similarities and differences between Turkish Gothic and Western Gothic tradition are considered to demonstrate the extent to which Gothic aesthetics may prove useful in illuminating important aspects of a particular cultural artifact. The essay concludes by outlining major converges and deviations between the two traditions.

The Shadow Plays of Asia Minor

The Karagöz and Hacivat shadow plays, products of Turkish and Ottoman folk culture, are among some of the most popular performances and forms of entertainment in Asia. The two male characters, Hacivat and Karagöz (or black eye), represent the duality of Everymen of a whole culture: the latter, hailing from the agrarian Asia Minor (Anatolia), is rough-necked, tough, rough, crude and illiterate, while the former, an intellectual from Istanbul, embodies the cultured, refined, and civilized Turk. Karagöz and Hacivat are believed to be historical characters who lived in Bursa and worked as a mason and a metalware worker respectively in the construction of a large mosque (Ant 2002, 56). The Ulu Mosque, construction of which began during the reign of Sultan Orhan (1324–1360), was completed during Sultan Bayezid's rule (1389–1402).[1] According to Muhittin Sevilen, the origin of Karagöz and Hacivat shadow plays can be traced to the *kaburcak* or *kavurcak* tradition of Mongolia, but their source may go back even further to China (Sevilen 1986, 4). Another possibility, based on the accounts of the well-known Turkish wanderer Evliya Çelebi, points to Egyptian sources. Whatever their source, it is certain that these shadow plays are authentic Asian works of art that draw from parallel traditions throughout the continent.

Alongside the camel skin and stick-supported figures of Karagöz and Hacivat are a host of other characters, and their narratives unfold against a white sheet. Human folly is a common theme, and is celebrated in a spirit of gay wisdom free from laws, restrictions, everyday preoccupations and seriousness. In this folk display of the carnivalesque and the grotesque, madness and obscenity parody reason and morality. The carnival-grotesque form of these plays marries the comic element with the Gothic. Eerie seriousness goes hand-in-hand with the laughter. Narrative exaggeration, hyperbole and excess are mixed with an aesthetic of the monstrous. Mockery is largely maintained through caricatures and highly stylized characters. In these plays, official borders are crossed and hierarchies are overturned. The negative elements of debasement and destruction are intricately intertwined with the positive element of renewal. In these plays, the marketplace, daily life, feasting and defecating are depicted, but sometimes in a Grand Guignol manner bordering on the theater of cruelty. Transformation is a common motif: on the one hand, the reversals of roles — men turning into women, and human beings into animals — metaphorize the brutality of human frailty and the instrumentalization of people by political forces. On the other hand however, transformation is also comforting to the individual because every time change occurs, there is a possibility of a new identity and a fresh start. It makes the various facets of life and survival bearable.

These shadow plays celebrate the body, the senses, the unofficial and inappropriate relations among human beings. Here, moral boundaries do not exist. The power of regeneration is achieved through madness and humour.

Grotesque laughter overcomes the fear of carnivalesque freedom and unfamiliarity, and the potential for violence and the inevitability of death are offset by slapstick. Ceremonies of death (vital motifs in these plays) are, for example, depicted by mock funeral conflagrations, and are often accompanied by ceremonies of rebirth, depicted by mock symbolic resurrection.

The shadows on the illuminated white curtain represent the microcosm of the multicultural and multiracial Ottoman Empire. Characters are Ottoman subjects comprising various ethnic and national identities such as the Jew, the Türkmen, the Albanian, the Armenian, the Arab, the Kurd, the Macedonian, the Greek, the Bosnian, the Bulgarian, the Circassian and the Georgian from the Caucasus mountains, and the Western foreigners, all of which are stereotypically configured.[2] Muslims, Jews, Christians, converts and atheists share multicultural and multi-religious lives on this "vast," unified soil. In addition, there are also incidental characters such as the girl without economic support, the sad spinster, the malicious mothers-in-law, the envious female gossip-mongers, the good-hearted outcast and whore, who contribute to the plotlines of the plays' narratives. Otherworldly characters also form an important element in these plays. Demons, witches, jinns, monsters, and the devil are both part of the main plot and the subplot(s). The presence of such creatures adds to the fantastic spirit of the Turkish shadow plays. In this seamless blend between the natural and the supernatural, grotesque and Gothic humor join together the forces of darkness and light.

Gothic Playfulness and the Familiarly Grotesque

What is obvious from the discussion above is that the notion of the Gothic, when applied to the Turkish shadow plays, takes on a configuration radically different from that of its Western cousin. While traditional Anglo-American Gothic tends to dwell on excessive representations of evil and transgressions, foregrounding narratives that build on the horror of obsession and an unstinting prevalence of the pathological, Turkish Gothic has a more redemptive and gleeful nature to it. The carnivalesque nature of the shadow plays is played out to its (il)logical extremity which collapses the horrible and the hilarious, so much so that the evidently Gothic and comic become indistinguishable.

In this section, in the interest of readers who may be unfamiliar with the Karagöz and Hacivat shadow plays, it will be useful to outline the plots of two of the more popular stories, coupled with a discussion of their "Gothic" dimensions while eliciting aspects of the carnivalesque-grotesque inherent in them. The play "Acrobats" ("Canbazlar"), begins with a prologue that consists of a call and compliment to the reader in place of a lover. Then comes the mystical note reminiscent of the Sufi tradition (*tasavvuf*): "What you see is the curtain, but the aim is to see what is behind it. Do not trust this world. See and know that this world is just shadow and illusion. Those who favor physical appearance and have not grasped the reality of God think that these secrets are metaphors. Look at the shadows on the cloth and take this as a message: make the ghosts and phantoms on this curtain your mortal world" (Kudret 263).[3] Such a note already suggests several "Gothic" possibilities to the story: first, it implies the power of fantasies to inveigle an unsuspecting individual into pursuing waywardness and destruction. Second, that reality is always already peopled by "phantoms and ghosts" suggests our "haunted/ haunting" existence, and that in the final analysis, humans are no different from "ghosts." But the metaphor of shadows upon the curtain suggests another "horror": because the Sufi injunction does not tell us what lies "behind" that cloth, it begs the question if to penetrate this fantasy screen would potentially "free" the subject from this world of illusion, or face the subject with his own void and emptiness. After all, meeting God can mean equally salvation or damnation. This ambiguity is an important element that maintains the carnivalesque–Gothic dialectics in these Turkish plays.

The play proper then begins, and almost immediately, comic-violence is introduced. The two men, Karagöz and Hacivat, are engaged in a fight because the latter has been "shamed" within certain social circles for associating with the former. Their fisticuff settles into a verbal contest of wit and knowledge which is full of innuendos and ludicrous irrelevancies. Meanwhile, another episode is occurring concomitantly in which a young girl is trying to seduce a gentleman with her valuables such as a fur coat, a watch, and a jar full of gold. This provides Karagöz with an opportunity to play the voice of reason and common sense as he observes this clumsy amorous interlude. Involved as a character in the various plays, he is on many instances also a voyeur, and a commentator (such as in this one). Constantly criticizing the girl for her naïvety at seduction, it becomes evident subsequently that she is no other than Hacivat's daughter who is giving away her father's wealth to a stranger. In the next act,[4] Karagöz meets a magician (*büyücü*), is intrigued, and proceeds to test the wizard's skills, but with the ultimate aim at cajoling the wizard into providing him with certain "trade secrets" to help him earn some money. Karagöz succeeds, and using the spell that he has been taught, he conjures a jinn (*Büyük Cin*) accompanied by an escort (*makam*). Excited about this newfound ability, Karagöz is desirous to show off to his friend Hacivat. But when the jinn appears out of a container, Hacivat begins to yell in horror. From the container also appear a foot, an arm, a hand and a snake, and then a fur coat, a watch, and a jar full of gold. These last three items, the two men realize, are the belongings of Hacivat which had been given away earlier by his daughter.

In act three, Karagöz sets out on a journey after securing his wife's permission with the promise of expensive gifts (it is customary in Ottoman society that before merchants embark on a business journey, a legal permit must first be secured from their wives). On his way, he meets three women, who wondered if Karagöz may be a jinn, a wild man, or even a monkey, due to his peculiar red cone hat. He compounds their curiosity when he tells them, in a jest, that he is protean and feasts on human flesh. The girls remain unfazed and continue quizzing this "monster" until they discover that he has been lying to them, after which they withdraw their hospitality, and Karagöz has to move on. A brief musical interlude occurs at this point, in which a second gentleman is introduced singing an invitation song to his beloved. He meets Hacivat and tells him that he is looking for an acrobat. Hacivat recalls that his good friend Karagöz is in need of a job (although Karagöz is no acrobat) and volunteers Karagöz for the job. The final act sees Karagöz tricked into an acrobatic performance by his "friend," and messing up the entire show. He is also killed in the process. Hacivat is sad but is more angry at his friend's clumsiness. He carries the dead man away, simultaneously lamenting his regret and beating the corpse at the same time. A funeral procession akin to the ancient Greek chorus marches to the centre of the stage-screen, but Karagöz suddenly rises from the dead and peeks out of the casket. Everyone flees in fear. The play ends in rejoicing, however, with Hacivat and Karagöz saluting and beating up one another again.

Even from the brief outline above, two salient aspects of the Turkish play stand out: that its narrative development is not only loose but does not follow any linear progression or lead to a climatic resolution, and that very profound moments of horror are accompanied by high comedy. "Acrobats" also showcases many stock characteristics of the Gothic: a family romance based on secrets, lies and the usurpation of the emasculated patriarch (a daughter secretly giving away her father's wealth); bodies in pieces, cannibalism, fierce spectral presences, exaggerated violence and death. But all of them are offset by the concurrent theme of regeneration: family restoration, rekindling of fractured friendships, and resurrection, all performed in a spirit of the carnivalesque. The motif of bodies in pieces is not only a crucial theme in the Hacivat-Karagöz plays, but structures the stories as well. That the various acts within a play unfold in a non-linear, disassociated manner — fracturing the "body" of the text — suggests this. Gothic writing is known for its fragmented narrative (with its deployment of the framed narrative, and multiple voices) which invites interpretative tensions that remain irresolvable, and the Turkish plays seem to reflect such a textual ambiguity as well, thus lending it a certain elective affinity with the Gothic.

Another aspect which the Hacivat-Karagöz plays share with the Anglo-American Gothic convention is an interrogation into the nature of duality. Hacivat and Karagöz are, to an important extent, each other's double: both are mutually dependent on each other, but their mutual dependence also promotes antagonism and violence. Like Frankenstein and his monster or Jekyll and Hyde, both Hacivat and Karagöz represent the split selves which are dialectically tied to each other in a grotesque-comic dance of fear and desire. This motif is very evident in the love-hate relationship both men have with each other; for instance, although Hacivat is deeply saddened by Karagöz's death, he is more incensed at the latter's incompetence because it implies his own failure. And when Karagöz comes back to life, Hacivat's happiness is also accompanied by brutality towards his double. But a more subtle deployment of this motif is also suggested in "Acrobats." Here, Karagöz, the magician and the jinn are also collapsed into each other, only to culminate in bathos when Karagöz meets the three women. Again, the potential horror that the sequence of this episode begins with — fragments of a body overflowing out of a container — is rendered ridiculous when, in the end, Karagöz is exposed as a fraud and the hospitality offered to him is withdrawn. His "victims" become the victimizers instead.

Finally, to return to the Sufi epitaph that opens the story, the various Gothic-comic elements of this tale build up to reinforce the dominant theme: the illusory nature of our world, and the extent to which men and women live to deceive others and themselves. As viewers are drawn to the slapstick ludicrousness of the two characters, they are compelled into questioning their own existential position and, in the process, begin to see the fragility of their enacted "fantasies" (which could mean both the plays themselves or the phantasies [punning on the word "phantom"] that have constructed and structured them). The only recourse out of this dilemma is to look beyond the screen of fantasy, but into what? As noted, to see God can lead to either good or evil, eternal salvation or damnation, reality (which, in Islam, has connotations of a reward of afterlife) or the void (everlasting punishment in *neraka*). That the Hacivat-Karagöz plays are also highly comic may suggest the aesthetics' means of defusing the terrible realization so that, despite the seriousness of the Sufi injunction, the point of the play is, in the end, all in the name of fun and folly.

This ambiguity between good and evil is made even more explicit in the play "Witches." If bestiality is merely a figurative trope which enhances the comedy in "Acrobats," in this second story, bestiality (occasioned by metamorphoses) becomes literalized and functions as an important motif of horror. Love as virtue is parodied when, in a fit of anger, an amorous couple turn to their respective female relatives who are witches to turn the other party into beasts. Hacivat and Karagöz, who try to intervene, are also subjected to a series of hilarious transformations (including a shovel, a vine, a donkey and a goat). There are two versions as to how the story concludes. In the first, everyone is restored to his or her original shape. In the second, Hacivat remains in the form of a goat, and is about to be slaughtered. Even when Hacivat's son recognizes that the animal is actually his father, he runs off to inform his mother that she can now marry another man. As punishment, the boy is in turn transformed into a frog by a jinn. Although by the end of the play most characters are restored to their original selves, Hacivat remains a donkey, this time under the care of this "friend" Karagöz. If "Witches" is read as a family romance, it has closer affiliations with the Gothic family romance in which children are antagonistic towards their parents, and husband and wife harbor unspoken resentments towards each other. Patricide and the discontinuity of patrilineal inheritance are familiar Gothic concerns, and these are played out in full relief in "Witches." At the same time, the metamorphosis motif in this tale suggests the porous and mutable qualities of the body and the ease in which it can be manipulated, hurt and abused. As the Gothic is about corporeal transmutation that reveals the frailty and instability of the Enlightened, moral subject, this Turkish play lends itself to many the stock Gothic devices that directly foreground such an ideology. Vices (hate, familial strife, jealousy) are exposed for their disguise as virtue (love, filial piety, friendship), and redemption (Hacivat the donkey is now cared for by his friend) — at least in the second version — is undermined by lifelong servitude (the donkey will now function as Karagöz's beast of burden).

In all these plays, despite the high comic dimensions, "horror" remains latent and unmitigated, spawning an endless cycle of such plays almost akin to the Freudian notion of repetition compulsion. Like the traditional Anglo-American Gothic stories which attempt to resolve the relentless excess and transgression with less-than-convincing conclusions, only to be reenacted all over again in the next Gothic installment, that the Hacivat-Karagöz plays are persistently told and retold may imply the impossibility of ever canceling out the dread that informs the deep structures of these tales, however comical and carnivalesque these plays may also be. It is as if the underlying philosophy in these plays is that life is an endless cycle of good and evil that culminates, not into some kind of existential closure, but into eternal ambiguity.

Middle Eastern and Western Gothic: Cross-cultural Transmutations

The word Gothic in the Anglo-American tradition is possibly linked to the Goths, an allegedly barbarian people from the Northern part of the European continent, and who are believed to have played a significant role in the collapse of the Roman Empire. As such the "Gothic" always carries a sense of the savage and the primitive threatening to spill into, and destabilize, the civilized and well-regulated (Punter 4, Cavallaro 7–8).

In terms of literary and cultural history, the Gothic is a recognizable movement. The Gothic tradition, with its characteristic representations of fear and horror, is approximately two hundred and fifty years old, and originated as a reflection of historical, social, and religious shifts occurring in Europe and the American continent at the turn of the eighteenth century. It was an era emerging from the dark Middle Ages and the Renaissance period, but the fear, anxiety, and dissatisfaction occasioned by Enlightenment rationalism and the displacement of religion as the authoritative mode of explaining the universe, provided the Gothic with perhaps its first inclinations. Both the French Revolution and the American War of Independence, coupled with intense urbanization and industrialization in Europe, resulted in an explosion of political and social crises. In England, the sensationalism of Victorian literature supplied a further impetus to the creation of the Gothic genre. In time, the Gothic became the platform upon which taboos were flaunted, and bourgeois prejudices and repressions are exposed. Unsurprisingly, because Victorian women constituted some of the most repressed individuals, Gothic narratives found their most important and influential practitioners in writers like Anne Radcliffe and Charlotte Dacre. As such, there has always been a vital connection between the Gothic novel in general and the evolution of perceptions about the subjugation of women and the covert social purposes of marriage and marital fidelity.

As a mode of expressionism, the Gothic exaggerates reality to reveal, ironically, how "shadowy" reality really is. In this respect also, the Anglo-American Gothic bears close affinities with the shadow plays of Turkey, which are deeply concerned with a reflection of reality as shadows on an imaginary slate (the white curtain). But that is the limit to the resemblances between Middle Eastern and Western Gothic. In Western Gothic, fear and horror are occasioned by a sinister "other." The equilibrium of an organized civilization is threatened by an externalized villainy, and harmony is momentarily disrupted until it is restored after encountering pain and suffering. Even though the Gothic is, ironically, a discourse that incorporates multifaceted forms of narration (poetry, shorter stories within longer ones, and so forth) and is thus a hybrid text, it nevertheless exudes primarily horror of the "other"; even with different narrative registers and values, this diabolic repertoire of the Gothic remains constant and unchallenged. As one theorist puts it, the

> Gothic has been and remains necessary to modern western culture because it allows us in ghostly disguises of blatantly counterfeit fictionality to confront the roots of our beings in sliding multiplicities (from life becoming death to genders mixing to fear becoming pleasure and more) and to define ourselves against these uncanny abjections, while also feeling attracted to them, all of this in a kind of cultural activity that as time passes can keep inventively changing its ghosts or counterfeits to address changing psychological and cultural longings and fears [Hogle 16–17].

In others words, the Gothic is useful in Western culture because it brings together two contrary states: the revulsion of, and excitement about "otherness" (horror, death, cross-gendering, the supernatural) that is always attended by modes of violence, either rhetorical, psychical or physical. That the Western Gothic persists in ever-changing guises attest to increasingly multiple forms of "otherness" which nevertheless encourage the same dialectics of fear and fascination.

But Turkish Gothic does not view self and otherness as opposites and hence, existing in tension. That there is fear is due to a tacit realization that there is no amelioration of evil, because it persists alongside goodness. At the end of the day, ambiguity is an accepted state of being and not a threat to alleged stability and coherence. Laughter is merely utilized as a balance to the horror inherent in the tales, but not, as mentioned earlier, to cancel it. As such then, aspects which are seen to threaten life and civilization, and which are then given negative connotations in the Western Gothic tradition, are untenable to the literary heritage of the Middle East. This is because such "negativities" (or evil) must be apprehended alongside goodness, truth and beauty which, together, form the meaning of the universe and existence. A logical extension to this philosophy is the acknowledgment of "otherness" within the self, and the stranger who is also a friend. This philosophy is, interestingly, a heritage of the history of the Ottoman Empire, a history which has, in my view, influenced the development of Turkish literature and what I see as Ottoman Gothic.

Because Anatolia (Asia Minor) is at the intersection of Asia and Europe, people from Europe, Asia and Africa made it a meeting point for trade and diplomatic relations. It was the land that encouraged and celebrated multiculturalism, and throughout its history it was popular amongst immigrants traveling between the three continents. Here, diasporic identities were created. Although a form of colonialism of identities also became inevitable, it was a colonialism based on settlement and taxation, rather than on the cultural erosion and psychic indoctrination of its migrant identities (for this reason, Western colonial discourse is not suitable for the Ottoman Empire). The divergent peoples gathering here are subjects of the Ottoman Sultan, and as such, became Ottomans by default before law. Diversity and variety were encouraged, placing equal standing on both the articulations of the so-called "colonizer" and "colonized." Even with Islam as the principal philosophy and the State's underlying political and social regulator, "Ottoman tolerance" continued to ensure the freedom of the State's multiracial groups and functioned as the binding force of these peoples for centuries (the Ottoman Empire remained united for more than six hundred years). The most important edict was to abide by the law and to be diligent subjects of the Sultan, who represents Allah and the Prophet Mohammed here on earth. If the Western concept of self is based on binary divisions and oppositions (an inheritance from Cartesian duality) and for this reason, has resulted in the notion of "identity" being reliant on the "other" as a framework against which the self is constructed, the long history of multi-racial interaction in Ottoman history somehow ensured that such a binaristic logic was avoided. As a land of mixed civilizations and peoples — all of whom go by an Ottoman nationality — cultural and racial borders were transparent and porous. Ideas were acknowledged for their specificity in time and space, so that no singular one could claim a universal position or be absolutely definite. Gender, for instance, was acknowledged for its fluidity and transgressive capacities. Unlike Western notions in which the male gender is perceived as active, courageous, and strong, and the female, passive, moral, and chaste, Ottoman men and women celebrated the slipperiness of gender identities and roles (for example, on the main characters in the play "The Stupid/Clever Doorkeeper" ["Abdal Bekçi"], *Zenne,* is a male crossdresser). The division within Ottoman houses into sections for women (*harem*) and men (*selamlık*) may seem, on the outset, to suggest a hierarchy, but was really to represent the equal claims to the house by both genders. This was due to the shamanistic history of the Turkish people that was descended from the steppes of Central Asia, where the highly respected and supernatural prerogatives of women required a separate space within the home. As such, in the Ottoman domestic ideology, matriarchal power is concurrent with patriarchal lineage.

If the Gothic is premised only on binary divisions and oppositions, then it makes sense to argue that in the Ottoman literary history, there was no tradition of Gothic of which to speak. But if such binarism is appreciated for its dialectical quality instead, then Turkish literature provides an interesting version of the Gothic, one which does not, for example, conflate death and chaos with evil, but sees such moments as indispensable aspects of life and the universe. In this sense, what is unfamiliar under the Western Gothic gaze and subsequently "othered," becomes integral and familiarly embraced by Middle Eastern Gothic. Summarizing what may be viewed as the Gothic in the shadow plays of the Karagöz and Hacivat narratives, but has been mediated by Ottoman culture and philosophy, will demonstrate the differences between Western Gothic and Middle Eastern Gothic tradition.

First, in the Karagöz and Hacivat plays, the stereotypes of grotesque bodies (dwarves, hags) and Gothic monsters (djinns, sea creatures) bear the metaphor of the (human) self's mirror image. Unlike in the Western Gothic, in which this image constitutes the ugly "other" which must be destroyed (for otherwise, it will destroy the self), in Middle Eastern Gothic, this image is acknowledged as the counterpart of the beautiful; as the repulsive other half of the Self, it too must be tolerated and embraced. This notion is especially important in appreciating the celebration of the grotesque in these plays. If physical beauty is highly prized in the West, the Ottoman culture — at least as suggested in the shadow plays (and in Turkish idioms) — appreciates the attractiveness of ugliness because it is believed that ugly people are better at drawing attention to themselves. As such, ugliness becomes an esteemed rarity, as opposed to beauty which is commonplace.

Second, Ottoman identities are fluid, contingent, multiple, and shifting. For this reason, in Turkish culture, thresholds are regarded as discomforting and exciting at the same time, for they afford a test of character, new prospects, and fresh opportunities for renewal. The essence of Ottoman Gothic, as such, is not so much a fear of the unknown, but the promises it can bring as well. Third, the migratory spirit of the Ottoman people has provided its literature with a sense of linguistic and geographical crossings and counter-crossings. "Home" can be anywhere, but once settled it becomes precious. The shamanistic tradition, as noted, has impacted the way in which gender ideology resists binaristic divisions and oppositions. Ottoman families and houses were neatly divided to demonstrate equal spatial stake in the home by both genders. The "head" of the household was not necessarily the patriarch. Hence, rather than a sense of entrapment and claustrophobia which the Western "Gothic" house metaphorizes (familiar in the Gothic family romance), the house in Turkish Gothic creates an ambivalence that has to do with the mystical (shamanism) and the mundane (patrilineage) cohabiting a single space. Rather than confining, such a space activates liberation.

Lastly, due to its carnivalistic disrespect of hierarchies and borders, the

Turkish shadow plays openly celebrate various forms of interstitial representations ranging from cross-dressing and homosexuality, to racial hybrids, class fluidity, and the childish adult (or mature child). In this narrative fantasy, time and space are overturned and confused; "abnormalities" or "deviations" are both suspect and playfully commemorated.

Notes

1. See Muhittin Sevilen's *Karagöz* (1990, esp. 1–23) for details.
2. For example, the Jew is a coward and a money-lover; the Persian is boastful and exaggerates all the time; the vagabond from Kastamonu, the regional city of the Black Sea, is illiterate and gullible; the crafty merchant from Kayseri seeks personal advantage and finds practical and cunning solutions whenever possible; and the Armenian is overweening.
3. I am using Cevdet Kudret's edition of the plays (2004) as my principle source.
4. In Turkish shadow plays, division into scenes and acts are uncommon, which emphasizes the nonlinear, non-connected form of storytelling. But for the purpose of this essay, I will use such a theatrical device to facilitate my argument.

Works Cited

Ant, Metin. 2002. *Oyun ve Büyü: Türk Kültüründe Oyun Kavramı* [*Games and Spell: The Concept of Play in Turkish Culture*]. Istanbul: Yapı Kredi Yayınları.

Botting, Fred. 2003. *Gothic*. London and New York: Routledge.

Cavallaro, Dani. 2002. *The Gothic Vision: Three Centuries of Horror, Terror and Fear*. London: Continuum.

Hogle, Jerrold E. 2006. "Introduction," in *The Cambridge Companion to Gothic Fiction*. Ed. Jerrold E. Hogle. Cambridge: Cambridge University Press.

Kudret, Cevdet. 2004. *Karagöz*, vol. I. Istanbul: Yapı Kredi Yayınları.

Punter, David. 1997. *The Literature of Terror. A History of Gothic Fictions from 1765 to the Present day*, Vol. 1. London: Longman.

Sevilen, Muhittin. 1986. *Karagöz*. Ankara: Sevinç Matbaası (Kültur ve Turizm Bakanlığı Yayınları [Publications of the Ministry of Culture and Tourism], 673).

Sevilen, Muhittin. 1990. *Karagöz*. Istanbul: Türk Klasikleri, [The Turkish Classics] (Milli Eğitim Bakanlığı Yayınları [Publications of the Ministry of Education], 2166).

About the Contributors

John Edgar Browning, adjunct instructor of English at Cumberland University, is the co-editor (with Dr. Caroline Picart of Florida State University) of a book about movies, games and comics based on Universal and Hammer *Dracula* films (McFarland, forthcoming), and is working on another book (with Picart) about *Dracula* and global identity in film. He has contributed as an editor and researcher to five other scholarly books on the topics of horror, holocaust, dance, and athletics, and has recently had an article on *Dracula* films published with *Film & History*. He is currently pursuing his Ph.D. studies.

Glennis Byron is professor of English studies and program director of the M.Litt. in the Gothic imagination at the University of Stirling, Scotland. She is the author of *The Gothic* (with David Punter, 2004), *Dramatic Monologue* (2003), *Letitia Landon: The Woman Behind L.E.L.* (1995) and various articles and essays on the gothic and on nineteenth-century poetry. She is also the editor of *Dracula: Bram Stoker* (a new casebook) (1999) and *Dracula* (Broadview 1998). Her present research focuses on the idea of the global gothic.

Kimberly Jew is an assistant professor of theatre at Washington and Lee University in Lexington, Virginia. She earned her bachelor's degree in English from University of California, Berkeley, her master's degree in English from Georgetown University and her doctorate in educational theatre from New York University. Her interests include modern drama, American and Asian American theatre, as well as stage directing.

Belinda Kong is an assistant professor of English and Asian studies at Bowdoin College. Her teaching and research focus on Asian American and Asian diaspora literature, with particular emphasis on the Chinese literary diaspora. She is currently at work on a book manuscript entitled "Writing Chineseness in the Age of Diaspora."

Amy Lai obtained her Ph.D. in postcolonial and gender studies from Cambridge University. She has lectured on film and media studies, cultural studies and literature in Hong Kong. Her essays have appeared in journals such as *Mosaic, Connotations, Tsing Hua Journal of Chinese Studies, Film International,* and *Jouvert*. She is the author of *Chinese Women Writers in Diaspora* (2007).

Carol Mejia-LaPerle is currently pursuing her doctoral studies at Arizona State University. Her research explores the intersection of gender and rhetoric in modern and early modern representations of female agency.

Sheng-mei Ma is professor of English at Michigan State University, specializing in Asian Diaspora/Asian American studies and East-West comparative studies. His publications include *East-West Montage: Reflections on Asian Bodies in Diaspora* (2007), *The Deathly Embrace: Orientalism and Asian American Identity* (2000), *Immigrant Subjectivities in Asian American and Asian Diaspora Literatures* (1998), *Sanshi zuoyou* (*Thirty, Left and Right*, a collection of Ma's Chinese poetry, 1989), *Chenmo de shanhen* (*Silent Scars: History of Sexual Slavery by the Japanese Military — A Pictorial Book*, bilingual edition, 2005), and numerous articles and book chapters.

Wendy O'Shea-Meddour is a British Academy post-doctoral fellow at Oxford University and is currently writing a book about Muslims in contemporary British literature. She teaches postcolonial theory and poststructuralist theory and specializes on the work of Kureishi, Rushdie, and Naipaul. Her work has appeared in books focusing on fundamentalism in literature and in journals such as *Textual Practice*, *The American Journal of Islamic Social Sciences* and *French Cultural Studies*.

Andrew Hock Soon Ng teaches contemporary fiction and postcolonial literature at Monash University, Malaysia. His publications include *Dimensions of Monstrosity in Contemporary Narratives* (2004) and *Interrogating Interstices* (2005). His essays have appeared in both journals such as *Mosaic, Concentric, Women's Studies, Women: A Cultural Review* and *Commonwealth Essays and Studies*.

Paula K. Sato is a Ph.D. candidate in French language and literature at the University of Virginia, where she teaches French and specializes in francophone Caribbean literature and New World studies. Her dissertation research focuses on the Caribbean and Sino-Caribbean counter-Gothic tradition.

Nieves Pascual Soler graduated from the University of Granada with a degree in English philology in 1989. She obtained her Ph.D. at the Complutense University in Madrid. Currently she is associate professor of North American literature at the University of Jaén, Spain. For some years she has been working on the effects of illness and imposture on the process of creation and has published her research in *Style, Mosaic, Revista Canaria de Estudios Ingleses* and *The Journal of Intercultural Studies*. She is working on a monograph on hunger and writing.

Wayne Stein, professor of English at the University of Central Oklahoma, teaches a variety of courses on film and literature. He regularly visits Asia and has traveled widely. He has presented papers on, writes, and teaches on several of subjects including kung fu films, the films of Kurosawa, cyberpunk film and literature, anime and manga, Vietnam War literature, and Asian American literature.

Hilary Thompson is a visiting assistant professor of English at Bowdoin College in Brunswick, Maine. Her recent work has examined Virginia Woolf's writing in light of Walter Benjamin's and Giorgio Agamben's theories of the state of exception. She received her Ph.D. in English language and literature from the University of Michigan in 1998, with major emphases on global literature, twentieth-century British fiction, critical theory, psychoanalysis, and feminist studies. She is working on an exploration of forms of messianism in modern fiction.

Ayse Didem Uslu is an academic at Beykent University in İstanbul. She is the author of numerous short stories and articles published in various journals, and has either published or edited five books (in Turkish) on American literature. Her fiction has earned her such prestigious national prizes such as the Haldun Taner Short Story Prize (1992), the Orhan Kemal Short Story Prize (1997) and the Inkilap Publishing House Novel Award (2002).

Tamara S. Wagner obtained her Ph.D. from Cambridge University in 2002 and is currently assistant professor of English literature at the School of Humanities & Social Sciences at Nanyang in Singapore. She is the author of *Longing: Narratives of Nostalgia in the British Novel, 1740–1890* (2004) and *Occidentalism in Novels of Malaysia and Singapore, 1819–2004: Colonial and Postcolonial "Financial Straits"* (2005). Her current projects include a book-length study of financial speculation in Victorian literature, and research on Victorian cultural fictions of the "shabby genteel." She is also editing a collection of essays on nineteenth-century consumer culture and a special issue on silver-fork fiction for *Women's Writing*.

Hongbing Zhang is an assistant professor in the Department of English and Foreign Languages at Fayetteville State University. He has published articles in such journals as *Journal of Modern Literature in Chinese* and *Language and Literature*. He is currently working on a project studying travel, space and cultural transformations in the late nineteenth- and early twentieth-century China.

Index